Fishing THE DELAWARE VALLEY

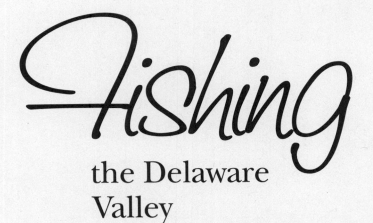

Fishing
the Delaware Valley

GEORGE H. INGRAM JR.

ROBERT F. MARLER JR. AND

ROBERT R. SMITH

Foreword by Joe Humphreys

Temple 🆃 University Press

Philadelphia

TEMPLE UNIVERSITY PRESS, PHILADELPHIA 19122

Printed in the United States of America

∞ The paper used in this publication meets the requirements of the
American National Standard for Information Sciences—
Permanence of Paper for Printed Library Materials,
ANSI Z39.48-1984

The authors gratefully acknowledge
the tireless work of Jan Brown Marler
in the preparation of the index.

Text design by Gary Gore

Library of Congress Cataloging-in-Publication Data

Ingram, George H. (George Herschel), 1939–
    Fishing the Delaware Valley / George H. Ingram Jr., Robert F.
Marler Jr., and Robert R. Smith ; foreword by Joe Humphreys.
       p.   cm.
    Includes index.
    ISBN 1-56639-588-7 (cloth : alk. paper)
    1. Fishing—Delaware River Valley (N.Y.–Del. and N.J.)—
Guidebooks.   2. Delaware River Valley (N.Y.–Del. and N.J.)—
Guidebooks.   I. Marler, Robert F. (Robert Franklin), 1932–
II. Smith, Robert Rutherford.   III. Title.
SH464.D38I54   1997
799.1′09749—dc21   97-20224
                                                                CIP

Contents

Foreword   *vii*

Introduction   *1*

Some Basic Principles   *7*

Freshwater Fishing in Northeastern Pennsylvania   *14*

    WAYNE COUNTY AND THE UPPER DELAWARE RIVER 14

    THE DELAWARE RIVER IN THE POCONOS AREAS AND

        THE KITTATINNY MOUNTAINS 58

    MONROE COUNTY 78

    LEHIGH AND NORTHAMPTON COUNTIES 91

    BUCKS COUNTY 97

    PHILADELPHIA 103

    MONTGOMERY COUNTY 108

    DELAWARE COUNTY 111

    CHESTER COUNTY 113

    BERKS COUNTY 116

Freshwater Fishing in Northern New Jersey   *119*

    SUSSEX AND WARREN COUNTIES 119

    HUNTERDON COUNTY 123

    MERCER-MONMOUTH COUNTIES 135

Freshwater Fishing in South Jersey   *137*

    BURLINGTON COUNTY 138

    CAMDEN COUNTY 145

    GLOUCESTER COUNTY 147

    ATLANTIC COUNTY 148

    CUMBERLAND COUNTY 152

    CAPE MAY COUNTY 155

The Delaware Bay   *158*

Coastal Saltwater   *165*

    PRACTICAL TIPS FOR SALTWATER FISHING 166

    THE JOY OF SURF FISHING 172

CAPE MAY COUNTY 174
ATLANTIC COUNTY 190
BURLINGTON COUNTY 204

Crabbing   208
Appendix   217
Index   236

Foreword

I was flattered when Bob Marler asked me to write the foreword for this book. We had just returned from a day's fishing on one of Tennessee's tailrace fisheries. Bob had used wet flies to take several trout that day, but that wasn't the first time I had watched him enjoy success on a stream; the first time had been a year earlier on a Pennsylvania water. That day he had taken trout on dry flies. Bob has established himself to me as a knowledgeable fly-fisher, so his fish-catching exploits on the Delaware and its tributaries can be believed—it's called credibility.

In the early seventies I fished the Delaware frequently, in part in preparation and research for my first book, *Trout Tactics* (Stackpole Press, 1980). As a trout fishery it was then an up-and-down river; the flow regulated by the dams of both the east and west branches was inconsistent. At times, water temperatures soared to nearly 80°F and chilled to the low fifties. High temperatures caused fish mortality. In spite of fluctuating temperatures, when the releases were consistent and the temperatures were in the mid-fifties and sixties, the fishing was excellent both day and night. I only wish that the river then was as good as it is now, thanks to an agreement on releases, and that this book would have been available to me then.

Of all the angling literature I've read, scanned, or browsed through, which has been extensive, none has been so comprehensive, detailed, and informative as *Fishing the Delaware Valley*. The authors' one hundred years of cumulative experience take you throughout the 14,000-square-mile Delaware drainage to its confluence with the Atlantic Ocean, along the New Jersey coastal area, with a compendium of helpful aids, suggestions, and facts garnered to assist the neophyte and the expert alike in the pursuit of fish, both freshwater species, such as trout, and the fluke or bluefish in saltwater.

To illustrate the authors' desire to assist the fly-fisher, an advised fly selection for the spring of the year on the Beaverkill, Willowemoc, Dyberry, or most of the trout-inhabited tributaries feeding the parent river, the Delaware, includes the blue-winged olive, the caddis, march browns, sulphurs, hendricksons, quill gordons, and, of course, the gold-ribbed hare's ear. Oh, yes, and don't forget a good stone-fly nymph imitation. What better direction could a fly-fisher be given, knowing what to fish, when, and where or, for the saltwater-fishing enthusiast, the signs to look for in selecting a good party boat or how to hire a charter boat on the Delaware Bay, Sandy Hook, or Cape May and what to expect from a good captain and mate. There is something for everyone, regardless of his or her piscatorial pursuits.

To enhance the how-to and where-to, anecdotes, such as the rescue of one author from a midriver boulder by an angler to whom he had just bragged about his accomplishments, add spice to the pages. Culinary adventures in cooking with mouth-watering recipes, some from the *New York Times,* like blackfish (tautog) stew or steamed whiting with scallions and ginger, add interest and variety. If you are a history buff, bits and pieces of history are dispersed among the pages, such as the early history of Honesdale and of Easton, Pennsylvania, and notes on historic sites along the way.

Equally as important as the angling hot spots is the directory to, and evaluation of, restaurants, shopping centers, tackle shops, and taverns. What better way to chart an enjoyable vacation or fishing trip than by simply knowing that there are dependable services in the vicinity you wish to visit! How many times have I been in need of a decent meal or a place to stay without a clue to what was available and had to drive miles out of my way to find them? Far more times than I wish to admit.

The fact that, as one author said, "Fishing is serious fun," and that it is a family activity was a paramount motivation for the writing of this book. Even for the nonfishers, there are places to go and things to see until the Izaak Waltons of the family return from the river.

What makes this book unique, so unlike anything on the market, is the authors' thorough knowledge of the subject. Would I follow their advice? You bet I would. And will I try those recipes? You can bet on that too.

—JOE HUMPHREYS

Introduction

"There is no such thing as luck in fishing. . . . Everything is cause and effect."
—a saltwater fly fisher, quoted in the *Philadelphia Inquirer.*

"Talent is energy and persistence and nothing more."
—HEINRICH SCHLIEMANN, who didn't fish (as far as we know) but who excavated Troy and Mycenae.

Why another book on fishing?

There are countless volumes on freshwater and saltwater fishing in New Jersey and Pennsylvania, and they have been written for every level of angler, from the beginner to the most advanced. Many of the authors are real experts, not only as fishers but also as authorities on bugs and baits, fish species and their habits, and the techniques and technology of fishing gear and boats. We'll tell you about some of these folks, and we'll provide you with a selected bibliography. We, too, know something about bugs and baits and all the rest, but we're far from being authorities.

Mostly, we know that folks who fish often and seriously, regardless of their talents, are usually thoughtful about what it is that encourages them to keep at it. We have frequently heard people say that the fishing was truly fine, even though they had caught nothing. There is no mystery here. To fish really well, a fisher practices just by going fishing. When "reading" the water and spotting fish, casting beautifully, and feeling the beauty of the day are all in balance, then merely not catching fish is almost unimportant.

We cherish the beauty of fishing. Some days are so lovely that they bring tears. Some angling experiences are hilarious; others are exciting, socially happy, or dismal downers. But for us, the sheer exhilaration of doing a thing well is the aesthetic reward for a day spent on a stream, a lake, a river, a back bay, in the surf, or out on the ocean. And, yes, it is good to catch and release fish, and the companionship of others who care about fishing is warming.

We know something more and it's a central reason for this book: we know that a fishing trip can be a pleasure for the whole family, even if the kids hate fish smells and a spouse fails to feel the earth move when perched on a river bank. This simple notion of pleasure is also important to the family member who loves to fish while uninitiated or unenthusiastic companions take in historical sites, a museum, or a fine meal. This book will guide you to some of the best such places located near good fishing.

One of us has a wife who loves to fly fish—for about two hours at a time. In the past, after those hours she would grump and then moodily sit in the car and read. But now she happily heads for a library, a historical location, a museum, or even a shopping center. She and her husband meet later for a glass of wine and dinner, and all's right with the world. Our simple solution to the "fishing problem" was one of the reasons for this book. Of course, you don't have to be married for our pleasure principle to apply, for any group may choose to play.

Despite the plethora of piscine literature, we have tried to create a book unlike anything else on the regional market. Our approach is that fishing is a major entertainment endeavor and a family activity that can be pursued within fascinating historical and culinary settings. We have tried to demonstrate that, most important, fishing is serious fun.

In this undertaking, we have attempted to speak to the novice as well as to the experienced angler, or fisher. And we should mention here that we often use the nonsexist British term *fisher*. One reason is that the first great book on fishing was written not by Izaak Walton, a great man nonetheless, but by Dame Juliana Berners, in 1496. Another, more contemporary reason is that the ranks of the fishing population are growing—and many of the newest members don't have male names. According to a study by the U.S. Fish and Wildlife Service, the percentage of anglers in the American population grew from 26 percent in 1980 to 27.4 percent in 1990—with the most rapid growth being among women. In 1980, about 38 percent of U.S. men went fishing, compared with 37 percent five years later. At the same time, the percentage of women fishers increased from 15 percent to almost 18 percent.

This book reflects, among the three of us, almost a century of fishing the Delaware Valley region. We hope that our modest effort offers reliable, practical, and amusing information for people who do not have the luxury of owning boats that can take them from the Delaware River to the Hudson Canyon—although we hope that these fortunate folk, too, will find something worthwhile here. We do not intend to be too technical because (1) fishing does not have to be complicated to be fun and enjoyable and (2) we're not all that technical either.

A note on geography: our "Delaware Valley" is an imperfect triangle, with the northern apex near Hancock, New York. That is where the East and West branches of the great Delaware River—the last major free-flowing river in the eastern United States—converge. The area includes both sides of the river as it flows along Pennsylvania, New York, and New Jersey, as well as nearby tributaries, lakes, and ponds. It includes the Delaware Bay and the New Jersey coast as far north as the Mullica River. Most of the time, we stay in our triangle but, if there is a special spot we have enjoyed outside the boundaries, we'll mention it. We have fished the lakes (reservoirs) of Hawaii for peacock bass, taken a subway and then a taxi to fish near Tokyo, pursued halibut in Alaska, watched Chinese friends use bamboo rods to cast into a fetid canal in Tianjin, and discovered an excellent saloon near the Madison River in Montana. Those places are too far afield for this book, although we may sneak in a reference to them here and there.

Our Delaware Valley triangle just happens to contain one of the nation's great historical, recreational, and scenic gems. It drains about 1 percent of America's land area but provides water to 10 percent of the nation's population. Sadly, according to environmentalists, the mighty Delaware also is the recipient of the country's sixth largest amount of toxic discharges from industry.

Things are not as bad as they were when runoff from upstate coal mines turned the Delaware black as pitch but, between 1990 and 1994, more than twelve million pounds of toxic discharges went into the river—legally— from such companies as DuPont in Deepwater, N.J.; BP Exploration & Oil, Inc., in Trainer, Pa.; Coastal Eagle Point Oil Co. in Westville, N.J.; Monsanto Co. in Bridgeport, N.J.; J.T. Baker Co. in Phillipsburg, N.J.; Occidental Chemical Corp. in Burlington, N.J.; Roche Vitamins in Belvidere, N.J.; Mobil Oil in Paulsboro, N.J.; U.S.S. Fairless Works in Fairless Hills, Pa.; and Franklin Smelting & Refining in Philadelphia.

A note on identifying roads: federal highways are referred to as U.S. 209 or U.S. 1. Major state highways are referred to simply as Route 17 or Route 191 and the context will make it obvious which state you are in, unless we are crossing from one state into another at which point we will say N.Y. Route 17 or Pa. Route 191. Most maps show a state highway as a circled number. More rural state-maintained roads are referred to as state roads, and are shown in the text as SR 1002 or SR 1037. Maps usually display state road numbers in a rectangle. The last step down the scale is township roads which are prefixed with TR in the text.

We have not attempted a complete and exhaustive listing of every fishing site in the fourteen thousand square miles that make up the Delaware

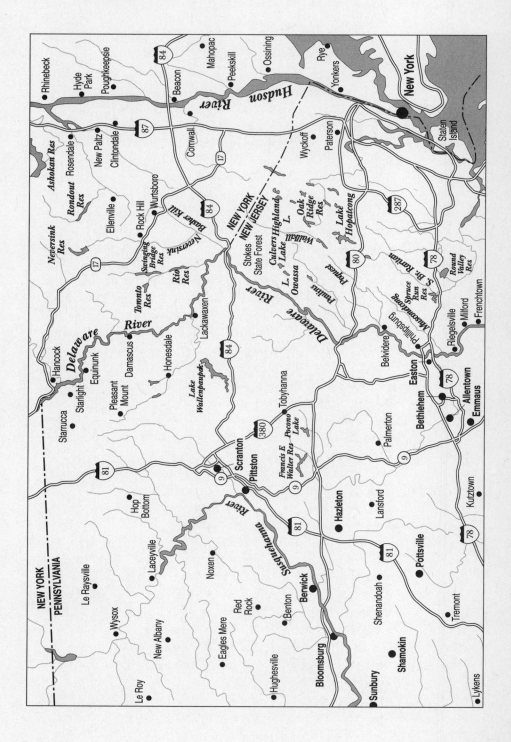

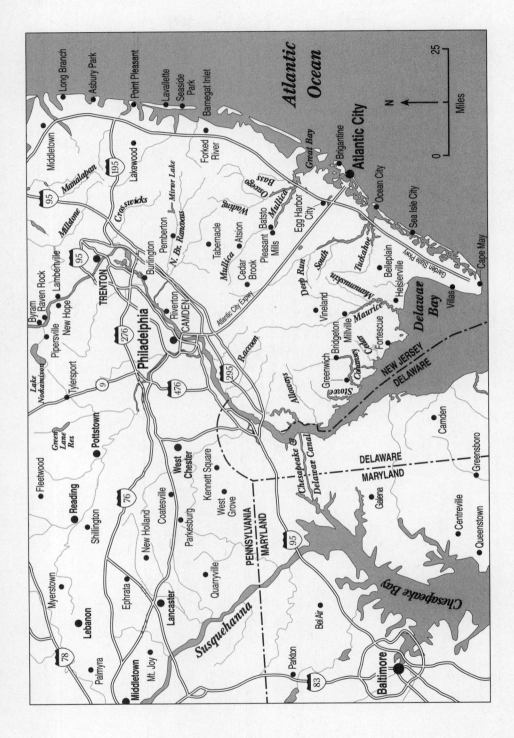

River watershed, plus the many more miles along the New Jersey coast. The Delaware River itself, especially the northern portion, is probably the sweetest freshwater fishery in the East, rivaling the finest waters west of the Mississippi; in our combined century of low-pressure fishing, we have not had the time to experience all of it. The sites we have chosen are those that we have fished and enjoyed over the years and to which we have returned again and again. The omissions you will find are merely the promises of future pleasures. We mention and frequently evaluate nearby birding areas, tackle shops, restaurants, rustic taverns, distinctive eateries (some with lousy food but fetching atmosphere), interesting historical or picturesque attractions, and even shopping opportunities.

Some of these locations may be only a few minutes from your home; none is more than three and one-half hours of driving from Philadelphia. We'll even pass along a good recipe from time to time, in the spirit of that wise *New York Times* outdoors writer, Nelson Bryant, who observed that, "Ideally, skilled hunters and anglers should be equally expert in cooking what was harvested, for it is at the table that reverence is to be paid to the creatures that have been slain."

Finally, at the end of the book is a list of sources for more information—regional books, magazines, maps, your daily newspaper, cyberspace, and organizations devoted to fishing and conservation.

Some Basic Principles

1. **Heraclitus was right**. Things constantly change. Some of the tackle shops, restaurants, taverns, fishing holes, and other places and sites in this book were there when we went to press, but they might be history now. Our report is a snapshot of the way things *were* when we wrote it.

2. **Use barbless hooks**. Barbless hooks make it easier to practice catch-and-release. Some trout streams in New Jersey and Pennsylvania require barbless hooks. You can buy barbless flies at many good fly shops, and just about any freshwater or saltwater hook can be made barbless by taking a pair of needle-nosed pliers and flattening the barb.

3. **Bodies of water can be lovely, but all are dangerous**. Every stream, pond, lake, river, marsh, inlet, bay, and stretch of pounding surf is a potential killer. The message is clear—water is dangerous. Young people should always wear life jackets around water. The 1996 theme of National Safe Boating Week put it succinctly: *"Life Jackets. They float. You don't."*

4. **Plan fishing trips when the crowds are scarce**. On saltwater and freshwater, the proliferation of thoughtless "jet ski" enthusiasts has driven many anglers from their favorite haunts. (If there ever was justification to arm fishers with stinger missiles, it is the arrogant navy of jet ski yahoos.) Fortunately, these disturbers of the peace don't rise very early in the morning. If you are going to fish an area that they have invaded, get out on the water early—before they get up—or later, after they've gone back to wherever they come from.

Thankfully, jet ski enthusiasts can't ruin fishing on small trout streams because they can't navigate them. Here the problem, early in the season, is the large number of fellow anglers jockeying for space on the water. This calls for a different strategy. Many of the fishers who crowd streams, ponds, and lakes on opening day of trout season are off to other pursuits a few weeks later, and the fishing pressure eases. The fish are still there, and you will enjoy yourself.

Another good time for serious trout fishing is autumn. Cool days, colorful leaves, fall stocking programs, and the absence of anglers—many of whom have replaced rods with shotguns for the hunting season—can combine to make golden days for fishing, if you're ready for it. "Trout season always sneaks up on me in the fall," Angus Phillips, the sterling outdoors writer for the *Washington Post* once confessed. "You wake up one morning and the water is cool enough for cold water fishing. Boom, there it is."

Recognizing this fact, the Pennsylvania Fish and Boat Commission asked its fisheries managers to recommend the best fall trout streams. Of the ninety streams the managers listed, at least seventeen are within the area covered by this book, and many are mentioned in the pages that follow. The streams and the Commonwealth counties in which they are located, according to the September 1996 *Pennsylvania Angler* magazine, are listed:

—Dyberry Creek, delayed harvest (Wayne County)
—Lackawaxen Creek (Wayne-Pike)
—Butternut Creek, delayed harvest (Wayne)
—Bushkill Creek, delayed harvest (Monroe)
—Bushkill Creek (Pike)
—Dingmans Creek, delayed harvest (Pike)
—Brodhead Creek (Monroe)
—Jordan Creek (Lehigh)
—Lehigh Creek, delayed harvest (Lehigh)
—Lehigh River (Lackawanna-Monroe)
—Tobyhanna Creek (Monroe)
—Bushkill Creek (Northampton)
—Pickering Creek, delayed harvest (Chester)
—Middle branch of White Clay Creek, delayed harvest (Chester)
—Hay Creek (Berks)
—Darby Creek (Delaware)
—East Branch of Perkiomen Creek (Bucks)

Fall is also a premier time for saltwater fishing. Many of the fish we pursue, like weakies, kingfish, blues, fluke, and stripers, are gorging themselves to begin their migration southward, and huge schools of little mullet are swarming in the bays and inlets. Sea bass fishing on the wrecks is excellent, too.

And don't forget the Delaware for fall fishing. "Autumn is the best time to fish the river," declares guide J. B. Kasper, who probably knows more about angling in the river than anyone else.

I discovered the beauty of Delaware River fall fishing—and the power of the Rebel "Crawfish" lure—on an ill-fated trip one October morning with Dave Plasket in his sixteen and one-half foot Cajun bass boat. We launched at Bulls Island, north of Stockton, N.J., headed north to just below the wing dam at Lumberville, and drifted back down the river. Dave is a tournament bass pro who has fished for bucketmouths from New York to Florida.

He was using traditional spinner baits, while I tied on a fall-colored brownish red crawfish. The action I had that day was incredible. I hooked into largemouth bass, smallmouths, bluegills, and even a channel catfish.

The bad news was that the water was low, and we drifted down the wrong side of an island, where the water was shallow. We bumped over rocks, and Dave couldn't put his 125-horse Johnson into the river to get us out of there. Soon we were far below Bulls Island, drifting down toward the nasty wing dam at Lambertville. Fortunately, we reached deeper water, Dave started the engine, and we cruised into a public dock near the Lambertville Station restaurant. I telephoned friends in nearby Stockton, and soon Jeffrey Leber drove up. Dave got a ride back to Bulls Island, where he retrieved his truck and trailer, and then he picked me and his boat up. — G.I.

5. **Watch tidal boundaries**. In New Jersey, there are specific areas where freshwater licenses are required, even if the water you are fishing is tidal. A lack of attention to detail could get you a fine. (See appendix.)

6. **Buy a freshwater license**. If you are taking youngsters freshwater fishing but don't plan to fish yourself, get a license anyway. Technically, you are fishing if the warden shows up when you are baiting a hook for your daughter or son—and you could get a citation for not having a license.

7. **Do You Need a Boat?** Do you? Of course. Everyone needs a boat. Nothing compares with the pleasure of being where you are not genetically equipped to be: on a lake, stream, or ocean. The more pertinent question

is this: do you need a boat for fishing? The honest angler—and there are a few—will admit that the answer is, "Not really."

Generations of anglers have fished by wading or casting from stream banks. Still, there are times when a boat helps. A boat is essential for fishing offshore on a large lake or out at sea. Some boats are built specifically for anglers. The modern bass boat, for instance, has evolved into a complex and relatively expensive fishing machine.

If you feel you must have a boat, consider a canoe. Inexpensive, stable as a wharf when you get accustomed to its motion, easy to car-top, at home in shallow water, the canoe is the ultimate fishing boat.

It's easy to acquire the skills needed to handle a canoe on small lakes and gentle streams. But you can spend a lifetime gaining the expertise necessary to handle a canoe on a large lake, in white water, or in the ocean. More than any other watercraft, the canoe is less intrusive and more a part of the scene. It becomes a part of fishing rather than a distraction from it.

Silent as the paddler's skill will allow it, unobtrusive to both fish and angler, as much a part of the woods as a log cabin, practical, and inexpensive, the canoe is the way to go if you must—absolutely must—have a boat.

8. **Ask the Landowner for Permission to Fish, and Clean Up Trash**. In our many years of angling, we have met more than a few crude jerks who crash through farmers' fences and stomp through fields, leaving in their wake an irresponsible collection of Styrofoam coffee cups, worm containers, beer cans, and tangled strands of monofilament. These yahoos do as much as possible to increase the miles of posted land, thus decreasing fishing opportunities for all of us. (The saltwater brothers and sisters of these slobs hurl empty beer cans from party boats.)

Trash, garbage, beer cans gleaming up at you from a creek bottom, and other things (including even the excrement that spoiled a trout fishing trip for us one Saturday morning along the South Branch of the Raritan River near Clinton, N.J.) are all sickening evidence of the earlier presence of slobs. We can't stop these creeps, but we can help diminish the effects of their selfish actions by being decent citizens ourselves. Here's a modest proposal: carry a plastic bag and clean up after the cretins. Help the landowner so that the landowner can help us fish. You may be surprised at the landowner's reaction.

9. **Taking Little Children Fishing**. Parents who want to introduce their young children to fishing would do well to take them to a local farm pond or lake where hungry sunfish and bluegills roam near the bank.

We have children and grandchildren of preschool age, and these little kids fish ponds and even the Delaware in safe havens with, of course, obligatory life preservers. You can turn sunnies, pumpkinseeds, and bluegills into monster fish by letting the kids use fly rods for two- and three-weight lines and, with a #16 or #18 Adams, just dipping the Adams in the water. Or take an ultralight spinning rod, add a bobber, and put on an earthworm. Wham! Dad, Mom, Grandmom, or Granddad becomes a hero by unhooking the fish. Make sure that you conspicuously release the fish, even if you have a kid screaming to keep it. Youngsters should learn early to respect life (except for the earthworm) and to kill nothing they will not eat.

My son was fishing by the time he was ten, but my eldest daughter was a late bloomer—which was OK. I think she was about twenty-five when we finally got her to go fishing. I once worked with a three-year-old named Barbara, using the fly rod dangle-and-dip technique on a wonderful farm pond north of Honesdale in Pennsylvania's Wayne County. Little Barbara caught and hauled ashore three substantial bluegills before her interest flagged, and I was proud of her (and of myself, of course).

But daughter Pam was a different matter. She had decided that she really wanted to fish—she really did. However, she honestly could not bear to touch, so help her soul, a living fish; in fact, I'm not sure she could handle a dead one, either, and it may be that her husband never had fish for dinner. It was hard to accept: my own child was anti-fish, even if she was pro-fishing.

And determined to fish she was. On an outing with her at the farm pond, I baited the flyline with a #14 Adams and showed her how to dangle it in the water. Pam deigned not to dangle; she wanted to cast. So I showed her the basics, and she began casting, in the process catching the bank, some grass, a couple of rocks, and a tree.

Meanwhile, I headed to a patch of reeds on the other side of a pond with a fly rod to fish for bass. Suddenly I heard her shout. "Good Lord, Daddy! I've got a damn fish! What do I do now?" I looked over and saw the little flopping bluegill, and I knew we had to confront the issue. I wasn't about to take that fish off the hook, and I told Pam that. "You've got to unhook it and return it to the water," I said in my best "tough-love" tone.

"Ooooooh, Daddy!" she cried. I just continued casting my artificial frog until I was distracted by a good strike.

After a major largemouth bass had snapped my tippet, taking my lure down to the pond's watery depths with him, I looked over at my daughter. She was sitting on the bank with that pitiful little bluegill between her feet, her toes clutching its little head. Gingerly, she was removing the hook, and we both knew she'd never be a surgeon. But she got the hook out and booted the fish into the pond. Pam smiled at me, and I still need to believe that that fish lived. —R.M.

10. **In fishing, never forget the importance of luck**. A time-worn cliché says that 10 percent of fishers catch 90 percent of the fish, which is hardly comforting to newcomers and inept anglers. Another way to look at the old saw, however, is that it's an exhortation to spend time on the water, because that's the only way we will improve. Still, we like the advice offered by Jerome Robinson in the January 1997 *Field & Stream* magazine. In his article, Mr. Robinson was leading his readers into an engaging report on moose hunting with an Ojibway Indian on the Quebec and Ontario border, but his words have special meaning for all of us, of varying levels of expertise, who prowl the lakes, creeks, ponds, rivers, surf, bays, and ocean for fish: "The longer you go without success, the closer you are to hitting a streak of good luck."

11. **When nothing is biting.** Fishing and birding are complementary and contemplative endeavors. When they're not biting, "they" might be on the wing. More than one frustrating fishing expedition has been rescued by the birds—and the Delaware Valley region is one of the richest birding areas in the East.

Your equipment is simple: a pair of 7×35 binoculars is all you need. You might spend as much for a pair of Zeiss or Swarovski glasses as you would on a good fly rod, but less expensive glasses by Nikon, Celestron, Pentax, Swift, Minolta, or Kowa will suffice. My two binoculars are made by Swift and Nikon, but I hunger for a pair of Zeiss Night Owls. Nitrogen purged, waterproof, and color-corrected, they brighten shadowy profiles in a way that seems almost magical.

The other essential item is a bird guide. Most of us cut our teeth on Roger Tory Peterson's *A Field Guide to the Birds East of the Rockies* (Boston: Houghton-Mifflin, many editions). We prefer Arthur Singer's illustrations in *Birds of North America* by Chandler Robbins, Bertel Bruun, and Herbert S. Zim (New York: Golden Press, many editions). The Audubon Society's *Field*

Guide to North American Birds (New York: Alfred A. Knopf, 1977, with subsequent printings) has better information than the others, but the photographs often seem unlike the birds in the wild, and the small, gray print is difficult to read while dodging rain drops, walking, or—a friend tells me—driving.

Although bird guides will help with identification, they do not help find the best locations. For that, a second book is necessary, and for us there is only one that fills the bill: John and Justin Harding's *Birding the Delaware Valley Region* (Philadelphia: Temple University Press, 1980.)

A word of caution: although anglers frequently engage in casual birding, birders do not engage in casual fishing. If you are going fishing, by all means take your guidebooks and binoculars; if you are going afield with birders, leave your rod behind. Many birders embrace their sport with a High Seriousness that makes no allowance for extracurricular endeavors such as angling.

Freshwater Fishing in
Northeastern Pennsylvania

WAYNE COUNTY AND THE UPPER DELAWARE RIVER

"In Pennsylvania, by the time the trout have started to learn something about Hendricksons, the hatch is gone; it usually peaks on one Wednesday and Thursday while I am a hundred miles away earning my wages, and then a heavy rain floods the river Saturday."
—DATUS C. PROPER, *What The Trout Said.*

Al Caucci, an excellent entomologist, author, fly-fishing teacher, and Temple University alumnus, agrees with others that the Upper Delaware River is the "Bighorn of the East." He writes, "Imagine productive, un-crowded cold rivers with wild trout that rise to flies on hot July and August days. This midsummer's dream is . . . just a few hours outside of New York City and Philadelphia, and not much farther from Boston and Washington."

In his article, "Delaware Summer," in the September 1995 issue of *Fly Fisherman* magazine, Caucci celebrates the Upper Delaware, notably the West Branch and the main stem of the river into which the West Branch flows. This article is a good introduction to the insect hatches a fly-fisher will meet on the Upper Delaware.

The West Branch of the river is truly a treasure, but neither it nor the rest of the Upper Delaware is easy to fish. Jim Merritt had it right in an article about Al Caucci in the February 1997 issue of *Field & Stream*: "The Upper Delaware is a lovely but fickle lady. I've been fishing it off and on for

15 years and have reluctantly concluded that it's a river on which I'll forever be paying my dues."

For some, like us, the large water was at first intimidating, and our ignorance (which, after all these years, continues to amaze us) held us back. Yet this is a great fishery. Despite certain heavily fished hot spots, the Upper Delaware will continue to thrive—if polluters, poachers, and thoughtless slobs in the fishing fraternity and sorority are held in check.

The East and West Branches of the Delaware join just south of Hancock, N.Y., the apex of our triangle. If you drive north on Pa. Route 191, you will come to a bridge crossing the river and leading into Hancock and N.Y. Route 17. You can fish just by the bridge if you like, but there are other, less crowded places. If you are unfamiliar with the Delaware, it's time to take an imaginary look at this great river.

If you stood on the Hancock Bridge and, with the vision of Superman, surveyed the river west, east, and then south through the Poconos to the Delaware Water Gap (or to Philadelphia, for that matter), you'd see nothing but productive, fishable waters. The river is reasonably clean, despite a few degraded sites—in fact, shortly we will take you past a sewage treatment plant on the way to a neat place to fish.

Your krypton-spawned super-vision would also reveal an astonishing variety of fishes: trout, catfish, stripers, panfish, bass of varying mouth sizes, muskies, suckers, walleyes, shad, and eels, and you'd see spectacular scenery in Pennsylvania, New York, and New Jersey. Old-timers will have narrowed their vision to favorite species and spots, but the prospects are truly awe-inspiring if you like to fish, eat, drink, and be entertained. We know places where you can drink champagne, among other activities, in a heart-shaped, king-size bed, but that's tacky. Besides, after catching a half-dozen trout, love is much better on a moss-lined bank.

WATER CONDITIONS ON THE UPPER DELAWARE

Water depths and temperatures on the Upper Delaware change quickly and erratically. For fishers new to the river, these water conditions are important. They are comparable to the tides and variable conditions on the lower river and along the shore. Don't be threatened; just know the conditions for the best fishing and for safety's sake.

There are several influential dams in New York, one at the Pepacton Reservoir (with a goodly population of brown trout) on the East Branch and one at the Cannonsville Reservoir on the West Branch. These two dams

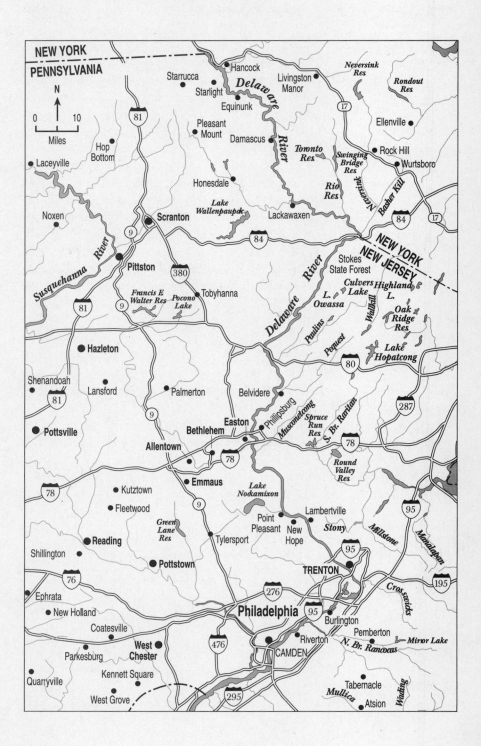

control water level in the East and West Branches and, ultimately, in the river's main stem. New York City takes a part of its water supply from the reservoirs, and the city's demand governs the water released by the dams. The water releases are erratic, yet those flushes are responsible for keeping the water in the East and West Branches at temperatures in the 40s and low 50s. Cool water is good for trout but not too good for the fisher in waders who falls in. If you have heart disease, please be particularly careful.

The March 1997 issue of *Fly Fisherman* reports that two new water control valves were recently installed in the Cannonsville Dam. We have been hearing about those valves for several years now. The valves are supposed to spread out peak water releases during the summer so that river conditions on the West Branch will remain steady. We aren't so certain. New York City still takes water regardless of what the trout need. The bottom line: when New York needs water from the reservoir, water releases downstream are reduced, and they are severely reduced in times of drought.

Luckily, the bottom of the Delaware is fairly easy to wade. There are the usual rocks, but anyone can handle them if the water is not too high. Be sure to wear chest waders and a belt, preferably warm waders with felt soles; the felt will help keep you from slipping on slimy rocks. Should you fall, the belt will trap air in the waders, and you'll have a better chance of floating. When the water is high, wading is difficult and so is the fishing. When the water is very low, wading is easy, and sometimes you can actually wade across the river, but the fishing is erratic.

If you plan to fish the Upper Delaware, you can call the National Park Service at (914) 252-7100 for a recorded message giving official water temperatures and gage heights that will tip you off about water depths at the Calicoon (New York side) access point, which is south of the East and West branches. A call to the U.S. Weather Bureau in Harrisburg at (717) 234-6812 or in Philadelphia at (215) 627-5575 will tell you what's going on at the Hale Eddy gage in New York.

According to Dwight Landis (*Trout Streams of Pennsylvania: An Angler's Guide*, 2d Edition, Hempstead-Lyndell, page 22), fishing is often best with a gage height between 2.0 and 2.5 feet. At 2.75 feet, there is some difficulty wading out very far; above 3.2 feet, you could get yourself in trouble if you don't work out about six hours a day. However, if the river is likely to be too strong for you, the hefty current when you first start to wade will let you know how careful to be. If we have frightened you, we back off. Fishing the Upper Delaware is not all that difficult. And if senior citizenship threatens to make you an alien on the river, then don't hesitate to use a wading staff.

We often do, and a fine fisher we know who has yet to see age fifty wears CO_2-inflatable suspenders all the time.

THE WEST BRANCH (WITH A DETOUR TO THE BEAVERKILL AND WILLOWEMOC)

"I'm tired of working from dawn to dark. . . . I'm just sick of it. I just want to go out to a trout stream and get away from it."
—Media mogul TED TURNER in 1996, after purchasing a 5,000-acre ranch in Montana.

We'll start with the West Branch of the river, and we are talking mostly about the trout fishing, which is about as good as it can get on the Delaware. You can begin by heading north out of Hancock, N.Y., on Route 17 to Deposit, N.Y. In Deposit, look for Route 4A, and take it south along the river to Hale Eddy. A New York fishing license is necessary at Hale Eddy, but it is valid on all water in the state and, thanks to a reciprocal agreement, in Pennsylvania and New Jersey wherever the Delaware is the border between the two states. (The reciprocity agreement is among the three states—New York, New Jersey, and Pennsylvania, wherever the river is a border.)

After fishing Hale Eddy with flies, lures, or live bait, anglers often return north in the late afternoon to the two-mile catch-and-release section just below Deposit, N.Y., and then cross the bridge in Deposit and come back south on Route 17, perhaps to wet a line in the water at the Hancock Bridge. In fact, for the sake of travel directions, we use Hancock and the Hancock Bridge as a kind of hub to a wheel whose circumference encircles the East and West branches, the Beaverkill and Willowemoc rivers, and the main stem of the Delaware down to about Equinunk. We will return to Hancock for reference before we speed out along another spoke of the wheel.

Resort
Before we leave the Hale Eddy area too quickly, we should mention the West Branch Angler and Sportsmen's Resort, (607) 467-5525, located on the Pennsylvania side of the river. Surrounded by the protected beauty of Pennsylvania State Game Lands, the resort has seventeen comparatively new cabins. The cooking facilities are elegantly complemented by L.L. Bean furniture. Guests have access to a good, private restaurant, and there's an excellent fly shop that carries top equipment and thousands of flies. A guide service is available, and fishers can rent canoes and rafts. There are

also hiking trails and a lodge with its own motel rooms. The resort is expanding, and Manager Larry Finley says the emphasis is on family recreation. In fact, the West Branch Angler and Sportsmen's Resort caters to non-fishing families as well as to fishers and expects to have a large swimming pool for the 1997 season.

Tackle

Driving south from Deposit, cross the Hancock Bridge onto Pa. Route 191 and start looking to the left for a tackle shop. This is the Delaware River Fly Shop (formerly Fur, Fins & Feather), now owned and operated by the West Branch Angler and Sportsmen's Resort. It's a good idea to stop at this nicely stocked shop before fishing the West or East Branch of the Delaware because whoever is working that day will know the right bait or fly to recommend, as well as conditions on the river, especially water depths and temperatures. You can telephone the Fly Shop at (717) 695-5983. For detailed information about water conditions, including the hatches, call the resort's Hot-Line at (607) 467-5565. If water conditions are really nasty, you can fish the famous Beaverkill and Willowemoc.

The Beaverkill and Willowemoc

As Dwight Landis points out in *Trout Streams of Pennsylvania*, anglers who come to fish the Delaware and find the water too high or too low often just head west on N.Y. Route 17 to the heart of fly-fishing. If inclined, you can quaff a quick one at the junction of the East Branch and Beaverkill River (Exit 90) at the Log Cabin Hotel and Bar. Keep going west on Route 17 to Roscoe or Livingston Manor, N.Y., to fish the Beaverkill and Willowemoc, both superior capillaries to the artery of the Delaware. You are now in historic fly-fishing country, so show some respect!

Access to the two streams is relatively easy, and parking is plentiful. Between Roscoe and Livingston Manor on the Willowemoc, there is a No-Kill zone restricted to artificial lures. Fishing is allowed year-round here. For more information, check with Fur, Fin and Feather on DeBruce Road in Livingston Manor, (914) 439-4476, or with The Beaverkill Angler in Roscoe, (607) 498-5194.

We have gone to New York in late spring and taken nice brook and brown trout on Blue-wing Olives, March Browns, Sulphur Duns, and the ever-faithful Gold-ribbed Hare's Ear for nymphing. We fished the Beaverkill close to Pig Pen Pool near Rockland and the Willowemoc between Akens Pool and Deckers Eddy. It was a lovely, slightly chilly day for early June. Fish were rising when we arrived at 10:00 in the morning, and by 7:00 P.M. we were still eager to fish; that is, one of us was eager. The others threw rocks to force one of us off the stream.

Attractions

As long as we are on this detour, we should mention that in mid-June youngsters can win prizes in the Annual Kids All America Fishing Derby at Water Wheel Junction (Livingston Manor) on the Willowemoc. The excellent Catskill Fly-fishing Center and Museum, (914) 433-4810, is also worth several visits by those who love fly-fishing and at least one visit by others. The museum features fly-fishing, its art and history. It covers the life of legendary fisher Lee Wulff and offers environmental education programs. Try also to visit the Roscoe O&W Railway Museum on Railroad Avenue. In addition to railroad exhibits, the museum has arts and crafts exhibits, a flea market, and a used-book shop.

Dining

In this area, enjoy some German food at Robin Hood Diner in Livingston Manor or Italian fare at Baimondo's Ristorante & Pizzeria in Roscoe; more upscale is the Beaverkill Valley Inn or the Oak Table, both in Livingston Manor, but you should make reservations. Other eateries and drinkeries at various levels of quality and ambience are plentiful.

Orvis is helping Trout Unlimited's effort to preserve the Beaverkill watershed. The March/April 1997 issue of Orvis News *had this to say about the project:*

You pull into Deposit, N.Y., on a slightly overcast, humid day in mid-June, ready to have at the monster trout that swim in the Beaverkill River. So you hurry to one of the better spots, and you're surprised at the number of anglers out on the water. Despite entire stretches of empty river, the more famous hot spots have anglers positioned elbow to elbow. That's because the fishing holes have become the only retreat for trout when water temperatures warm to unbearable levels. You gear up, tie on a blue winged olive, and head down to the river, only to discover water levels precariously low and water temperatures frighteningly high. You turn your eyes toward the overpass that rises above you. Route 17 meanders along the greater part of the river, and polluted runoff from that highway spills directly into the river at incredibly high temperatures. There are no rises—not a nose in sight. You switch to a nymph, and still nothing. By noon, you give up, frustrated and confused.

Orvis's CEO, Perk Perkins, has called the Beaverkill "a fundamental piece of our heritage, and to turn our backs on this most storied fishery would be unforgivable." The company has initiated a $75,000 challenge to its customers to help Trout Unlimited with Beaverkill projects. Accordingly, Orvis and The National Fish and Wildlife Foundation will match every customer donation on a 2:1 basis. The result will be that every $100 tax-deductible check becomes a $300 gift to Trout Unlimited. Send donations to Trout Unlimited/Beaverkill Restoration Project, Department RS, Orvis, Historic Route 7A, Manchester, VT 05254.

BALLS EDDY

When the water is down on the West Branch of the Delaware—as it usually is in May and June—we return from the detour to the Beaverkill and Willowemoc. For easy public access on the West Branch, head for Balls Eddy. If you are driving south on Pa. Route 191, a hare's breath below the Hancock Bridge, you'll find the aforementioned Delaware River Fly Shop. Across 191 from the Fly Shop is SR Route 4014 (Winterdale Road). Follow it west for about four miles, past some three miles of private land that prohibits public access to the river, past the ramshackle Riverview Inn, past Al Caucci's Delaware River Club Fly-fishing Resort (on your left), to a well-marked entrance to Balls Eddy (on the right).

Balls Eddy is a delightful place to fish for trout, even if the truck traffic rumbling on the New York side occasionally intrudes on the peace and beauty of this popular public access site that's maintained by the Pennsylvania Fish and Boat Commission.

The water flow and temperature here are determined in large measure by the people at Cannonsville Reservoir, whose releases affect the fishing. Regular anglers know that a surge of cold reservoir water will turn off feeding trout. There are days when nothing—absolutely nothing—will entice a trout to your hook.

There is plenty of free parking, a boat launch, and toilets that are typical of state parks. At the Buckingham access south of here, however, the toilets are fouler, and the last time we tried the ones at the Damascus access even farther south, there was retching all around. At Balls Eddy, there is also a big shady tree at the river's edge for hot summer days when the trout aren't biting on anything and all you want to do is take a nap while listening to the water in the early stages of its long, long journey to Delaware Bay.

Fishing at Balls Eddy is with whatever bait the fisher or fish prefer. Bait-casting gear with spinners or minnows will bring trout to the creel, but our preference is fly-fishing with artificial flies. We must confess that, on occasion, out of frustration we have resorted to ultra-light spinning gear with small spinners.

Brown trout and rainbows are the main objectives at Balls Eddy, and essentially they are battle-hardened natives. Please don't kill them. They fight hard, and they are beautiful. Take photos, get witnesses, or tell lies, but please don't take them home. Release what you catch.

The first time I fished Balls Eddy I knew little about the river, and there I was, fishing alone. It was May, and earlier in the day I had been down on the river at Damascus, fishing unsuccessfully in a crowd of people for shad. After that, I worked the Delayed-Harvest section of the Dyberry Creek south of Cold Spring and caught several large stocked rainbows and one ugly Palomino. I wanted a witness to whom I could brag.

Flushed with pride, I drove to Carole's bar in Equinunk for a cold beer, then moved north on Pa. Route 191 to take on Balls Eddy.

There I tied on a Prince nymph, stomped into the river at the boat launch, waded out about fifteen feet, flung out my little nymph, and hooked into a honey of a fish, which I released.

I had two fishless witnesses, and I bragged. Two hours later, however, I had not had another strike, despite a hatch of Hendricksons. I tried just about every springtime fly in my box: Hendricksons, Blue-winged Olives, Blue Quills, Quill Gordons, a variety of caddis flies, and a larger variety of nymphs. When no one was watching, I even tried an assortment of Wooly Buggers. Nothing. Nada. Zip. By about 5:00 P.M., I was almost in tears. Besides, my two witnesses had by now caught several trout, and they were smiling condescendingly at me.

To escape their company, I ignored the rising water and started for the riffles about 100 or so yards south of the boat launch. Knowing that the current was increasing slightly, and that I was ignorant of this new-found stretch of the river, I nonetheless blundered downstream.

After about a dozen good casts, I caught a little eight-inch brown on a black Gold-ribbed Hare's Ear nymph. Life had improved, but only for about 10 minutes. I looked at my watch and suddenly realized that I was going to miss a date with my wife. In fast water about knee deep, I headed toward the bank. Then I felt—and think I heard—the weak knee go "pop." Down I went, my rod taking off downstream with me tumbling after. We both hit a large rock, and I held on dearly to both rock and rod.

My waders runneth over, and I was afraid of losing my rod or my life, and maybe both.

"Help!" I began. Then much, much louder, "Help me!" I was seriously scared, but my witnesses never heard me. (They told me after they retrieved me that they laughed when they saw the smart-aleck go down.)

After a change of clothes, I contritely took the witnesses to the Fireside Inn on Route 191, near the village of Dyberry, where they saved me again. My waiting spouse was in a gentle rage—a most dangerous variety—but my kindly witnesses, simply because they were there as my guests, imposed courtesy all around. By dinner's end, we were all in good spirits, and even today I exchange Christmas cards with the witnesses.

The moral of this story? Learn humility and know and respect the river. Be kind to witnesses. Brag if you must, but do it with a measure of humility. And never, ever keep your spouse waiting. —R.M.

Up to my waist in the Delaware, I paused in my inept fly casting near the Balls Eddy launch ramp to watch a man pull a one-person canoe to the riverbank.

Then he pushed the craft halfway into the water and loaded into it a sleeping bag, cooler, and several black plastic bags. His wife, who had driven up with him in a car, gave him a kiss. The man slid into the canoe, eased out into the Delaware and began to paddle slowly as the current embraced him.

"How far you going?" I asked when he drifted by me.

"All the way to Bristol." That's Bristol, Pennsylvania, below Trenton.

"Wow," I said. "That far. You know, I always wanted to do that."

"So did I," he said with determination, "and that's why I doing it now." —G.I.

SOME COMMENTS ABOUT FLIES AND HATCHES

"Fly-fishing is a wonderful diversion. On vacations Dad and I, the whole family, would go to the casting pool."
—Classical guitarist CHRISTOPHER PARKENING
(*New York Times*, November 3, 1996)

For fly-fishing, there is a large variety of insects on the Delaware River. It pays to know something about "matching the hatch," and Charles Meck's *Pennsylvania Trout Streams and Their Hatches* (Backcountry Publications, 1989) can help novice fishers and those new to the river. The Landis book we mentioned earlier, *Trout Streams of Pennsylvania*, is also very useful. But for this section of the river, the best book is *Hatches II*, by Al Caucci and Bob Nastasi.

A legend on the Delaware for his fly-fishing is Ed Van Put. We know him by reputation only, but there is a useful article on this gentleman by Jim Merritt in the April 1993 issue of *Fly Rod & Reel*. We suggest novices take notice.

According to Merritt, Van Put represents a point of view that we endorse: use generic flies. You don't have to be an entomologist to fish for trout successfully in any water, even the difficult Upper Delaware. We suspect that Van Put knows the bugs in the Delaware as well as anyone else. But, like many fishers, he depends regularly on several generic flies that imitate nothing specifically. Yet, because they don't know this, the trout often assume those flies are familiar, tasty morsels.

If you are just starting out on the Delaware, try a #14 or #16 Adams as the dry fly of choice or, if the persnickety fish are ignoring dries, a #14 Zug Bug, Pheasant Tail, Prince, or Gold-ribbed Hare's Ear as the nymph of the day.

When the water is deep and the fish aren't hitting dry flies, try a Hare's Ear wet fly or a Lead Wing Coachman wet. With these wets, use a small split-shot weight attached 10 or 12 inches above the fly. Cast across and upstream, lift the rod tip slightly, and let the fly sink as you strive for a "natural" drift with the current. Mend your line as needed to keep it drifting naturally, but give the rod the slightest jiggles as the fly heads downstream. Keep the tiny jiggle—really tiny—going, for you are imitating the birth of a bug. Joe Humphreys taught us this trick on the Watauba River in Tennessee. We tried it and wham! We always try it now.

Having said all that about generics, we must point out that around the first of May the Hendrickson hatches begin to appear on the Delaware, and knowledgeable fly-fishers eagerly look forward to them. The Adams is an acceptable substitute, but we promise you more fun—and hits—if you tie on a Hendrickson.

We have found that other fishers on the water readily share information about what the fish are up to. After good-natured greetings there is usually an open exchange of information. None of us has ever been rebuffed or treated rudely, and we concluded long ago that folks who fish the very public Balls Eddy are kindly disposed.

Resort

After a good day, no matter how many fish you've caught, head back south and east along SR 4011. On the right is the ramshackle Riverview Inn; stop if you must, but to miss it is no loss. It will be a serious loss if you do not investigate Al Caucci's Delaware River Club Fly-fishing Resort, (800) 662-9359, which is also on the right as you drive toward Pa. Route 191.

We have dropped by the resort perhaps a half-dozen times and found that the philosophy there is similar to that in this book. This is a family resort that can provide two miles of private access to the West Branch, but endorses fun for everyone. Caucci's fly-fishing school is famous, accommodating the beginner or the experienced. Visitors can stay in the campground with their own equipment or rent cabins with maid service. There are also motel units.

Patrons may rent canoes, hire a guide, purchase tackle, and buy a book. For children and nonfishers, there are swimming pools, kids' playgrounds, a game room, ponds, and hiking trails. Caucci is often there to teach bugs and casting, and we must report that he once chose Temple University, although we have yet to ask him if he knew Bill Cosby. If you do nothing but visit the Resort for a few minutes, take a close look at a copy of *Hatches II* by Caucci and Nastasi.

From Caucci's Delaware River Club, head back east to Route 191 and the Delaware River Fly Shop. About one mile south of the Fly Shop, where 191 meets Route 370 in Wayne County, is a relatively new access area. It's so new that it has no name, but some folks are calling it the Shehawken Launch. In fact, Shehawken Creek parallels 370 roughly from Starlight to Preston Park, and you might want to give it a try. The entrance to this new access is only a dirt road off to the left as you head south on 191, with a "Pennsylvania Fish and Boat Commission" sign. The dirt road dead-ends at a parking area. When you stand on the Pennsylvania bank, you are just north of Junction Pool—just above the junction, that is, where the West Branch meets the East Branch to become the main stem of the Delaware.

Enjoy yourself here. This access opened in 1995, and people are still discovering it. There is plenty of room to fish, and there are plenty of fish for those with a little skill and more patience. From the bank at the parking area, a fisher can walk north or south with ease, in the water or out of it. Spin casting and bait casting with live minnows will produce a strike if you reel in fairly slowly, letting the current carry your "wounded" bait. We have also used Mepps spinners and rooster tails here with some success.

Fly-fishers can expect roughly the same hatches as they encounter at Balls Eddy, but in July and August try terrestials, too: grasshopper patterns, small beetles, and red and brown ants. If fish are rising in the late afternoon, watch the hatch carefully; if the Caddis flies and Blue-winged Olives fail and you don't go home angry, then tie on a Light Cahill or Blue Dun. If these fail, too, leave and go get a beer. Or tie on a #16 Adams, and later take a photo of the 20-inch brown trout you will have caught. Sure.

This is a story that turned serious.

I was at the new access for the first time, and as usual I talked to a fisher about what was happening on the water. He showed me the flies he'd tied up for this trip, and he told me a couple of conventional whoppers about the fish he'd caught. He said there was a giant trout just to the south of the parking area. He told me, too, that there was a positively stunning young woman fishing there with her mother. She was a novice with a little talent, but I should be sure to watch her, he said with an unappealing grin.

I went where he had directed me, but I saw neither a huge trout nor a young beauty. There was an older woman fishing diligently—and well—with a spinning rod, and I watched her hook a small rainbow and release it. Downstream about thirty yards, I began my casting, still glancing about for the girl when, almost negligently, I hooked that monster trout on a #18 Adams. This fish was huge by my modest standards, and I was almost sick with excitement. It even tore off enough line that

*it got into my backing, and that let me know I was well hooked even if
the fish wasn't. I fought that trout for about 10 minutes, and several
watchers gathered.*

*The fish broke off my #6 tippet because, for a moment, I foolishly
dropped my rod tip and let it point at Moby Dick. As soon as the rod was
not bent, it lost its spring, and the trout easily broke a too-taut tippet. I
reeled in the limp line, looked back at my audience, shook my head, and
then suddenly saw the girl. I was, in fact, stunned. She was truly beautiful, and from the distance, radiant. She was wearing shorts, a loose
T-shirt, and dirty sneakers for wading. She moved with grace. Her smile
was large, very large, and I was intensely feeling my failure with the fish
when I heard her laugh. I don't recall seeing beauty as instantaneous in
its impact; there was a hint of exoticism mixed with the childish, a touch
of the Oriental, perhaps, but strangeness certainly. I just reeled in and
slouched on back toward my car.*

*She was ahead of me, and when I arrived at the path to the parking
area, I saw that she was standing in the water, talking to her mother, the
woman with the spinning rig who had caught the rainbow. The girl was
laughing and nodding at me. I tried to nod, but she continued to laugh.
That laughter, I suddenly realized, was not derisive. Up close, the laughter's silver brilliance dissolved. She laid her head on her mother's shoulder, and the older woman held the girl's hand as they walked up the path.
The girl was still laughing. Her mother looked at me and said quietly
that her daughter was not laughing at me, that she had behaved that
way since she had been a child, and she was still a child.*

*Hand in hand, they walked up the path. As they disappeared, I
heard that laughter once more, and I fogged up. I still do. But I'm glad
I was there to feel it all, even my own foolishness. Sometimes, going fishing can be awfully important. —R.M.*

THE EAST BRANCH OF THE DELAWARE

Special Dining

The Delaware's East Branch joins the West Branch just below the Hancock Bridge at Junction Pool, but the best route to get a decent fishing spot
is N.Y. Route 17, heading east out of Hancock. Before we get the fishers to
the water, however, we suggest the gourmets take time to visit Ray Turner
Jr.'s Delaware Delicacies Smoke House in Hancock, (607) 637-4443. Call

ahead for directions and then go on a spree and buy smoked fish and fowl. Our favorite is the trout filet, but the salmon is fine, and we're told by folks who can down 'em that the eels are best. Dandy! You can even get live eels here. Smoked turkey, duckling, and Cornish game hens make up the fowl offerings, and all three are delicious. We like to bring along olive oil, tomatoes, fresh basil, Stilton or Brie, and the best bread and best inexpensive Chardonnay, and head for the woods for a family picnic. If you have the opportunity, talk with Ray Turner. He is a fascinating philospher, naturalist, and chef.

Junction Pool

Now, after the picnic, let's get to that sewage treatment plant we mentioned earlier. The plant does not much adversely affect the river, but it's a geographical check point as we head toward Junction Pool.

The Pool is a good fishing spot, especially for trout. Drive out of Hancock on N.Y. Route 97 and cross a bridge over the East Branch. A little less than a mile west of the bridge, look for a road to the right that takes you to a factory named Bard Parker. These folks do not want to see you; their property is posted. So, turn left at the factory entrance and look for the sewage treatment plant. You can park near the entrance to the plant. Then follow a path along the plant's fence until you reach the river. This will put you on the main stem of the Delaware, so walk upstream to Junction Pool, fishing along the way.

East Branch

From Hancock, N.Y. Route 17 east will take you to the town of East Branch and the junction with N.Y. Route 30. If you stay on Route 17, you'll land in Roscoe and the Livingston Manor—but we've been there. Take Route 30 to Downsville and the Pepacton Reservoir. From the town of East Branch to Downsville, Route 30 parallels the water, and there is easy access to the river's East Branch. The hatches here are really prolific, but if you have any doubts about access, be sure to ask the landowner for permission.

Pepacton

Pepacton is a 7,000-acre impoundment that is one of three water-supply reservoirs for New York City. At certain times, the water level in Pepacton must be lowered to reduce the potential for flooding downstream. This step was authorized, for example, in February 1997 by the Delaware River Basin

Commission, which manages the nearly 14,000-square mile area. Swollen to 99 percent of its capacity by heavy rains, Pepacton, with nearly 140 billion gallons of water, had to be bled. In the spring of 1996, the huge snowfalls and rains led to what *Trout*, the magazine of Trout Unlimited, called "trout habitat destruction of the most brutal kind." Flooding caused a great deal of havoc to the Upper Delaware's East Branch area, but what happened afterward was even worse. Here is how Peter A. Rafle, Jr., editor of *Trout*, described it in a deeply disturbing article, "A Bulldozer Runs Through It," in the magazine's Winter 1997 issue:

"On tributary after tributary, crews began to remove the vast quantities of gravel and cobble that the flood waters had deposited in the stream bottom. What was left, in many cases, was something that looked more like a Louisiana levee than a mountain trout stream. As bulldozers plowed down the center of the channel, berms were constructed on either side—in some places to a height of ten feet or more. The stream-bottom itself was scraped off, replacing the plunge pools, riffles, and pocket water with a featureless channel." In at least two dozen Delaware tributaries, Rafle wrote, the "bulldozing ranged from stretches of a few dozen yards cleared of flood debris to reaches hundreds of yards long channelized in a fashion that would have done the Army Corps of Engineers proud."

You get the picture. Trout Unlimited and other conservationists went to war with the oxymoronic New York State Department of Environmental Conservation to correct the damage.

But let's return to Pepacton. There is a lot of fishing available there from the banks or, more effectively, from a boat. You will be fishing for large brown trout, so bring tackle that can go deep.

At this point on the East Branch, the reader should reflect on just where he or she is situated. Think for a moment on your good fortune: you have for exploration the Catskill Mountains and Catskill Park to your south. You can keep going along Route 30, stopping, of course, to fish until you find Route 28 and follow it for about thirty-five miles to scenic Ashokan Reservoir, where the natural beauty is free. From Ashokan you are just a few miles from the Hudson River, from the "Great War" airplanes at Rinebeck, and within striking distance of the entire Hudson Valley.

But if at Pepacton you decide to head for the Beaverkill and Willowemoc, take Route 30 back west and follow it to the junction with Route 206, then south on 206 into Roscoe, Rockland, and Livingston Manor, where you can again fish your heart out. The prospects are fine indeed, and a family with fishers and youngsters can spend a wonderful vacation in the area.

Dining

However, if you return to Hancock, it's time for a cocktail, dinner, and a pleasant place to sleep. We suggest you drive a little farther, across to Pennsylvania, and try the Starlight Inn at Starlight, Pa. Take Route 191 south to 370, make a right, and follow the signs to the inn. It's best to call ahead for reservations, (717) 798-2519 or (800) 248-2519, and you could well plan to spend to stay for a night, a weekend, or a week. This is a good place with plenty of amenities, good food, good libations at the Stovepipe Bar, and sensible prices—and it really is on a lakeside, so there is more for the fisher and the family.

The inn has its own row boats, sailboats, and canoes for the lake, which is impressively clean and clear, with plenty of panfish. Tennis, swimming, biking, and hiking are available and encouraged. Boats and bikes are free to guests. In winter, the ice fisher may want to send the nonfishers out skiing on the inn's own network of ski trails. (Or send them to ski Elk Mountain, in neighboring Susquehanna County.)

Starlight Inn has nicely appointed rooms, circa 1900s, in the Main House, and there are a variety of cottage rooms, along with the three-bedroom house. But we believe the food is central. The hosts, Jack and Judy McMahon—who had the good sense to send both of their children to Temple University—have set a high standard of quality. You will find smoked trout and smoked Cornish game hen, and if you have read carefully or visited the aforementioned Delaware Delicacies Smoke House in Hancock, you will know that Ray Turner, Jr., is the source of these delicacies. Also at the Starlight, the black bean crepes are excellent, and for us the roast leg of lamb is on the push list. Get the homemade desserts. Drink the espresso and sip the Cognac. Die happy and wake up in fishing heaven!

You might like to try the Starlight Lodge, (717) 798-2350, also in Starlight, of course. This is a bed-and-breakfast inn within a large log structure, and hosts Pat and Beth Schuler claim that a stay in their lodge is a unique experience. The country breakfast is assuredly unique, and the lodge caters especially to fly-fishers. There is also the Nethercott Inn Bed & Breakfast in Starucca, a 100-year-old Victorian building furnished in antiques, (717) 727-2211.

If none of these suggestions for food and lodging are appealing, contact the Penn York Bed & Breakfast & Lodging Association, P.O. Box 746, Hancock, NY 13783, for a listing of other places, all of which are within a fifty-mile radius of Hancock.

BUCKINGHAM

If you follow Pa. Route 191 south from Hancock for about six miles, you will see a small sign on the left for the Buckingham access. Route 191 actually parallels the river from Hancock to Equinunk, but public access to the river along this stretch is almost impossible. Most of the land is private and posted, and parking along the highway is difficult, except for a couple of places—and at those places you practically need mountain-climbing experience to get down to the river. In general, forget it unless you are fortunate enough to get a landowner's permission to cross the property. Above all, do get permission before crashing through.

Buckingham is a nice public access point; when the water is down some, you can wade the width of the river. But there are occasional rough, rocky areas—and river holes—that demand your care. The fishing is good here, up or down the river. We have had our best success nymphing for trout with bead heads or weighted flies, but Blue-winged Olives are good through the spring and summer. If you catch it, the Green-drake hatch is fine—usually in late May or early June.

Although we have been told that the best smallmouth bass fishing is south of Callicoon, we know better. Hellgrammites at Buckingham along the New York bank have worked well for us on a fly rod, and live baits, minnows, and crawdads, are great with spinning or bait-casting gear.

EQUINUNK AND LORDVILLE

Dining

From Buckingham, head south on Route 191 for about two miles to the little town of Equinunk, home of one of our favorite watering holes, Carole's Bar. The official name is probably the Equinunk Inn, but after after 15 or so years of patronage we know it simply as Carole's, namesake of the owner, operator, bartender, and sometimes cook, Carole Dennis.

Coming from Buckingham, make the only left in Equinunk you can make off Route 191; go the equivalent of a block (see the mobile homes on the left) and then turn left into the parking lot. There is no sign, but you won't miss it.

Once inside, you might be tempted to be outside again. Don't leave. The clientele is not exactly the jet set, but you have found good drinking companions and storytellers. Try to be worthy of them. Also inside is a pool table, a jukebox with country music, a sign advertising "boneless chicken" (hard-cooked eggs), and incredible—and priceless—antiques hanging from the walls and ceiling in every direction.

One frigid April day when snow was blowing, we met an old fellow in Carole's who could not have weighed a hundred pounds. He was then well past bedtime in his drinking. We learned that he had been arrested so many times for DUI that he had lost his car and probably would not live enough years to get another driver's license. He had come into Carole's from the surrounding hills driving his lawn tractor. But now the snow was too heavy for an old man on a lawn tractor. Would we take him home? Of course we would and did. —R.M.

Carole collects antiques, and she has old lanterns, signs, posters, bottles, farm implements, and Christmas decorations that have been hanging for a long time. These things are fascinating, even with their original dust. Don't try to buy them. She won't sell. But she might be able to find something similar if a person is really interested. And if Carole won't deal, there is an antique shop on the corner of Route 191 and SR 1023.

There is a pool table, but if a player must move to the east side of the table for a shot, you who are sitting at the bar could get jabbed with a cue. Don't leap; just smile. The player will always apologize. Carole will cook a pizza or burger, but she's a much better bartender. She's got a wry sense of humor and an infectious laugh, and if you are decent and kind, she might give you permission to cross her property out back to the river. We hope you earn the privilege.

Fishless, frustrated and thirsty, we make the walk from the river, stow our gear, and enter the sanctuary of Carole's Bar.

As we sit down on the stools, Carole pulls out a metal tray with ice cubes and a 20-inch natural brown trout reposing on them. "You guys

*wanna see a trout? Take a look at this one!" she tells us, informing and
teasing at the same time.*

"Who caught that?" asks a regular.

"Cos—and he got this for me today out back."

*While the Philadelphia crowd gawks at the largest brown trout since
we fished Lake Ontario, the local says, "What did he catch it on?"*

*"I dunno," says Carole, putting the metal tray and its spotted deni-
zen back into her beer box. "He comes here every afternoon and ties flies
at the bar and goes out there to the river."*

*"Carole," pleads the local. "You tell Cos to leave me somma them
flies tomorrow, you hear?" —G.I.*

Once you get permission to go "out back" (don't count on it), gear up
in the parking lot (use chest waders; hip boots won't help much here), and
from the back of the bar walk straight to the Delaware. You will be just north
of the spot where the Equinunk Creek enters the Delaware, and on a pleasant spring, summer, or early fall day, this is a good place to be. Wade down
to the junction of the creek, and you might hook a trophy brown trout,
especially in the spring. Further down, by the cliff, some big smallmouths
and walleyes are known to lurk in late October and November.

If you wade upstream a hundred yards or more, you will do well in the
summer and fall. But if the water is up, wading can be difficult. If the river
is moderately low, then wade toward the New York side and fish the opposite
bank for trout. Keep an eye on the riffles and watch for jumping fish and
for rises in the seams and pockets. If you are getting skunked, go on back
to Carole's and wait for dusk, especially in the summer, and return to work
nymphs and wet flies. Late afternoon and night fishing can be very productive, but wade carefully.

A Hellgrammite or #12 or #14 Gold-ribbed Hare's Ear on a sinking tip
fly line might produce a good-sized smallmouth bass or a major brown
trout, as we have learned from experience. When the nymph is on the bottom where it should be, either species is a possibility. In addition, in late
spring shad fishing is a good bet at this location.

A word of caution: watch out for the U.S. National Park Service. These
young, humorless, uniformed people have been known to float down the
river in canoes. Armed with 9mm handguns, they seek out potential felons
who are foolish enough to fish without licenses. In most of the river bars on
the Upper Delaware, NPS personnel aren't welcome—and you will be as
welcome as an anti-gun advocate if you're a supporter of the Service. One

afternoon in Carole's, we saw a tipsy young man invite any "NFS lovers" in the bar outside for a friendly fistfight. Of course, during the summer months, some nasty drunks sometime float the river, too, and even the independent folks of the Upper River recognize the need for some law enforcement.

Most folks, other than locals, fish this section of the Delaware on the New York side, at Lordville. To get there, come out of the parking lot at Carole's bar and turn left, heading east. Cross the new Lordville Bridge and park in the lot. (If you come south on N.Y. Route 97, turn right onto Lordville Road and travel several miles to the bridge.)

Work the deep pool at the bridge, or continue three-quarters of a mile below the bridge and fish the riff. For more fishing, look for the dirt road just beyond the railroad tracks near the bridge. Turn right onto the dirt road (there is a dead-end sign), and it will lead you to an access point after about three miles, where you can park and walk to the river.

If you are in the Equinunk area for the opening of trout season, you might want to spend some time on the Equinunk Creek. The Pennsylvania Fish and Boat Commission stocks the creek before Opening Day from the creek's mouth at the Delaware to the point where TR 724 intercepts SR 4007, about four miles upstream from the mouth. For us, the best time to fish this once-fine trout stream is a week or two after Opening Day. The fish are hatchery raised, with deformed fins and such, but they will fight. In the first week of the season, the trout will eat virtually anything you throw in, which is depressing. After a couple of hours on the Equinunk, you will probably want to return to the Delaware—or to Carole's bar.

Other Attractions

The small town of Equinunk is an interesting and historic place. There is a general store for gasoline, groceries, and knickknacks. Across the street is an antique shop. We regularly spend time in the Equinunk Historical Society, Route 191 and Pine Mill Road, (717) 224-6722. In fact, we liked it so much that we joined. Individual membership is $5, family membership $12. The displays, featuring local historical materials, include arts and crafts, photos, books, historical documents, and a Native American dugout canoe in the basement. Here is American material culture in its raw form, and we believe this to be a modest but first-rate local historical society. The volunteer docents are very good. The Equinunk Historical Society is also restoring the Joe Hill Sawmill nearby. Those who visit the lavish and wonderful Independence National Historical Park, far down the river in Philadelphia, should see what a small, dedicated group of local citizens have accomplished in Equinunk. (Some of our Japanese friends actually preferred the little historical society to the big Historical Park in Philadelphia.)

One final note: try to arrange a visit to Equinunk during the town's once-a-year fire company barbecue, featuring chicken and shrimp. It usually takes place late in July.

EQUINUNK TO DAMASCUS

Once you leave Equinunk heading south on Route 191, the highway leaves the Delaware River, which flows east by southeast to Callicoon. Route 191 takes you south and a little southwest to the tiny village of Rileyville (where the Grange Hall hosts an occasional, but usually good, flea market). At the stop sign in Rileyville, you can go west on Route 371 to find your way to Lower Woods Pond, Upper Woods Pond, and the intriguing Dyberry Creek. Or you can head east on 371 to Damascus on the Pennsylvania side of the Delaware and Cochecton on the New York side.

Meanwhile, if you want to fish somewhere between Equinunk and Damascus, you can do it easily, but you must use N.Y. Route 97, which leaves the main stem of the river about three miles south of Hancock and doesn't return until Long Eddy.

Long Eddy and Hankins

There is a boat launch at Long Eddy, and Ginger's Country Restaurant offers reasonable victuals. But the fishing is best about a half mile south of Long Eddy, where Basket Creek empties into the Delaware. Route 97 south of Long Eddy will take you to Hankins, where there are several canoe rental outfits. Access to the river is difficult, but ask at the canoe rental establishments, and have a meal at the Hankins House. Keep going south on Route 97 and you will arrive in Callicoon. You can also get there by driving south on Pa. Route 191 and taking a left on SR 1016. Cross the Little Equinunk Creek and follow Route 1016 to Callicoon. (There's a Callicoon, Pa., and a Callicoon, N.Y., on the other side of the river.) If it happens to be springtime, park at the Little Equinunk on the Pennsylvania side, gear up, and march up or downstream.

The Little Equinunk

The Little Equinunk is stocked before opening day in April, and we have fished it without finding too many other fishers there. In fact, we have fished it from Duck Harbor Pond, just south of SR 1016 on Route 191, to a point about a mile north of the bridge where you parked.

Here we have caught more native trout (feisty little fighters, usually brown trout and an occasional rainbow with bright colors) than stocked fish, and that's unusual. We used tiny black midges (#22 and #24) on an Orvis 1-ounce fly rod with a double-taper, 3-weight line and a #7 tippet. On that rig, those little fish felt twice their size. There are monsters in the Little Equinunk—when you create them yourself!

Hollister Creek

After leaving the Little Equinunk and continuing eastward on SR 1016, you will pass Snyder Pond, which feeds Hollister Creek, on the left. Follow the creek, first on the right and then on the left, to Callicoon. Before the season opens, Hollister Creek is stocked from TR 670 downstream for about a mile and a half. There are also a few native trout, but we know that by hearsay and not personal experience. Hollister Creek is narrow and therefore not much fun for your typical, fly rod-challenged person.

Callicoon and Cochecton

Once in Callicoon—either the New York or Pennsylvania side—you will have a convenient access point for the Delaware and for launching a boat. On the New York side there's Callicoon Creek upstream from the access point. If you fish this productive stream, be sure to have a valid New York State license. Otherwise, fishers licensed in the Keystone State should try the riffles in the river downstream of the Callicoon Bridge for trout and smallmouth bass. (You'll also find shad here in the spring.) Then, after a day's angling, fishers often retire to the Autumn Inn or to Club 97, both on the New York side, for sometimes fair fare.

If you leave Callicoon on N.Y. Route 97, you will arrive in Cochecton and the Cheers Bar. The access for boat launching is the province of the New York Department of Environmental Conservation, and the site is a favorite spot for putting in canoes and rafts.

Dave Plasket and I discovered Cheers Bar after a day's outing on the Delaware, but we hadn't counted on the bear story, which wasn't a tale told by Faulkner. It was recounted by a local farmer, and it remains embedded in my memory:

"My neighbor was havin' trouble with a bear, and he asked me to help him git it. So one morning I laid out there with my rifle. Now, I really didn't want to shoot no bear, but I wanted to help my neighbor, so I waited. Not long afterwards, I seen this big black bear comin' out, and I shot him dead. Now what would we do? My friend says, 'Let's get him over to the barn so we can gut 'em and hang 'em up.'

"So we got the tractor and drug him over to the barn. My neighbor says, 'Let's get 'em inside and throw a line over one of the joists.' So we drug the bear inside. My friend tied a rope around the bear, then threw the line over the wooden joist. We both got on one end of the rope and pulled. We pulled, and we pulled. We'd just about got the bear up when the joist broke, and the roof come tumblin' down on us. That damn bear cost him a heck of a lot of money, and almost cost us our lives!" —G.I.

Damascus

From Cochecton, cross the river again into Pennsylvania and you will be at Damascus, which offers boat launching. The Damascus launch is best in the spring because the water is generally too shallow for an easy launch in the summer. But the Delaware at this spot is easy to wade, and the fishing, north and south of the bridge, is promising, with plenty of eddies, riffles, and flats. On a fly rod we have taken some nice smallmouths with Hellgrammite imitations, and on ultra-light spinning rod we have done well using deep-diving crankbaits, especially crawfish imitations, and Mepps's Aglia. Panfish are everywhere. Damascus is an excellent spot for springtime shad fishing, but we have had less success with the trout population.

It was late spring, and I'd promised the Dean that I'd take him shad fishing on the Upper Delaware. When we drove up to the public access at Damascus, there were probably 15 anglers north of the bridge to Cochecton, casting shad darts into the river without any success. The Dean and I gathered our gear and slipped on our waders. He decided to try his luck on a little spit of land south of the access site. I went to the other side of the bridge, where all the other anglers were podded up. They gave me scant attention when I arrived. I stood on the bank for several minutes, watching what my fellow fishers were doing. Then I tied on a large white

*and red shad dart at the terminal of a nice Pflueger rod I have used in
both saltwater, for fluke, and freshwater, for shad. I made one cast just
north of the bridge foundations and retrieved the lure. I made a second
cast. Bang! I had a large roe shad on my line and brought it onto shore,
much to the surprise of the Dean, and to irritation of the hapless anglers
who had caught zilch. —G.I.*

If you plan to use a boat to head south of Cochecton-Damascus, we say
don't. Don't do it unless you are an accomplished canoeist, capable of stopping in front of a haystack before moving laterally left or right. Skinners
Falls, a couple of miles south, and close to Milanville, is one of the most
dangerous rapids on the Delaware. You won't fish there, and you may have
to fight for your life there. Instead, go just south of Skinners Falls to fish for
plentiful smallmouths and an occasional walleye in the fall. You can use
N.Y. Route 97 or, on the Pennsylvania side, come south from Damascus on
SR 1004 to Milanville and continue south on SR 1017, which can take you
to the bridge over to Narrowsburg, New York.

FISHING AND PLAYING ALONG PENNSYLVANIA ROUTE 371

*"One of the best places to fish in spring is a good farm pond, but it's a
hard deal to land. Farm ponds generally are private, difficult to get
permission to fish, and in this era of ever-expanding suburbs, just plain
tough to find."*

— ANGUS PHILLIPS, *The Washington Post*

Before continuing south on the Delaware, consider the Dyberry Creek and
surrounding areas in Pennsylvania's Wayne County, including Lower and
Upper Woods Ponds, the Fireside Restaurant, the Red Schoolhouse, the
town of Honesdale, and the annual Wayne County Fair. But first take a fishing trip along Route 371.

From Damascus, follow 371, through the little town of Rileyville at
Route 191. There's a small restaurant at the corner that has gasoline pumps
that work sometimes. A quarter-mile farther on 371, keep an eye peeled to
find the road to Rose Pond and thence to Duck Harbor Pond. (An easier
access to Duck Harbor Pond is from 191 north of Rileyville.) Heading west

on 371, the next stop is Alder Marsh Brook, which crosses 371 on its way to feed the East Branch of the Dyberry. Despite reports of native brook and brown trout, we have never had any success on Alder Marsh Brook.

Immediately after Alder Marsh Brook is the bridge over the East Branch of the Dyberry. A fisher can drive across the bridge and turn south onto SR 1023, which parallels the East Branch until 1023 dead-ends at SR 4007. SR 4007 then parallels the East Branch to the point where the East and West Branches of the Dyberry join to form the creek's main stem.

Except for a posted section south of the bridge at 371, the East Branch is readily accessible. It really is a pretty stream, and it is stocked four times a year, with the final stocking in mid-May. Spring, then, is the season for the best fishing, but when there have been wet summers, we have caught fish throughout the trout season, and frequently we have played small wild browns.

Continuing westward on 371, your next stop is Lower Woods Pond, which is north of the highway. Look for a small sign on your right. Lower Woods is attractive, but it is not stocked with trout. Largemouth bass and panfish are promising, however.

A little further west is the tiny crossroads village of Cold Springs, or Cold Spring, as it appears on some maps. At the southwest corner of the crossroad you will see one of the nation's smallest chapels (white, of course), with the longest sermons in the east, or so we have been told. At the intersection, look for a small sign that says "Upper Woods Pond," and make a right turn.

Upper Woods Pond is in the northern section of State Game Land 159. Maintained and stocked with rainbows by the Fish and Boat Commission, Upper Woods is well worth a visit. There may be, in fact, some kokanee salmon from a stocking experiment that ended in 1990. Upper Woods Pond also has a boat launch, plenty of parking, and toilet facilities. It's a lovely area, and we regularly picnic there.

Fishing on Upper Woods Pond can be great, but you really need a boat (no internal combustion engines are allowed); a canoe is just fine. Be sure your boat is properly registered. Trout fishing is especially good along the north and east banks. Along the south bank you can go very deep—up to eighty feet or more. Despite the plentiful fish, fishing pressure here is not too intense because not many outsiders visit the Pond. Local people, however, are pleased with this gem. Ice fishing is also a good possibility, as long as you do it when it's legal.

It was February, and my daughter Pamela reminded me that I had never taken her ice fishing. So we packed our gear and drove up one Friday night from Philadelphia to a trailer a group of us were renting in Wayne County. Next morning, we headed to the nearby Upper Woods Pond, which was covered with a thick sheath of ice. But there was something wrong—this was Saturday morning, and not a single soul was out on the ice fishing.

We collected our gear, including a manual ice auger, tip-ups, a spoon with holes to keep our fishing holes ice-free, and some light rods. The ice cracked slightly as we walked out, solitary anglers in pursuit of cold and hungry fish underneath. Upper Woods was beautiful, white and ice covered under a bright blue sky. I drilled several holes and showed my daughter how to jig at different depths.

Suddenly a Pennsylvania Fish and Boat Commission jeep pulled up at the boat landing, and the fish warden walked toward us. I assumed he wanted to check our licenses, so I greeted him warmly.

"Catch anything?" he asked matter-of-factly.

"No sir, we just got here," I told him, turning around so he could inspect the valid nonresident license on my back.

"Well, I'm afraid you're in a little bit of trouble. This area is closed for trout stocking. You're in violation of the law."

I shuddered. It was like getting my first speeding ticket.

"Damn!" I blurted out, more angry at my own stupidity for not checking the regulations. "I wondered why there weren't any other fishermen out here when we arrived."

"That's usually a pretty good sign," the warden said, with just a hint of a smile on his face.

So, my lesson cost me $25. The warden, by the way, was a decent guy. He could have fined Pam, too, but chose not to. —G.I.

Continuing west on 371, the next stop after Cold Spring is the Middle Branch of the Dyberry. Just before a bridge over the creek is a parking lot on the left for the State Game Land. The Middle Branch has been disappointing for us. It is not stocked, and we have lusted after native trout, only to return home frustrated. But other fishers have succeeded.

After about three-quarters of a mile west of the Middle Branch, Route 371 crosses the West Branch of the Dyberry. Because of posted land, there is virtually no fishing at this point on the West Branch. A short distance away, Route 371 comes to a screeching dead end at Route 247. A left turn onto 247 sets you on your way to a good country meal at the Red School-house Restaurant.

Dining

We must tell you up front that the Red Schoolhouse has always been one of our favorite country eateries. The food is rich (saturated fats and cholesterol), usually tasty, and reasonable. There are pool tables, a horse-shoe bar, and a jukebox. Hunters and fishers are welcome, but most of the people who regularly patronize the place live nearby, and they know what they are about. Farmers gather in this large, plain building for cold beers and conversation, but if you are visiting for the first time, then order the Ace of Hearts, a buffalo steak, for $8.95. The Buffalo Burger, with fried onions, is the best one this side of the Bison Burger served up by The Fire-place Restaurant on U.S. 6, three miles west of Tunkhannock. Of course, more traditional food is there for the asking, and there is a salad bar.

THE DYBERRY CREEK PROPER AND THE WEST BRANCH FROM THE SOUTH

Cold Spring, you'll recall, is located at the tiny chapel where Route 371 crosses SR 4007. Turn south from 371 onto 4007, which passes the summer home of Metropolitan Opera star Paul Plishka before coming to the south-ern section of State Game Land 158 and the East Branch of the Dyberry, where the road meets SR 1023. As a geographical marker, look for a sign directing you to a rifle range. Continue south on 4007 (you may have to dodge a few wild turkeys) to the bridge crossing the West Branch of the Dyberry. Just before this bridge, there is a dirt road on your right that will take you on a bumpy, muffler-squashing ride to the lovely Tanners Falls. We have more to say about this place below.

Dyberry Proper

If you cross the bridge on 4007, you will shortly cross a second one that spans the main Dyberry before reaching the upstream end of the Delayed-Harvest, Fly-fishing-Only section of the creek. (If you drive further south to

the next and third bridge, the Mary Wilcox Bridge, you will be at the end
of the Delayed-Harvest section.)

*My son had come in from California to go deer hunting with me and my
friends in Wayne County. It was the Monday after Thanksgiving, the
traditional start of the season in Pennsylvania. But George had another
monkey on his back. "I've got to go fly-fishing, Dad!" he told me on
Friday, after we had arrived from Philadelphia at our trailer in Cold
Spring. It was about 28° outside, but how could a responsible father
refuse a son's request to go fishing? I gave him a fly rod, and we drove
down to the second bridge over the Dyberry, where the road was blocked
because workmen were building a new span over the creek. When George
got out of the car, snow was beginning to whip across the adjacent fields.
But he wanted to fish, had to fish. He went to the bank and began casting
with that easy, natural cast that I'd always secretly admired. Construction workers on the bridge saw him, and as the white flakes flew, they
broke out in a spontaneous burst of cheers and applause for a kid who
just had to go fishing. I sat in the heated car until George returned, red
from the cold but happy just to have fished. —G.I.*

After you cross the second bridge, you will pass a small private pond on
the left; then keep your eyes to the right and look for several mail boxes on
that side, with a dirt road opposite the boxes. You won't readily find this
northern end of the Delayed-Harvest section unless you are careful. Once
you home in on those mail boxes, however, you're in business. Park as
best you can, walk behind the mail boxes, and slip down to the creek. You
have arrived. From the mail boxes, fish downstream with a fly rod for the
Delayed-Harvest area, and fish upstream with your favorite equipment for
open fishing in a stocked stream.

The Dyberry has received some bad press over the years, especially
since the drought of 1988 when whole sections completely dried up, wiping
out most of the trout. At that time, we watched gray herons and hungry
raccoons catch and devour trapped fish. It was Darwinian ugly. And the first
time we saw the thrashing and splashing that marked an American eel killing a trout, we went after the eel in the riffles; that sight was not nice, either.

The eels come up from the Delaware, up the Lackawaxen River, and into the Dyberry. Charles Meck, who also comments on the 'coons, eels, and herons in his *Pennsylvania Trout Streams and Their Hatches*, wrote that the serious trout fisher would choose the Delaware and Lackawaxen Rivers over the Dyberry. As he put it, "Why place stream improvement devices on the Dyberry, when the fantastic Delaware is only ten miles away?"

We disagree, but we don't want to argue, because there is plenty of room on the Delaware for people the Dyberry doesn't need. After spring stocking, we know that fishing pressure on the creek is indeed heavy, but the Delayed-Harvest, Fly-fishing-Only section escapes some of that intensity because most folks prefer spin or bait casting, especially with live minnows and worms. Too many want to keep what they catch, but the rules say that fishers in a Delayed-Harvest zone can't keep fish until after June 15.

My wife and I were driving to dinner along the East Branch of the Dyberry one spring evening. Just north of the road to Tanners Falls we spotted a fish hatchery truck that was pulling over to dump its cargo into the stream. Behind the hatchery truck was a small caravan of about a half-dozen cars and pick-up trucks, and they darted to the road's shoulder when the hatchery truck parked. We were being offered an opportunity to see the Fish and Boat Commission in operation.

We parked also. At least 12 men jumped from their cars and trucks, tumbled down the bank to the water, and began fishing. The men from the hatchery truck (which probably came from the State's hatchery on 371, west of Cold Spring) dumped buckets of wriggling trout into the pool that the fishing fools surrounded. As the trout were "stocked," the human predators were yanking them out. These guys were keeping every fish, even as they glanced guiltily at the hatchery employees.

Here on Dyberry Creek, old Satan was at work; here was evidence of the psychological truth of original sin. At that moment, we believed these guys were fundamentally corrupt. If they had licenses and kept no more fish than their limit, they were within the law. But the obvious disdain for sportsmanship and, more depressing, the demonstration of raw greed were awful.

When I talked to the driver of the hatchery truck, he told me that it was usually the same group. But, he said, similar things take place all over the State. George Ingram and I had seen something like it on the Little Kettle Creek in Potter County when the hatchery workers emptied trout into the pool in which we were already fishing. We were surprised at such luck, but the fun soon wore thin after several carloads of men appeared. George and I kept one trout for dinner (which was cooked over a campfire in a rainstorm while we listened on a battery-operated short-wave radio to Radio Baghdad), but after that we both stopped keeping any trout.

My wife asked the hatchery truck driver if there wasn't a better time of day to stock the creek. He said he could not always stock in the morning to avoid—his word—the "cruds," and anyway someone always tipped them off to the schedule.

"Watch them," he said, "they're sharks."

We saw them stuffing fish into creels and plastic bags—and one big fellow was shoving fish into the top of his waders!

The driver pointed to one man and explained that they had gone to school together. The man, he said, wasn't rich, but could easily support his family. Yet the SOB had two huge freezers filled with trout and deer meat, for he poached deer out of season. The man, he said, was proud of himself and bragged about his "accomplishments."

My wife said she wanted to leave, and we did. —R.M.

The Main Stem of the Dyberry

Except for the gluttons, the Dyberry is accessible and pretty. The Fly-fishing-Only section has over-branching trees for cover, and is marked by riffles and pools that hold fish most of the year, and sometimes all year. We have caught trout through January, and on the West Branch south of Tanners Falls, we have taken natives fairly regularly throughout the fishing season. During dry summers, water temperatures can rise into the 70s by mid-June, but if there is average to above-average rain during the summer, many of the pools remain cool enough to support surprising numbers of fish.

If you enter the creek behind the mailboxes we mentioned and head south for the Fly-fishing-Only section, you'll come to a riffle about ten yards below the mailboxes. Begin your fishing from the west bank in the pool just below the riffles, and if you do not notice any hatches coming off the water, use a #16 Adams or a #10 or #12 attractor as a dry fly. Attractors or stimulators are versions of sorts of stone flies, and they often work here. We haven't seen all that many stone flies on the Dyberry, but the trout strike attractors and stimulators in what seems like anger. But also look for Sulphurs, Hendricksons, Quills (Red, Gordons, and Blue), March Browns, and Caddis flies.

For nymph fishing—and the creek can do a booming business in nymphing—use versions of the Gold-ribbed Hare's Ear, notably the natural Hare's Ear with a bead head. A bead-headed Prince or Pheasant Tail works well, as does the Slate Drake nymph. There is no need to use strike indicators, which are usually neon-red foam things that are squeezed onto the fly line about two to eight feet behing the nymph, depending on stream depth. Just keep a fairly tight line as you seek the most natural drift with the current, or use a large attractor as a strike indicator with your nymph tied to the end of the tippet. Be sure to keep your fly close to the east bank and get down deep, with lead-less split shot if need be, so that you lose a nymph or two on a submerged log that by now is at least 90 percent snagged fishhooks.

Early in the season, streamers will work on the Dyberry, especially a Mickey Finn, Grey Ghost, Dace, or Muddler Minnow. Throughout the season, Red and Brown Ants and small Beetles will catch fish.

If you wear good sunglasses and get on your knees and stalk carefully, you can see trout feeding. Try it, unless some head-blown nut driving past on the road above you flings down an empty beer can, or unless you break your fly rod or something.

It was Christmas 1994, and I'd given myself a present: an Orvis HLS 1-ounce fly rod. Matched with a medium-priced reel and 4-weight fly line, I spent the winter looking at it. On decent days, I'd take it outside, tie on a tiny fly, and cast it into the snow flurries, waiting patiently for spring to arrive.

It happened to be a tough winter for the weather and for work, and I never got a chance to use my Christmas present until March, when Richie Lutman, Dave Plasket, and I made a trip to the Delayed-Harvest section of the Dyberry Creek, where fly-fishing is permitted virtually year-round.

We drove to the creek in Richie's big Bronco. With great expectation,

I pulled my new rod from its metal tube, attached the reel, threaded the fly line through the guides, and tied on a black nymph as a starter.

Richie was gearing up too. I put on my insulated chest waders because the water was still frigid. I placed my rod in the crack of the back door of the Bronco, and turned my attention to the waders. I have to confess that, when I left that expensive rod there, with the butt on the ground and the tip pointing to the sky, I had a fleeting sense of doom. But the feeling was only a nanosecond, because I trusted Richie.

I can still hear the door as it began to be slammed shut, and I can still hear me trying to cry out, as in a bad dream, "Richie, no!" and I can still hear the sickening crunch of the rod as it was destroyed in the slam of the Bronco's door. There was a long silence, punctuated by Richie's mea culpas. I almost cried.

Fortunately, Orvis stands by the company policy of replacing broken rods. "Looks like this one died a virgin," said the clerk at the Walnut Street shop in Philadelphia when he saw the clean cork handle. Within a few weeks, I had a new 1-ounce. But Richie Lutman won't go near any of my rods anymore. —G.I.

If you continue wading south, exploring as you go, various pools and riffles will appear, and fallen trees along the banks promise a strike. Several hundred yards downstream the creek narrows, followed by a deep pool next to a fallen tree; in high water, be careful to stay along the east bank. There are few, if any, fish in this pool, but if you wade on down about twenty-five yards there is another deep—very deep and dangerous—pool that holds fish. You should fish it from the western side, but use the east bank to get around the pool. That's easier said than done, especially after the grass and underbrush have grown up in the summer. But once around the pool you can make it to the Mary Wilcox Bridge and the end of the Delayed-Harvest, Fly-fishing-Only zone.

Return to the mailboxes and head north, upstream. Now you're no longer in the Delayed-Harvest zone. Nonetheless, this is a good place to fish at the start of trout season. In April, many other fishers will join you, especially on weekends, yet the fishing is good enough to justify the trip.

About two hundred yards upstream from the mailboxes is a deep pool just beneath a small falls. This pool is stocked heavily, and fishing is usually done with worms and minnows, which are scorned by the fly-rodder. There is, in fact, no reason for scorn whatever your bait. If you are fly-fishing in a crowd, go deep with weighted Wooly Buggers, Muddler Minnows, or Mickey

Finns. Otherwise, use an Adams or even a Royal Coachman. Matching the surface hatch early in the season won't help much here because the fishing pressure keeps trout down.

We like this entire section of the Dyberry, and for simple fishing pleasure the creek is first-rate. Into May and June, we have enjoyed the quiet, especially in the section from the mailboxes south. While fishing we have stood almost eye-to-eye with deer and gray foxes; we have talked to raccoons, chipmunks, and squirrels, and spotted all sorts of birds, including kingfishers, bluebirds, yellow finches, wrens, and wild turkeys. Once we dodged hummingbirds because we feared they were huge bees. (Emily Dickinson would have chuckled at us.)

Occasionally along the Dyberry, there are larger animals.

Early in my career as a Dyberry fisher, I waded south, nymphing carefully as I went. In less than an hour, using March Browns and Slate Drakes, I had caught and released about a dozen worthy browns and rainbows. It was a splendid day, bright sunlight splashing through the trees, with only the water and the birds making any sound. I was alone and at ease and pleased with the world and myself.

As I fished downstream, I discovered the first deep pool by a fallen tree. I was exploring a little when I heard what sounded like a large limb breaking off a tree. If you camp much, you know the "crack-in-the-forest" sound I'm talking about. Anyway, just after that "crack," I heard a loud thump, and I had to check it out. Scrambling up the bank, I stared into the woods, and no more than twenty yards away I saw a bear cub.

This little guy was sitting on the ground amidst the splinters of a large but rotten branch, and—I swear it—that cub was shaking its head, as if to remove cobwebs. It had fallen out of the tree when the bough broke, and I got to witness its embarrassment. In chest waders, I was on my knees on the crest of the bank, fly rod in hand, and in a state of wonder that I was chosen to see the show. Then I thought, "When baby bear falls, can the dam be far behind?"

As with Young Goodman Brown, the mere thought produced the thing in itself. Mother Bear came lumbering to her cub and spied me. I was not Ike McCaslin in Faulkner's "The Bear," and I didn't linger to

see the ticks on the bear's legs. Despite rod and waders, I was down that
bank, across the creek, and into the trees before I had a new thought—
which was to cease fishing for the day. I drove to the Fireside Inn and
had a turkey sandwich and drank more than one. —R.M.

Dining

We must comment on the Fireside Inn, (717) 253-0141, in more detail.
It's located on Route 191, north of Honesdale and just north of the village
of Dyberry. (After you leave Dyberry Village, keep your eyes to the right and
high up the road embankment.) The Fireside is a good place to know about
when you're on the Dyberry because it is easily accessible from the East
and West Branches of the creek and main stem. It's also a good place to
know about if you enjoy a big horseshoe bar with a large variety of beers,
including some nice German brews, a pool table, a variety band on weekends for dancing, and decent, standard American cooking (the meat-and-
potatoes kind). The variety of sandwiches is large, and so are the sandwiches themselves.

The Fireside is a family place, and owners Joe and Debbie Ranner intend to keep it that way. They cater to the local communities, to the families
and staff members of nearby children's summer camps, and to the crowd of
hunters and fishers. But Joe is especially partial to race cars. NASCAR is
evident throughout the bar area, and Joe himself has a racing car he drives
for the fun of it.

After more than a decade of patronizing the Fireside, we can report we
have always been treated with kindness and respect. One night stands
out in particular. George Ingram, Pat Staub, and my wife Jan and I
arrived with our tired and fussy infant, Mary Beth. George and I had
been fishing the Dyberry with minimal success, and we were also tired
and fussy. We had no reservation, and we were apprehensive about
Mary Beth's performance at dinner. Pat and Jan were apprehensive
about George's and my performance.

The head waiter, Jeff, is the Ranners' son-in-law. Without a request
from us, he took over everything, seating us in the empty back room where
we could enjoy privacy and not worry about the baby. He served the
Fireside's special vegetable appetizer platter, took drink orders, returned

with a huge blanket, and made a soft bed on the floor for Mary Beth. We enjoyed a quiet, leisurely dinner while Mary Beth happily slept. Such unsolicited kindness is rare today. —R.M.

For fishers at the Mary Wilcox Bridge (the south end of the Fly-fishing-Only section), parking is easy along SR 4009. There is a well-stocked pool at the bridge, but wading upstream can be a bit difficult because of fallen timber. There are paths that lead around obstructions, so persevere.

Little more than a quarter-mile south of the Mary Wilcox Bridge, SR 4009 dead-ends at TR 456. A left turn onto 456 brings fishers immediately to another bridge, which crosses a very nice pool that the Fish and Boat Commission stocks lavishly. The problem is that anglers fish it just as lavishly, and there are crowds at this site early in the season. The pool is fished out quickly, so we suggest that the eager angler of summer wade south for about one hundred yards. One may not catch much on this little jaunt, but it's a pretty walk.

TR 456 runs east into Route 191 and dead-ends. A left turn leads north to the Fireside Inn and back to Rileyville on Route 371. A right turn will take you to the General Edgar Jadwin Dam (with no water; it's there for flood control), then to the Wayne County Fair Grounds, and finally to Honesdale, the Wayne County seat.

The West Branch of the Dyberry and the Story of Tanners Falls

Perhaps the best place to begin fishing the West Branch is Tanners Falls. You might recall the first bridge you passed coming south on SR 4007 from Cold Spring. This bridge actually crosses the West Branch just where it flows into the main stem of the Dyberry. If you wanted to, you could park here and wade south in the main stem to reach the mailboxes at the beginning of the Fly-fishing-Only section.

But just a few yards north of the bridge is a dirt road heading west. Technically, this intersection is known as Tanners Falls, and that's what most maps label it. But local people refer to Tanners Fall as the pretty falls that you'd come up on if you took the dirt road west. This road is SR 4017, and it leads about a half-mile up the side of the mountain to the falls. A deep pool below the falls invites fishers, quiet meditation, and the occasional illegal swimmer.

Above the falls, an old and battered iron bridge—a worthy symbol for Commonwealth of Pennsylvania bridges in general—crosses over the West Branch. After you park, walk onto the bridge and look about. Beneath you and downstream are the falls, remains of the foundation of an old mill, the plunge pool, and the all-but-hidden exit of the West Branch from the pool. Upstream is quiet water between steep banks; there is a blocked service road on the east bank, which you may hike for the view but not for ready access to the stream.

To fish the plunge pool and the West Branch downstream, a fisher should take the relatively easy climb down the east side of the falls. The Fish and Boat Commission stocks the pool twice in the spring—once before opening day and once in April. However, we have taken fish through mid-summer. We suggest fishing the plunge pool along its east bank and especially the bank south of the falls and to the east of the West Branch's exit downstream.

In the absence of a trout rise, sink a nymph (Pheasant Tail or Hare's Ear will do) or a couple of nymphs on a dropper, and fish it close to the south bank. Work them under the sticks and debris, and be patient. If there is no strike, then strip in line in quick but very small jerks. But if you see trout rising or sucking in emergers or midges from the surface, try to match the hatch. Chances are that a tiny, #22 black midge will bring some action, but a fisher with little interest in bugs can fling out a #16 Adams and occasionally score. We have been told that small silver spinners on light or ultra-light spinning gear will also take fish at Tanners Falls. If, however, you do the Goat Dance on the iron bridge, you should improve your chance of success markedly.

The Tanners Fall plunge pool inspired the invitation to the Goat Dance. (If you have to ask what it is, you'll never learn it. But check out *The Ginger Man* by British author Kingsley Amis.) This incident occurred before the somber events recorded further below.

I had been fly-fishing along the swirl of the current in the pool and had caught a couple of nice trout when I heard voices above. I looked up and saw a fellow emerge from the path. This blond youngster was a Greek god or maybe Billy Budd, and he was wearing only a pair of cut-off jeans and sneakers. It was when his companion emerged from the bushes that I almost did the Goat Dance; she was clothed in little more than a Bull Durham tobacco sack without the string. Mercy! The two of them embraced lightly on the rocks and, even as I was fishing, they dove into the

pool. They came up in an embrace, then smiled and waved at me, so I tried to forgive them their bad manners. I guessed they hadn't seen the "No Swimming" sign, and I surmised they didn't know a trout from Leviathan.

Anyway, I stubbornly began to cast again, ignoring the hanky-panky but fully aware that by then all the fish were all the way to Philadelphia. Yet I really wanted to fish, and here's what happened: I cast my fly too far into the pool just as the pair dove in again. This time, when they came up, I had hooked more than fish. I had caught the girl by the top of the Bull Durham sack, and as she broke the water's surface, the hook and line pulled her top down.

The girl wasn't hurt. They both laughed as they walked to ankle-deep water and he removed the hook from her meager top, which was now at her waist. I looked away, offering embarrassed apologies.

"No problem, man," laughed the unabashed Billy Budd. "Like, we were all over your turf. We're cool. Not to worry. Good luck with the fishin', man."

Here was a different kind of grace under pressure. As they re-treated—she still topless—I smiled back and waved before returning to my watery "turf." —R.M.

Nice scenery but little excitement are in store for the fisher who heads south from the falls and down the mountain to the main stem at SR 4007. Here the West Branch is narrow, with arching trees and overhanging bushes, and the creek bed is rocky, with rock steps alternating with small falls and shallow pools. It is probably best to use hip boots for this venture because the hiking on dry land is not always easy and occasionally impossible.

For those who do not crash through the underbrush and stomp through the water, and who are willing to keep a low profile and walk on their knees so as not to spook fish, there is an opportunity to land feisty native browns and rainbows. Small wet flies on light tippets—Hare's Ears, March Browns, or Lead Wing Coachmen, for instance—will do as well as anything. Let them drift under rocks and ledges, and stay alert.

The area around Tanners Falls is usually quiet and inviting, provoking vague reveries of life in an earlier century. The invitation to meditation, however, was once an invitation to death. Not too many years ago, a young woman who worked as a counselor at one of the children's camps in the area was enjoying her day off at Tanners Falls. As the newspapers reported later, she was a popular and religious girl who visited the falls alone to read her Bible.

She was raped and shot to death at the falls. The police have never charged anyone, although there continue to be rumors about suspects. The girl's parents have not given up the search for the murderer. When you drive up the dirt road to Tanners Falls, you will pass, near the top and on the left, a small cross. It is usually decorated with flowers, and it is a reminder of the girl and her brutal death.

You can leave the gloom of the falls to fish the northern section of the West Branch by driving across the old iron bridge on SR 4017. In less than a quarter of a mile, SR 4017 intercepts TR 554 on the left. SR 4017 bears to the right to follow along the west bank of the creek, and you are now into State Game Land 158. The going is tough, especially in wet weather, and four-wheel drive is best, although we made it once in a 1985 Crown Victoria. Don't try to park and climb down the steep bank to the creek, because there are only a few better ways to break your neck. Keep going for a little more than a mile until you come to a small bridge. Off to the right is a road leading to a parking lot for the Game Land, and from the lot you can easily make it to the bank of the West Branch.

We have fished this section only two or three times, but it is nicely secluded and very woodsy. Even if we have not taken too many fish, we have seen plenty. We shall return. Author Dwight Landis writes that one can fish upstream from the parking lot for about four miles before coming to posted land—and that's a hike to look forward to.

HONESDALE: THE COUNTY FAIR

Driving south on Route 191 from the Village of Dyberry, stop at the nice lookout on your right at the top of the mountain. From this vantage point you can look down on the dry Jadwin dam and the entire area. Back in the car, the alert driver will spot the Dyberry Creek on the right, running parallel to 191. Soon you will come to the Wayne County Fairgrounds, where you can park and fish the creek. It is stocked here and the trout are readily taken. Just remember you are close to Honesdale, and as you move south, "civilization" is a barrier to much fishing fun.

At the Wayne County Fair, the fun comes once a year around the first week in August. If you have never been to a county fair, go to this one. We like it better than the highly touted Bloomsburg Fair, although it is smaller than the one in Columbia County but, in its fashion, more intimate. Take the children and go on an empty stomach (perhaps with a cast iron liner). The food is something a writer should not describe—from funnel cakes, French fries, pizza, fried potato cakes, sauerkraut, burgers, hot dogs, ump-

teen kinds of sausages, coleslaw, waffles, grilled corn on the cob, and, finally, too many country desserts to contemplate. It is not all good, but much
of it is. Just watch your intake of cholesterol.

The fair offers all the traditional rides for youngsters of all ages, from
little guys to jaded teenagers and to the old guys having surreptitious fun
riding shotgun with the little guys. Along the midway, every game of chance
or "skill" is a delightful cheat, and there are stalls upon stalls selling Americana made somewhere in Asia. There are also scores of other stalls featuring
local businesses and agencies. (We are always pleased with the Game Commission's forest displays and demonstrations.) In addition, you can find
stoves, plumbing fixtures, books, paintings, and sculpture (yes, you can
even find flamingoes for your winter lawn). Take a tour of the most recent
models of mobile homes. After all, compact living is a challenge and a vir-
tue, which is something we hope to discuss with Henry David Thoreau when
we pass on.

In the evening, you can catch the musical shows with famous and not-
very-famous country musicians. There is even a little hard rock, but forget
Bach. We have been in and out of country music halls all of our lives, and
some of the County Fair groups are first-rate. If you can't take the music,
then listen to the power noise of the tractor pulls.

And finally, go see all the animals in the competitions. Some of the
products of 4-H members are spectacular, but nothing was more affecting
than the youngster who was delighted to have won a blue ribbon for her
beautiful sow, but who broke down with uncontrollable sobbing when the
pig was sold off at auction.

The Wayne County Fair is as fetching as a circus. It is certainly easier on
the purse, and the freedom to wander about is a pleasure.

Dining

If you miss the fair, you can still stop by the fairgrounds for a visit to
The Villa Restaurant located there. It's a good mom-and-pop Italian restaurant, and the calamari with marinara sauce is especially tasty with a bottle
of Chianti classico. The Villa is one of Honesdale's better restaurants.

HONESDALE: THE TOWN

On the way into town on Route 191, look on the left for the Clearwater
Seafood store. We have always found the fish and shellfish to be fresh and
the proprietor honest. If you can cook what you buy without much delay,
then stock up.

Route 191 becomes Honesdale's Main Street. Just after Thirteenth Street, on your left, is Day's Bakery. This is a first-rate place for breads, cookies, and other goodies. We know a Honesdale expatriate who travels all the way from Burlington County, N.J., just to savor the cream puffs from Day's. Curiously, you can also buy a new Buck knife here.

The stoplight on Main Street, where it intersects with U.S. 6, offers other options. The old Wayne Hotel is on the northwest corner, and the ancient bar is worth a look, but both the bar and the restaurant have seen better days. Across the street from the hotel, however, is an eye-opening historical display by the Honesdale Protection Engine Company #3. From the street, visitors can see a rotary steam fire engine that Company #3 purchased in 1875 and used until 1936. That old engine is still in operating condition, but just resting silently there, it inspires us, along with other children.

A westward turn at the light onto U.S. 6 leads to the County Hospital, a beer distributor, and to Prompton State Park for nice picnicking and for bass fishing on Prompton Lake. The West Branch of the Lackawaxen River parallels 6 on the south side and joins Van Auken Creek west of the junction with Route 170. Van Auken Creek and the West Branch are stocked with trout, but this section of the Lackawaxen is ugly with commercial development and the attendant crud.

As you move south through the Main Street-U.S. 6 stoplight and over the bridge, you are literally on top of the Lackawaxen River, about four blocks upstream from where the Dyberry joins the river. So go fish! No joke, you can fish. Early in the trout season, you'll see anglers in waders working the water eastward. The ambience is not that of isolated woodlands, but you can catch a batch of trout here in the shadow of the picturesque courthouse and a couple of churches. The Fish and Boat Commission stocks this section, and it is a place to wet a line while the rest of the family shops, takes a ride on the Stourbridge Rail Line, or visits the Wayne County Historical Society.

Honesdale is a small and attractive town that suffers a little from traffic congestion, especially on summer weekends. Local folks blame it all on New Yorkers and Jerseyites. Whatever the reason, driving through Honesdale at times can be a real ordeal. Pedestrians crossing Main Street within the marked crosswalks have the absolute right of way; no matter what, cars and trucks must stop. You have been alerted.

We do warn readers that during the Wayne County Fair driving through Honesdale is a true ordeal. Bring food and water (perhaps a tent and sleeping bags). Nevertheless, we really like this town, its shops, friendly people, and interesting history. We recommend a visit, especially for a train ride on the Stourbridge Line and for a visit to the Wayne County Historical Society.

The town of Honesdale is a nineteenth-century product of anthracite; it was a central shipping point for coal, and especially for coal destined for New York City. Philip Hone, mayor of New York and subsequently the head of the Delaware and Hudson Canal Company, was largely responsible for the construction of a canal that would carry coal from Honesdale to the city. In 1829, the Canal Company under Hone's leadership imported one and possibly two steam locomotives from England to replace mules that were used to haul the coal from the mines to the canal. One of these engines, named the Stourbridge Lion, was the first locomotive to run on American rails—a major first in American railroad history. But the Lion, after several test runs along the tracks, proved too heavy for the rails, and that ended that; the mules were re-hired, the engine's boiler saw service in the company's shop, and in 1889 what was left of the Lion ended up at the Smithsonian Institution.

Today, visitors to Honesdale should not miss the train ride on the Stourbridge Lion, something of a monument to the old days. The excursions lead from Honesdale to Hawley or to the Delaware River at Lackawaxen, where riders can tour the Zane Grey Mansion at the confluence of the two rivers. The Wayne County Chamber of Commerce, (717) 253-1960, which sponsors the line, has all sorts of variations. In the summer, be certain to take the children for the train robbery excursion. There are special trips for fall foliage, for Christmas, Easter, and Halloween, and there is an elaborate evening that includes dinner in Hawley at the Settler's Inn and a show at the Ritz Theater.

Bang! Bam! Bang-Bang!

With six-shooters blazing, the outlaws galloped from the woods and ambushed our train along the banks of the Lackawaxen River. It looked like an old Gene Autry movie, with bandits on horseback racing alongside until they forced the engineer to halt. Youngsters aboard the Stourbridge Line were wide-eyed as the ten-gallon galoots made a desperate attempt to free their gang leader, who was being transported to jail by the sheriff. But after a fierce gun battle outside the train, the sheriff—

with the welcome assistance of a faithful Native American deputy—prevailed, and the bandits were defeated.

Again.

It happens regularly along the route from Honesdale to the town of Hawley, and the little kids love it. The truth is, we adults who grew up with the Lone Ranger, Hopalong Cassidy, and Ken Maynard find it fetching, too. —G.I.

To discover more about Mayor Philip Hone, the history of coal, and the story of the Stourbridge Lion, take the family to the Wayne County Historical Society and Museum at 810 Main Street. This institution flourishes under the direction of Ms. Sally Talaga. For information about hours and nominal admissions fees, call Talaga at (717) 253-3240.

Before we leave Honesdale, we must mention the Himalayan Institute, (717) 253-5551. If you have had a bad day, month, or year for fishing and are contemplating dynamite or hand grenades to ensure finally a suitable catch, then you really need the institute. Here you can enjoy classes in meditation, yoga, diet and nutrition, self-rejuvenation, and biofeedback. If you want to probe deeper, there is a ten-day holistic therapy program. Depending on your state of mind and on your degree of seriousness, these things might work. To find the institute, drive to the north end of Honesdale on Route 191 and bear left onto Route 670; go through the small town of Bethany and then look for the sign on the right side of the highway. If you miss the institute, you will come to the Red Schoolhouse at the junction of 670 and Route 247. The therapy at the Schoolhouse, you might recall, is different from the Himalayan sort.

Tackle

For fishing equipment and information, Northeast Flyfishers at 923 Main Street, (717) 253-9780, is the place to go. The shop, managed by owner Rick Eck, is a dealership for Orvis, and the Orvis goods typically sell at Orvis catalogue prices. The clerks are kind and knowledgeable. Several doors south is Northeast Firearms, a gun shop for your hunting needs, but it is not associated with Northeast Flyfishers. In addition, there is another sporting goods store, Northeast Sports, which isn't associated with the other two.

If you're looking for a guide to fish the Delaware River, call the Chamber of Commerce for recommendations or try licensed guide Anthony Ritter, the proprietor of "Gone Fishing," at (914) 252-3657 in Narrowsburg, N.Y., where he has a home, or at (212) 866-6398 in Manhattan, where he has his commercial art studio. Ritter is probably unique; he is a city kid who fell in love with the Delaware and, according to our experience, has mastered the river.

Dining

Restaurants are sprinkled around Honesdale. The peripatetic fisher will discover the over-priced Townhouse Diner and a couple of good sandwich shops, but not much that really commands attention. Overlooking the town is Jack Trainer's, which is worth a visit. So is the much-above-average Main Street Beanery, (717) 253-5740. South on U.S. 6 is Cordaro's, where many local people go, Two Guys from Italy, and the Stourbridge Lion Inn. At least you won't starve.

Lodging

Nor is there outstanding lodging. On the south side of town near Route 191 and the railroad tracks is the Fife & Drum Motor Inn, (717) 252-1392, which has inexpensive and adequate rooms, plus a bar and a restaurant. For bed-and-breakfast, one might try Olver's at 1415 Main Street, (717) 253-4533. But for the good stuff in food and drink, we prefer heading south on U.S. 6 to Hawley (more about that later).

If you come back from an Upper Delaware fishing trip with a mess of panfish or trout, this recipe, from the editor of *Pennsylvania Angler and Boater* magazine, is great for fillets. The number of fillets will depend upon the size of the fish you catch:

Art Michaels' fried fish strips

(From the *Harrisburg Patriot*, April 13, 1994.)

Fillets, cut into 1-inch-wide strips
1/2 tsp. salt
1 beaten egg with 1 teaspoon water
1/3 cup fine bread crumbs
1/3 cup grated Parmesan cheese

1 tsp. dried basil
1/4 tsp. black pepper
2 tsps. vegetable oil
2 tsps. butter or margarine

Dip fillets in mixed flour and salt. Dip in egg, then roll in mixture of crumbs, cheese, basil, and pepper. Set aside on wax paper to dry.

Heat oil and margarine or butter in a heavy skillet. Cook strips until brown on both sides, about 10 minutes total, depending on thickness.

THE DELAWARE RIVER IN THE POCONOS AREA
AND KITTATINNY MOUNTAINS

From Honesdale, it is easy to reach a variety of interesting places and challenging fishing. A Pennysylvania map shows that Narrowsburg, on the New York side, is east and a little north of Honesdale and that one can drive south of Honesdale on U.S. 6 to Pa. Route 652 and thence east to Narrowsburg on the Delaware River, and that's where we are headed now. Then we will move down the river to Lackawaxen for good fishing on the lower end of the Lackawaxen River and for visits to several special sites. After that, it's back to Hawley, Pa., for tasty food and happy antiquing.

Once in Narrowsburg, it is a good idea to check in at the National Park Service Information Center. The Rangers there can tell you about the fishing but also about the interesting Fort Delaware and its colonial background. The fort is located a little north of the town on N.Y. Route 97.

George Leber and I were cruising in my car around Narrowsburg, where three decades before he had spent many idyllic summers at his uncle's place along the Delaware. We drove through the streets, with George recalling places and locations, including a barely remembered tackle shop because we wanted to buy hellgrammites to fish the river for smallmouth bass.

He asked me to pull up outside a house where two older men were painting the siding.

"Excuse me," George said, "but I'm looking for Smith's tackle and bait store. Do you know where it is?"

From his ladder perch, one of the old men looked down at him just a little skeptically.

"Smith's closed down years ago," he advised us.

George felt dumb. "I'm sorry," he said, "but I haven't been around here for thirty years or more."

The old man smiled and said gently, "Son, you ought to pay us a visit more often!" —G.I.

Dining and Lodging

If you plan to spend a night in town, you might try the Narrowsburg Inn, (914) 252-3998, which was built in 1840 and has the reputation of being the oldest continuously operating inn within the entire Empire State.

The accommodations were recently remodeled, with new beds all around. In total, there are only seven rooms and a suite, which means that you should make reservations well in advance. If you want a private bath, take the suite; the seven rooms share three baths. Perhaps the best thing about the inn is its food. The salmon is good, the grilled duck is fine, and the chef prides himself on the steak au poivre with a Cognac cream sauce. There's an ample dessert selection, with cheese cake leading the list. You can also find comfortable lodging at the Ten Mile River Lodge, (914) 252-3925, Narrowsburg Holiday Inn, (914) 564-9020, and Wolfe's Pioneer Motel, (914) 252-3385.

For committed anglers, Narrowsburg is a central point. The town has two very good launch sites, one on the New York side and one on the Pennsylvania side. Both are close to the Narrowsburg Eddy, which, according to J.B. Kasper, in *The Delaware and Its Fisheries*, is very deep, ranging from 85 to 100 feet. That means structure for boaters who, with a little experimentation, can take smallmouth bass and walleyes. North and south of the launches, shore fishers and waders have a relatively easy time of it, thanks to the many riffles, flats, and shallows rapids. When the shad are running, this is a good spot to be.

Although it wanders away from the river as you drive south, N.Y. Route 97 is a godsend heading north from Narrowsburg all the way to Callicoon because it is close to the Delaware, and the stops along the way offer excellent fishing opportunities. It is worth remembering that the further north you travel from Narrowsburg, the more trout you'll encounter.

For those who want to leave the Delaware and venture into rustic New York, a short side trip to Lake Superior State Park will do the trick. From Narrowsburg, take N.Y. Route 52 to the junction of N.Y. Route 178. Turn right on 178 and drive about eight miles to the park. From Damascus/Cochecton, follow 78 east to the park. Lake Superior State Park is not developed very much, but that is a large part of its charm. It is a lovely place for a picnic, a park where children can run off energy while adults regain theirs.

PIKE COUNTY

From Narrowsburg south to Masthope, access to the Delaware is limited. N.Y. Route 97 approaches the river at the town of Tusten, where several streets head down to the Delaware. Then 97 pulls away from the river for two or three miles until Kunkell Rapids, just north of Lackawaxen. After this, the highway stays close until Port Jervis, where 97 ends its life at U.S. 6.

On the Pennsylvania side, things are a little more complicated. If you are coming out of Narrowsburg, take Route 652 a short distance to SR 1006 and turn left. Then almost immediately turn left again onto SR 0652 to the river, if the road is open. A better bet is to take a left off SR 1006 onto SR 1015 or SR 4003. Go left off either of these roads onto SR 1014 (Honesdale and Masthope Plank Road) and follow the signs to Masthope.

Lackawaxen and the Lackawaxen River

From Masthope, you can follow along the river to Lackawaxen, where you will discover the Zane Grey Mansion, the Roebling Aqueduct (now a bridge), which foreshadows Roebling's Brooklyn Bridge, and the very restful Minisink Battleground Park. Along the way from Masthope, access to the river is not always easy, so whether you come down on the New York side or the Pennsylvania side, be certain to get permission to cross private property. But find a way to get to the river, for, as Zane Grey wrote in his first published story, "A Day on the Delaware" (1902): "At the lower end of the big eddy below Westcolang Falls, the Delaware narrows, and there commences a two-mile stretch of eddies, drifts, falls, and pools that would gladden the heart of any angler" (*Tales of Fresh-water Fishing*, New York: Grosset & Dunlap, 1928, page 2).

Above the town of Lackawaxen, the Lackawaxen River, which we first met in Honesdale, empties into the Delaware. This lower Lackawaxen is stocked with trout all the way from west of Hawley at Middle Creek to the Delaware, and the best fishing is along this lower section. We have had good fishing just at the mouth of the Lackawaxen, where it enters the Delaware.

There is a boat launch here for the Delaware, and the Zane Grey Mansion is on the bank and above the launch site. A fisher can readily park and then wade into either the Delaware or the Lackawaxen. In the Delaware, there are all the panfish you will ever need, but also there are walleyes, smallmouth bass, and trout. This lower section of the Lackawaxen is best for trout, but there are plenty of bass in there, we promise. Hellgrammites and crawfish imitations are effective for bass and the occasional trout. In the spring trout take Blue-winged Olives, Red Quills, Quill Gordons, Hendricksons, and Adams. Go deep throughout the season with the Hare's Ears, Drakes, Muddler Minnows, Wooly Buggers, and Mickey Finns. Stone fly and Caddis imitations are off and on all season, and in the fall terrestrials, especially Beetles, are effective along the shore line.

During the shad run, the pool in front of the Zane Grey Mansion is a very popular place for fly-rod and spinning gear. Incidentally, if you use a fly rod for shad, try krill imitations. If you can't find the krill or can't find out how to tie them, then call on old Thom Rivell in his Fly Fishing Tackle Shop on Route 507, Greentown Plaza, Greentown, Pa. 18426; the phone is (717) 676-4446.

LACKAWAXEN RIVER

Tackle

In Lackawaxen you can pick up most of your fishing supplies at the Angler's Roost and Hunter's Rest at 1 Scenic Drive, Lackawaxen, PA 18435, (717) 685-2010. Charley and Dimitri Zaimes operate the store.

Plenty of fishers are devoted to this river, which is challenging whether crowded or not. To go fishing, you can take Route 590 east out of Hawley as it parallels (more or less) the river to SR 4006; there are several roads along the way that head south to the river bank. Leave 590 and follow SR 4006 toward the town of Kimbles, where there is a bridge and where you are close to the Pennsylvania Power and Light Company's power plant. SR 4006 follows the river closely through Bayoba and on to Rowland, where it rejoins Route 590. You then can follow 590 along the river to the town of Lackawaxen. From Hawley to Lackawaxen, there is parking along the river, but increasingly there are no-trespassing signs. The future does not look altogether promising for open fishing.

Here is a major caution! The Lackawaxen River can be a dangerous river to wade. First, the Pennsylvania Power and Light Company (PP&L) operates a hydroelectric power plant upstream from the town of Kimbles, and the plant, which uses cooling water from PP&L's Lake Wallenpaupack, releases up to 46 million gallons of water per hour into the river. Read that again: 46 million gallons per hour. The result is sudden rises of the river's level that can catch an angler unawares and—believe it—can drown the unsuspecting fisher. From that power plant to the Delaware, the Lackawaxen River becomes one big tailwater.

Second, the bottom rocks and shale can be very slippery. Bob Marler, who used to take risks and is notable for several splendid dousings, went down one day in less than five minutes after wading in as a river rise was under way. Sudden water rises in a normally swift river with a slippery bottom mean you could miss supper—and all subsequent ones. Take seriously the signs that warn anglers that the river level changes rapidly, and, as most commentators on this stretch of water tell readers, avoid fishing the side of the river opposite your vehicle; if there is a rise in level while you are on the wrong side of the river, you won't easily cross back to your car. In this case, however, you'll miss only one supper.

Here is the good news. PP&L has a hot line for the Lackawaxen and Lake Wallenpaupack. Call (800) 807-2474, twenty-four hours a day, to get information about changes in the river's water level and about the operating status of the power plant.

We simply had to give up fishing for the day. The rain and thrashing wind during this wretched last week in April were vicious, and any bugs left from the morning's meager Hendrickson hatch were by now drowned, smashed, or electrocuted. It was terrific weather. Maybe you recall Robert Frost's grimly fine sonnet, "Once by the Pacific":

> *The clouds were low and hairy in the skies.*
> *Like locks blown forward in the gleam of eyes.*

Well, that's how it was on the Lackawaxen, and we leaned hard into the wind and were blown soaking into our Ford Explorer. The rain was horizontal across a black sky, and we could drive scarcely ten miles per hour at three o'clock in the afternoon.

The headlights had ignored the man we almost hit, but we did see him in air as he leaped, arms flailing and rain gear flapping, into a huge puddle. We spun to a stop, and he emerged muddy and drenched but unhurt. He was not angry at us, and he laughed quietly when we apologized. We took him in, of course, and offered him a lift to wherever he was going. He was, he said, going back to New York, going anywhere to get out of the area and away from the storm and his "friends." He had a silver flask and offered fine bourbon all around; that bourbon was special, probably a single-cask product of about 110 proof. It was proof of his good taste. We all sipped sparingly but very appreciatively.

He asked to ride with us to Hawley. He and his erstwhile "buddies" were staying at the Settlers Inn, and he meant to have a final go at the two of them. The three had driven down in his van from New York City, fishing along the way. When the rains came, he gave each of the other two a set of keys to the van so that anyone could climb in and out of the weather. This was their second day on the Lackawaxen, and the other two had spent much of their time climbing "out of the weather" and into where that bourbon was.

Before we almost ran him down, he had been fishing toward the bank opposite his van. When the PP&L released water, the river's level rose too fast for him to return to the van, so he emerged on the opposite bank and looked over toward his vehicle. His buddies were there. In the silent pantomime imposed by the roar of storm, they waved, toasted him with their silver flasks, danced around laughing, and then drove off in his van.

"Did they just steal your van and leave you?" I fairly yelled.

"Well, that's the look of the caper," he murmured. "I guess it started as a practical joke, but they didn't come back. Maybe they are asleep some place, but for me the joke has turned to ashes. I hope they didn't wreck my van. I had decided to hike and hitchhike to Hawley when you guys came along, and I'm glad you almost hit me. That way, I get this ride. Now, I can surprise them, one way or another. Here, have another sip."

We had another and pulled into the parking lot of the Settlers Inn. He spotted his van right off, and we parked alongside. He got out and quickly checked for dents and scratches. The rain belted him, but he did not go into the building. He thanked us, got himself and his gear into his van, and started the engine.

"Aren't you going into the hotel?" asked one of our fellows.

"No, no," said our new friend. "I have decided to donate my suitcase and stuff in the room to my friends. I am headed home now. If you guys see two jackasses hitchhiking toward New York, let them trudge." With that and a wave, he drove off.

Someone had better be prepared for rage.
There would be more than ocean-water broken
Before God's last "Put out the Light" was spoken.

—R.M.

LACKAWAXEN

In decent weather the town of Lackawaxen is pleasant for fishers and nonfishers alike. A family can happily spend one or several days here, and we strongly support the Narrowsburg-Lackawaxen-Hawley triangle as an unusual vacation area for fishers traveling with nonfishers. Aside from the fishing, there are the three major attractions in or near Lackawaxen that demand attention: Zane Grey Mansion and Museum, John Roebling's aqueduct, and the Minisink Battleground Park. All three are significant symbols in American cultural history.

Zane Grey

Zane Grey, although still remembered, is far less read than he was fifty or sixty years ago. Do you recall *Riders of the Purple Sage* (1912), probably his most famous novel, or *The Last of the Plainsmen* (1908), probably his best novel? For years during the first half of the twentieth century, Zane Grey was celebrated as the quintessential Western novelist. Even Owen Wister's *The Virginian* (1902), a wonderfully seminal book in its way, has sometimes taken second rank to Grey's works.

Zane Grey was born in Zanesville, Ohio, in 1872, as Pearl Zane Gray; later he changed Gray to Grey and dropped the Pearl. He attended the University of Pennsylvania on a baseball scholarship, but the popular writer of cowboy fiction became a dentist in New York City. Apparently, he hated it all and sought solace in writing, although his early work scarcely sold. He began playing semipro baseball in New Jersey. Through his baseball travels, he discovered the Delaware River and also his wife-to-be, Lina Elise Roth. In 1905 he and Lina, called Dolly, married and bought the house at Lackawaxen. There the two lived regularly until 1918 as Grey slowly achieved success as an author; he kept the house until 1929. For anglers, his life in Lackawaxen is also significant for his profound interest in fishing in general and the Lackawaxen and Delaware rivers in particular.

Apparently Grey knew every flat, riffle, and pool in the area, and he fished with humor, intensity, and that bragging humility that we appreciate. If you plan a journey to Lackawaxen, first look through Grey's *Tales of Fresh-Water Fishing*. The collection gives a sense of what the two rivers were once like, yet it remains contemporary. Look over the early works (personal narratives and essays), entitled "A Day on the Delaware," "Fighting Qualities of Black Bass," "Black Bass—Artificial Lure," "The Lord of Lackawaxen Creek," and "Mast Hope Brook in June." In your own travels, you will recognize landmarks mentioned in these pieces, and that's fun. But you won't catch as many big fish as Zane Grey caught.

Later in the day of your travels, be certain to stop at the Zane Grey house. It's a full vision of an earlier time, and it offers a quiet pleasure.

The Roebling Aqueduct

Hart Crane, the tormented poet who celebrated the Brooklyn Bridge, led a twisted life that stands in sad contrast to the stately beauty of that suspended wonder of the East Coast. In *The Bridge* Crane wrote of the bridge as "thee":

> O Sleepless as the river under thee,
> Vaulting the sea, the prairies' dreaming sod,
> Unto us lowliest sometime sweep, descent
> And of the curveship lend a myth to God.

The "curveship" that encloses in freedom the myth of America begins, interestingly, in Lackawaxen.

At Lackawaxen John Augustus Roebling, a German civil engineer, built the Delaware Aqueduct, which opened in 1848 and remains in use today as a bridge over the Delaware. This structure, the oldest existing wire suspension bridge in the United States, is the forerunner of the Brooklyn Bridge that Roebling and his son Washington would build in the 1880s.

Roebling's aqueduct, one of four crossing the Delaware, was a solution to a major problem: timber from the upper Delaware Valley floated down the river to Trenton and Philadelphia, and coal from out of Honesdale and the mountains of northeastern Pennsylvania was delivered to New York City via the Delaware and Hudson Canal in canal boats, which crossed the Delaware from Lackawaxen to Minisink Ford in New York; logs and canal boats often collided violently at a place where you—the contemporary fisher—might be flinging out a plastic string with a fishhook on the end. There were fights of the Mike Fink sort, death, lawsuits, and bitterness. Then, too, the canal boats had serious troubles with high water and ice jams in the Delaware.

Roebling's Delaware Aqueduct, along with the three smaller ones, was the solution to the problem. The directors of the Delaware and Hudson Canal hired Roebling in 1847, and he took to the air. He designed an aqueduct that would carry the canal boats *over* the Delaware and *over* the timber. So just there, in the avoidance of conflict, was a grand step toward the development of the Brooklyn Bridge.

Drive across the aqueduct on your way to Minisink Battleground Park (on the New York side) and look closely as you go. We still get caught up in wonder at this 150-year-old structure carrying modern automobiles; we can see here hints of the Brooklyn Bridge, and we can feel touches of Hart Crane's emotion.

Minisink Battleground Park

Minisink Battleground Park is a quiet park today. The hiking trails are inviting, and the facilities are clean. It offers a pleasant diversion for the fisher who flails and fails. However, the park was once a bloody place, and, if you visit, you can discover the facts behind a large massacre during the Revolutionary War.

In 1779 a large band of Mohawks and Tories raided Port Jervis, then called Minisink, burning and sacking the settlement. As the victorious band headed north, a group of fewer than 200 settlers attacked the Indians and Tories. There was little in the way of successful revenge here, for most of the attacking settlers were killed. Mike Sajna neatly embellishes his interesting book, *Pennsylvania Trout and Salmon Fishing Guide* (Portland, Oreg.: Frank Amato Publication, 1988, page 147), with historical information. He writes that the commander of the outnumbered settlers, a Major Woods, escaped with about two dozen of his troopers because he accidentally used the Masonic distress signal. Apparently, Chief Joseph Brant of the Mohawks saw the signal and let Woods and his men live.

Dining and Lodging

For food and drink in the Lackawaxen area, anglers rest at the Cuckoo's Nest for a sandwich and a beer or for dinner. As the T-shirt proclaims, "The Cuckoo's Nest Does It Best." For dinner, try the Lackawaxen House, (717) 685-7061. Others have gone to the White Owl Tavern in Welcome Lake, which is, well, "rustic." For bed and breakfast, you can't beat the lovely Roebling Inn on the Delaware, (717) 685-7900. The inn is all but next door to the Zane Grey House. Once, but no longer, you could have tried Jungle Jim's.

It was early May, and I was introducing my son George to shad fishing at the confluence of the Delaware and Lackawaxen Rivers in Pike County. We hadn't caught anything, so I suggested moving eastward, up the Lackawaxen, near a pile of rocks that George could safely stand on and cast into the river while I retreated to the comfort of a bar called Jungle Jim's, which is no longer there. Dad was halfway through his first Budweiser when his breathless son burst into the bar with a wriggling four-pound fish dangling from his line. "Dad! Dad! I got one!" he yelled, eyes as wide as full moons. One of the grizzled old-timers at the bar turned around and calmly said, "Son, you'd better get that bass back in the water 'fore the warden sees it. Bass season don't start for three more

weeks." With the bass still flopping from the line, father and son ran back to the river and released the illegal catch. —G.I.

Hawley

Hawley, the county seat for Pike County, is a small Poconos town that offers anglers and nonanglers excellent food, good lodging, and bountiful antique shops. The Stourbridge Lion out of Honesdale stops here, and so do folks from all over the East Coast who want to fish or to shop for old stuff. And the town lives in the history of journalism, for Hawley was the birthplace of the late *New York Times* reporter, Homer Bigart.

Today when I travel through Hawley I always think of the privilege I once had of sharing a cab with Homer Bigart. Although I was familiar with his by-line in the Times, *I really had no idea that I was in the presence of a great man. Bigart had been a legendary journalist, covering breaking news throughout the world, including the murder of Charles Polk in Greece. Now his career was in a graceful decline, and he was reporting police news in Gotham. As a reporter for the* Philadelphia Inquirer, *I was dispatched to New York City one Saturday afternoon to cover the arrest of a murder suspect who lured his victims into his tobacco shop in center city. I had no idea what I was doing, but I struggled on. From Pennsylvania Station I jumped into a cab to take me to the precinct where the arrested man was waiting for arraignment. Bigart jumped into the cab with me, and when he discovered that I was a fellow reporter, he suggested we share the cab. It was a memorable ride, as this gracious old-timer pointed out landmarks ("That's Cooper Union, where Lincoln gave his address") to the 26-year-old kid from Philly. Embarrassed to learn that he knew more about the local political scene in Philadelphia than I did, like Huck Finn, I promised to do better. —G.I.*

From Hawley, a fisher can be on Lake Wallenpaupack in ten minutes, while the spouse is making that first purchase in an antique shop. Or, for the kids, its a quick ride on Route 590 east to Hamlin and thence four more miles east to the Claws 'N' Paws Wild Animal Park, (717) 698-6154. From experience growing up in the South, we normally by-pass such places. However, Claws 'N' Paws is not one of those roadside "zoos" that has a snake, alligator, pitiful parrot, and mangy lion. This park is well stocked and includes a petting zoo, an Indian wildlife area, woodland trails, three shows daily, and a picnic area. If a small, private zoo appeals to you and your youngsters, then this is the place.

The Dorflinger Glass Museum is off U.S. 6, a few miles north of Hawley, at White Mills. The collection of Dorflinger glass is impressive, and the museum hosts a variety of summer concerts (from country to classical) at the Wildflower Music Festival, (717) 253-1185. It gets better: the museum is located in the Dorflinger/Suydam Wildlife Sanctuary, which offers about 600 acres for exploration along extensive walking trails.

Antiquing

We suspect, however, that Hawley was put on this earth as the location for shopping for antiques. We have visited in the area more than forty shops of various sizes and quality, but we cannot even try to cover them all. Determined visitors manage to find plenty of them, and discovery is part of the fun. You will catch some bargains, but not too many; these dealers are knowledgeable, not bumpkins. There is some used furniture that tries to be antique, and there are reproductions that masquerade as old stuff. But experts tell us that there are nice things and rare things in some of these shops. Prices are generally a little lower than those in cities.

We suggest that you start with the Hawley Antique Exchange, (717) 226-1711, where you encounter more than twenty shops under one roof. The Exchange is located on U.S. 6 between Hawley and Lake Wallenpaupack. In the Country Classics shop, you can find Janet Kane, who manages the Exchange; she can tell you about the shops. For guidance in your antiquing around the area, visit with Linda Slocum when she is in her shop, Linda Slocum Antiques, (717) 226-8853. Without pushing her own things, Linda can suggest where to find what, and she can discuss antiques in your price range. Further, she is familiar with restaurants and lodging in the Hawley area; if pushed a little, she can comment on the fishing scene. If she can't comment, her husband certainly can. He is Tony Ritter, the Delaware River guide we mentioned in our discussion of Honesdale.

On the south side of Hawley on U.S. 6, you will almost run into Castle Antiques and Reproductions. Just after you turn left off U.S. 6 toward the large sign on the Castle, which announces the place, you will drive past several small shops that are worth a visit. The Castle itself is a huge building with a large collection of material that at first will take your breath away.

Breathe again. The eclectic collection is interesting but, upon reflection, doesn't altogether come up to the initial impact. We are pleased with some of the kitsch we have bought at the Castle. However, the main business of the Castle is the manufacturing of reproductions of antiques, which they ship widely. You can find solid furniture here, but most was made last year or last week.

For people who would like to expand their searches for antiques beyond the immediate Hawley area and need information in advance, we recommend writing to the Antique Dealers Association, Inc., P.O. Box 884, White Mills, Pa. 18473. The association serves Wayne and Pike counties in Pennsylvania and Sullivan County in New York.

Dining and Lodging

As we have said, there are good restaurants in the Hawley area, a couple with comfortable lodging, that have satisfied us over the years. Simple, homemade Italian food is served at CC's Cafe off Main Street in Hawley; good food, dull restaurant name. Local folks like the cafe.

When we are flush, which is rare enough, we try to move upscale. However, the better your taste (whatever that may mean), the faster the bills leave the wallet. Here, we think, is a compromise establishment that does a good job with the elegant at affordable prices; the owners call it "affordable elegance." We are suggesting Michael and Dorothy Fenn's Grand Cafe in their Falls Port Restaurant and Hotel, (717) 226-2600, an establishment that is almost a century old. The antiques are Victorian, but the service is modern and courteous. Be sure to try the lobster ravioli. For heavier fare, order a steak and recall what certified Angus beef tastes like. If you need a hotel, here is a good one. The twelve rooms upstairs, all remodeled in the last five or six years, are filled with antiques and are comfortable. Rates are reasonable. The Falls Port is in the center of town, at 330 Main Avenue (U.S. 6), across the street from Teeters Furniture store.

Behind the Castle Antiques, you can find the Old Mill Stream, (717) 226-1337, an inn on Falls Avenue that has twelve hotel rooms with private baths and ten condominium units that boast two bedrooms and one and a half baths and that can accomodate up to seven people. The restaurant used to be the Turbine Room, but that is now being replaced by the Cascades Restaurant; the restaurant is scheduled to open after this book's publication date, so we cannot comment on the fare.

Further upscale, the Settlers Inn, with eighteen rooms, all with baths, is a top restaurant and inn. As you enter Hawley on U.S. 6 from the north and near the Lackawaxen River, where the Stourbridge Line has a stop, you can't miss the large Tudor revival establishment, dating from 1927, on the right. You need reservations for meals, (800) 833-8527; without them, we have been rebuffed noon and night. Still, as *USA Today* put it, "The cozy bar specializes in beers from the region, and patrons quaff them in front of the living room fireplace amid pre-1920 furnishings." That beer is first rate.

The inn appropriately features trout in multiple recipes. They have their own smokehouse and do good things with it, using fish from the nearby Blooming Grove Trout Hatchery. If it's on the menu when you are there, try the Angler's Trout, a baked fish with spinach and wrapped in bacon. In fact, the inn graciously contributed its recipe, which we give below. With their own bakery and one of the owners as the dessert chef, the Settlers Inn serves excellent breads and superb desserts. So, after a tough day fishing the Delaware, Lackawaxen, or Wallenpaupack, with a spouse suffering from a tough day in the antique shops, we relish such food in such surroundings. We should, maybe, don a necktie, but we don't.

Settlers Inn angler's trout

(Our thanks to the Genslingers of Settlers Inn for the recipe.)

First is the stuffing for *each* boned trout (with head removed):

1 spring onion, chopped fine
3 chopped spinach leaves
a dash of dry sherry

1/2 teaspoon tamari (aged soy sauce)
a pinch of black pepper

Toss the above ingredients and stuff the fish. Spiral wrap two strips of bacon around the trout, with bacon ends beneath the fish. Add a splash of water to a baking sheet (or to a frying pan if you are cooking over a campfire). Bake for ten minutes at 400 degrees; then place two thin slices of lemon on top of the fish and bake a couple minutes more. When the bacon is crisp, drain the excess moisture and sear with a splash of white wine. Plate and serve.

Sautéed watercress and oven-roasted red potatoes are a good accompaniment for this dish.

Lake Wallenpaupack: A Quick Introduction

A trip of a few miles west of Hawley on U.S. 6 brings an angler to a potential paradise of fishing, the 5,700-acre Lake Wallenpaupack ("the 'Pack") with its fifty-two-mile shoreline. Route 507 branches off U.S. 6 and follows the southern shore in Pike County, and Route 590 follows the eastern portion of the northern shoreline in Wayne County. Secondary roads come and go and are readily discovered. If you would like a tour of the whole thing, try the *Spirit of Paupack*, (717) 857-1251, at Tanglewood Lodge on Route 507, near Tafton; the *Spirit* is the largest excursion boat on the lake.

The 'Pack is the largest man-made lake in Pennsylvania. However, it is not yet a paradise, and for half the summer or more we stay far away. We do not enjoy all the power boats, some of which are large enough to scare an admiral. The boat traffic is very heavy and very loud. The lake was built in 1926 to provide water for the generation of electicity. Pennsylvania Power and Light owns the lake, and the water that flows from Wallenpaupack to that hydroelectric power plant on the Lackawaxen River determines the rise and fall of the river's level and of the lake's level, too.

Wallenpaupack is indeed beautiful, but it is surrounded by vacation homes and communities that, for us, devalue that beauty. We have similar difficulties with sprawling ocean-shore vacation communities. We go to the beach, but always there is the disappointment that hangs on until we are on the water and out of sight of land. By contrast, as a youngster we loved such places, and we doubt that there are many teenagers (from age 13 to 100) out there who, with a throttle controlling more than a hundred horses in the stern, would relinquish the thrill of speed for the quiet of a cove and a rod and reel. It's partly the generation gap. We may not enjoy lake and ocean communities, noisy, noisome motors, power skis, and float tubes, but, aside from reasonable laws and limits, we do not propose putting a stop to other people's pleasures.

Spring, fall, and winter on the 'Pack, however, offer gentle fishers opportunities for huge brown trout (how about seventeen pounds!), stripers (more than thirty-four pounds!), walleye, large- and smallmouth bass, muskie, and panfish including crappie and perch. The lake is especially well known for the trout, striper, and smallmouth bass populations, but experts are increasingly reporting a rapid growth in the numbers of largemouth bass—big ones. Wallenpaupack has, over the last couple of decades, developed a large crop of weeds and aquatic vegetation around the shoreline. The result has been an explosion in the fish population. If you fish there, you will succeed.

With shore fishing limited, to succeed in a big way on the 'Pack a fisher needs a boat. A canoe will do, but unfortunately, even a small motor is an advantage. There are five launch sites around the lake. PP&L operates four launch sites adjacent to its four campgrounds—Wilsonville, Caffrey, Ironwood Point, Ledgedale—and the Fish and Boat Commission has a launch site off Route 590 a little north of the Wallenpaupack Dam. The dam is at the eastern end of the lake and is close to Hawley. In fact, if you approach the lake from Hawley on U.S. 6, you will come to the dam and should drop in at PP&L's Visitors' Center. There you can gather up the information on the four launch sites and the campgrounds.

If you need more information, call the Lake Superintendent's Office at (717) 226-3702 for a brochure. Angler's Aid offers a subsurface structure map of Lake Wallenpaupack that also shows roads, creeks, campsites, and villages; contact International Map Co., 547 Shaler Blvd., Ridgefield, NJ 07657, (201) 943-6566 or 943-5550. For a good overview of when to fish for what and what bait to use, see Darl Black's "Don't Overlook Lake Wallen-paupack," on page 4 of the September 1996 issue of *Pennsylvania Angler*. We have borrowed some information on PP&L from Black's article.

Anglers who visit Lake Wallenpaupack should know that, just beyond the southwest end of the lake, there are several trout streams worth a try. It's beyond our scope to cover them in detail, but read up on them in Charles Meck's and Dwight Landis's books and scout them in Howard Wm. Higbee's extemely detailed *Stream Map of Pennsylvania*, updated and published in 1991 by Vivid Publishing, Inc., in Williamsport, Pa. We mention three streams that stand out: the West Branch of Wallenpaupack Creek, Jones Creek, and Butternut Creek. All three are stocked streams, and the West Branch and the Butternut both have Delayed-Harvest, Artificial-Lures-Only sections.

Just a few miles south of Lake Wallepaupack on Route 390 is the Delaware State Forest, which encompasses Promised Land State Park, where Lower Promised Land Lake is stocked with trout. The larger Promised Land Lake provides bass, panfish, and pickerel and offers excellent fishing for youngsters with bobbers. Both lakes are restricted to electric motors, and that is a very nice feature. Promised Land is a good location for family camping; there are family campsites for tenting, and rustic cabins are available, but you usually have to reserve the cabins ahead of time. There is a sand beach with swimming.

Dining and Lodging
There are various kinds of restaurants around Lake Wallenpaupack. Hot dogs and hamburgers are readily available, but there are several interesting places we will note.

You can enjoy a nice view of Lake Wallenpaupack with your meal at Ehrhardt's Lakeside Restaurant, (717) 226-2124, on Route 507 before the intersection with 390. For good Italian food and take-out service, there is Perna's, (717) 226-3108, on Route 590 just west of Hawley. The Inn at Peck's

Pond, (717) 775-7336, located on Route 402 off U.S. 6 south of Hawley, has a standard menu that the chef supplements daily with various specials, and the children's menu offers burgers, chicken tenders, and pizza.

And, finally, you can live it up at The Inn at Woodloch Pines, (800) 572-6658 and (717) 685-2661, east of Hawley on 590. The inn is, in fact, a clean, first-rate, family resort with strong support for children. You can find plenty of entertainment, indoors and out; for example, there's racquetball, handball, tennis, indoor/outdoor pool, hiking, movies, and children's crafts. Here you can enjoy tasty food, with a Sunday and Tuesday smorgasbord, good service, and varied fun at night, from dancing to full-scale floor shows featuring Broadway musicals. Call ahead for upcoming shows and times and for the schedule for the smorgasborg.

PIKE COUNTY: THE DELAWARE RIVER FROM LACKAWAXEN TO THE TWO BUSHKILL CREEKS

Before we move further south from Wallenpaupack country into Monroe County to explore the waters west of the Delaware River, we should first continue down the Delaware from Lackawaxen to the well-known Little Bushkill Creek and Big Bushkill Creek.

Barryville, New York

From Lackawaxen to Barryville, N.Y., the Delaware is much as it is around Lackawaxen, except there are no major tributaries to empty water into the river until Shohola, Pa., where Shohola Creek empties, across the river from Barryville. Smallmouth bass, walleyes in the autumn, and panfish are the major species, but, during the spring shad run, fishers tend to focus mostly on the shad. Cedar Rapids can cause novice boaters some trouble, but the eddies through the section are rich in bass. Just below Barryville is Shohola Rapids.

Shohola Creek

Shohola Creek, which begins about thirty miles to the west of the river, is something of an enigma to anglers new to the area or who fish but intermittently. Charles Meck and Dwight Landis tend to ignore the stream, but Mike Sajna in his *Pennsylvania Trout and Salmon Guide* likes the stream especially for its beauty and natural setting in State Game Land 180. Shohola Creek is stocked from the point where Route 739 intersects I-84 to Lake Shohola, a distance of about four miles. Then, from the other end of the lake at lovely Shohola Falls it's stocked to the boundary of the Game Land.

In July some years ago, we fished the southern portion near the bridge over the creek at Route 739 and got severely skunked. Yet it is a very pretty stream, indeed, and we have meant to return for an early spring trip, especially to see once again Shohola Falls and the subsequent chasm that Sajna rightly emphasizes.

Dining and Lodging

In Shohola, Pa., you can dine or have a beer at Rohman's Inn. If you are in town any day from Wednesday through Sunday, try something different for dinner; eat at Le Gorille on Twin Lakes Road, (717) 296-8094, where gorilla and monkey decorations dominate. It's really unusual, and the carefully prepared food (all fresh and environmentally proper) is very good, but make reservations. Across the river in Barryville, there is the Barryville Hotel and Reber's Castle Inn for food and lodging.

As you head south from Barryville toward Port Jervis, N.Y., you will have to rely mostly on N.Y. Route 97; the Pennsylvania side of the river offers little in the way of improved roads, except for the short stretch of SR 1017 between Matamoras and Millrift. The town of Millrift marks the end of the Upper Delaware Scenic and Recreational River. Between Matamoras and the town of Milford, Pa., on U.S. 209 is the northern end of the Delaware Water Gap National Recreational Area, which continues down the river to the south of Stroudsburg. And U.S. 209 in Pennsylavania is the easiest route south to the Gap at Stroudsburg.

Pond Eddy

Fishing the Delaware from Barryville south to Matamoras/Port Jervis is to continue with smallmouth bass, walleye, panfish, and shad. For structure there are several small islands and the confluences of several streams, most notably Pond Eddy Creek at Pond Eddy. Anglers fish Pond Eddy deep (about thirty-five feet) for walleye, and there are occasional trout that enter the river from Pond Eddy Creek on the Pennsylvania side. You can find adequate lodging and food at the Best Western Inn and the Edgewater Restaurant in Metamoras at U.S. 6 and U.S. 209.

Pond Eddy Creek

Pond Eddy Creek, although it is not stocked with trout, is worth a visit because of the native browns and brookies. The creek is located in State Game Land 209, so the surroundings are natural for the most part, and fishing, once you can find the creek, is serene. Out of the village of Pond

Eddy, N.Y., on N.Y. Route 97, take the bridge across the Delaware and turn right at the railroad tracks. Follow along the tracks until you can make a left turn leading across the tracks. Drive slowly to save your muffler, and end up in the Game Land. Park and walk to the creek.

From Matamoras to Milford, the Delaware offers excellent shad fishing. At the downstream end of Mashipacong, Minisink, and Namanock Islands, fishers will discover walleye, and with a canoe anglers will land plenty of smallmouth bass. Further south is the Dingman's Ferry area of the river, which is perhaps the most popular shad fishing area on the entire Delaware. Local guides have assured us, however, that the walleye and smallmouth fishing can be as good as it gets. The boat launch site at Dingman's Ferry is very popular. You can wade the flats and surface fish for smallies, however.

Dining

After a day's hard fishing, head on back to the especially attractive town of Milford—featuring antiques and book stores—and have drinks and dinner at the pleasant Tom Quick Inn ("Tom Quick the Indian Slayer"), 411 Broad Street. For lunch, you must have a sandwich at the Water Wheel Cafe and Bakery, 150 Water Street. Good, inexpensive stuff. The best dinner we have had in Milford was at the Black Walnut Inn on Fire Tower Road, (717) 296-6322. The inn is a lovely place to stay for a night or a week, but the public is welcome for dining. Everyone told us to try the duck; we did, and we will again.

Dingman's Creek

Dingman's Creek, which has its confluence at Dingman's Ferry, does not receive much attention, yet the trout fishing is good, and the scenery, with five dramatic waterfalls, is worth a day for the whole family. From U.S. 209, go west on Pa. Route 739 to Dingman's Falls and to the Visitors' Center for information about fishing places and about the entire area, including the Delaware Water Gap National Recreation Area. The upper section of Dingman's Creek has a Delayed-Harvest, Artificial-Lures-Only section that is in George W. Childs State Park, so there are picnic areas. With the spectacular waterfalls and the conveniences of the state park, the area is a real find for the entire family.

Wallpack Bend

Friends of ours have argued that the area that includes the portion of the Delaware from Dingman's Ferry through Wallpack Bend is one of the great freshwater fisheries in the United States. That's a stretcher perhaps, but the area is unique for several reasons. Close to the border of Pike and Monroe Counties in Pennsylvania, the Little Bushkill Creek empties into the Big Bushkill, which then flows into the Delaware near the village of Bushkill at Wallpack Bend. On the Jersey side, Flatbrook Creek also flows into the Bend. Both creeks send trout into the Delaware, especially in high water. About two and a half miles north of Wallpack Bend on Route 209 is the confluence of delightful Tom's Creek. Wallpack Bend itself is the most famous bend in the river, and the cliffs rising above are dramatic.

J. B. Kasper, in *The Delaware River*, writes that the Bend provides premiere walleye and smallie fishing and that the numerous eddies, deep pools, points, ripples, and other structures offer inviting and very rich opportunities. Finally, between Dingman's Ferry and Wallpack Bend, the river is secluded because of meager access points. Fishing pressure is fairly light, but you need a boat for the float trip that will produce the most fish.

Tom's Creek and the Two Bushkills

Dwight Landis, on p. 32 of his *Trout Streams of Pennsylvania*, has published a very useful map of Tom's Creek and the Big and Little Bushkills. It clearly shows Wallpack Bend and where the creeks empty into the Delaware, and it shows the important roads and highways. Landis's maps are invaluable, and trout fishers new to the area will do well to refer to his book.

Tom's Creek is not stocked; its brook and brown trout are natives, but they are protected by a two-mile, Catch-and-Release section within the Water Gap National Recreation Area. Despite its rocky stream bed, we have enjoyed fly-fishing this creek. If others come along, there is a pleasant picnic area.

The Big and Little Bushkill Creeks in Pike and Monroe Counties are not to be confused with the Bushkill and Little Bushkill Creeks that are south in Northampton County; those creeks join and then enter the Delaware at Easton, Pa.

The Little Bushkill in Pike County joins the Big Bushkill just south of the village of Bushkill, and then they flow beneath the bridge on U.S. 209. The Little Bushkill is a fine, woodsy stream that is worth fishing until June, when it begins to warm up. Two miles of the lower creek from the mouth to just below Bushkill Falls are stocked, and the upper section of about a mile in the Delaware State Forest is also stocked. To get to the upper section, take the Bushkill Falls Road toward Bushkill Falls and thence past the entrance of the Tamiment Resort and Conference Center, which is a large 2,200-acre Pocono resort. After passing the resort entrance, continue for about two miles, then turn right onto the first road on your right. Park and walk down to your right to the creek. We have not fished this section for many years, and we have relied in part on Landis for our directions.

While you are at the Little Bushkill, you could visit the very commercialized Bushkill Falls, (717) 588-6682. The Bushkill Falls, along with the other seven falls, are okay, but of course you will want to see the fudge kitchen and play miniature golf! Good grief!

The Big Bushkill, which actually belongs in our Monroe County section below but is retained in this section because of its association with the Little Bushkill, is a great stream, provided you don't break a leg among all the rocks and boulders on the stream bed. We enjoy the quiet fishing with slow wading with a staff in wide water, and friends of ours insist on at least one trip to the Big Bushkill every spring. Like the Tobyhanna Creek, the Bushkill has the dark red or brownish water that comes from tannic acid, but the color doesn't much affect the trout; however, the warm water of summer affects them, so fish there in the spring.

The Big Bushkill has a lengthy, Delayed-Harvest, Fly-fishing-Only section that extends for about six miles through the Resica Falls Boy Scout Camp. To get there, take Route 402 north from Marshalls Creek, which is north of East Stroudsburg on U.S. 209. Follow the signs to the Scout Camp, and park at the camp store, where you should contribute some bucks for a permit. To fish the upper part of the Delayed-Harvest section, return to the bridge over the creek on Route 402. Turn right onto Firestone Road and drive about a mile or a mile and a half to the fire road on your right. From here you can walk to the creek, but, if you do fish this section, be sure to walk upstream to the impressive water falls.

To fish the lower, stocked section of the Big Bushkill, follow U.S. 209 into the village of Bushkill. Then take TR 301 over the bridge at the mouth of the Little Bushkill Creek to where TR 301 dead-ends at Winona Falls Road. Turn left, immediately cross over the Big Bushkill, and park after the bridge.

Typically, we tie on the Quills in early spring; then switch to March Browns, Caddis flies (olive and tan), and Light Cahills (especially at sunset). That is pretty much our arsenal, but we have heard that just about every fly in the catalogs works. In fact, we watched a kid catch a lunker on a bright salmon fly, so you can try big attractors or stone flies if you want to.

Dining

In the town of Bushkill, there is a good Italian restaurant with a big bar, although the prices are a little stiff. Try Petrizzo's Italian-American Restaurant, U.S. 209.

MONROE COUNTY

"Often, I have been exhausted on trout streams, uncomfortable, wet, cold, briar-scarred, sunburned, mosquito-bitten, but never, with a fly rod in my hand, have I been in a place that was less than beautiful."
—CHARLES KURALT

The Delaware River: From Bushkill through the Delaware Water Gap

South of the town of Bushkill and Wallpack Bend are Depew Island and Poxono Island. These two structures provide anglers with excellent walleye fishing in the deep holes just below them. The flats around the islands offer up smallies and panfish.

The Delaware north of the Water Gap is interesting and rewarding fishing because of the four islands that promote surface fishing on the flats around them. Tocks, Labar, Depue, and the large Shawness Islands have created typical structures that invite waders in search of smallmouth bass and panfish. But below the islands are the deep holes that harbor walleye and muskie. The Delaware Water Gap itself has very deep water, and in addition to the walleyes, smallies, and shad, anglers are increasingly landing stripers.

The Water Gap is a narrow cut in the ledge that underlies the region. The Delaware accelerates through this gap, producing a great natural beauty that, surprisingly, was improved by one of the works of man that was never constructed.

In 1962, Congress authorized construction of a dam across the Delaware at Tocks Island, a few miles north of the Water Gap. In anticipation of the lake that would have been created by the dam impoundment, the Delaware Water Gap National Recreation Area was created. Although this recreation area was officially designated, environmental groups, including Trout Unlimited and many local organizations, successfully opposed construction of the dam. As a consequence, we have a park-like area offering wonderful fishing, boating, and camping—and the Delaware remains one of the few major free-flowing rivers in the nation.

The Gap is easily reached from either the east or west by taking Interstate 80, which crosses the river at a toll bridge. From the north or south, Route 611 is the fastest approach.

You may launch a canoe or boat at the recreation area. On the New Jersey side, wading is a good option. There is a wide variety of fish here—brown trout, smallmouth bass, walleye, innumerable panfish, and shad in season. A good way to get started fishing the Gap is simply by standing around and watching what the local anglers are doing. We have found that silver spinners, cast a short distance from shore and retrieved parallel to it, can be particularly effective.

The Appalachian Trail crosses the river on the I-80 bridge, and offers two memorable day hikes. On the New Jersey side, follow the white rectangular trail blazes from the I-80 bridge along the service road. Continue on the road, walking parallel to I-80, past the Information Center to the I-80 underpass. A parking area on the right offers access to the red-blazed trail to Mt. Tammanny. The trail ascends moderately and offers views of the Gap in both directions. At the summit, the blue blazed trail descends gradually to the Appalachian Trail, making an interesting loop.

On the Pennsylvania side, the Appalachian Trail rises quickly and spectacularly for more than 1,100 feet, with memorable views of the river. To reach it, take Route 611 into the village of Delaware Water Gap. At the intersection of Main Street and Mountain Road, the trail is marked by a large sign erected by the Commonwealth. The trail follows Delaware Avenue, and there is on-street parking. Follow the traditional Appalachian Trail blazes (white 2 x 6-inch rectangles on trees, power line poles, or rocks). To avoid walking back down, it's necessary to continue on the trail for either 4.7 miles, where a four-wheel drive road crosses it, or 7.2 miles to Fox Gap, where Route 191 crosses the trail. It is easy to spot a car at this intersection for the return journey.

A cautionary note about drinking water: there are no springs, wells, or faucets on this stretch of trail, so you must carry your water. Two of us once carried sufficient water on an overcast day in June and enjoyed a half-day hike. On a bright day in late summer, however, we were parched when we reached our car, and each of us consumed a one-liter bottle of Gatorade that had been cooking in the bright sun on the car's rear seat. The taste is difficult to capture verbally. French vintners have never achieved anything close to it. The moral: take more water than you think you will need.

It isn't difficult to find housing to meet your taste in the Gap area. Camping is available at the recreation area on the New Jersey side of the river. In Pennsylvania, our favorite is the Mountain House in Delaware Water Gap. It has catered to anglers and hikers for years. A bed-and-breakfast and several motels are also available. West of town, at the I-80 exits, are motels for those who prefer the aroma of Diesel fuel and the sizzle of 18 wheelers on hot macadam.

The Information Center at the Delaware Water Gap National Recreation Area, (717) 588-2451, can provide information about trails, fishing, and boating. For information about the Appalachian Trail on either side of the river, consult the *Appalachian Trail Guide*, Volume 4, *New York–New Jersey*, and Volume 5, *Pennsylvania*. They can be purchased at sporting goods stores or directly from The Appalachian Trail Conference, Inc., P.O. Box 236, Harpers Ferry, West Virginia 25425.

The first time I encountered the Water Gap I was in a canoe. There were eight of us in four canoes, and we set off from Port Jervis, New York. It was mid-May, but the temperature was 38 degrees. The water was heavily silted, and in many places it rolled over the banks. This obviously was not the time or place for a swim.

We alternated paddling positions and, on this morning, I was in the stern. This is a position which confers most of the privileges of a Fleet Admiral on the bridge of his flagship.

The river had standing waves as it moved over and around unseen obstacles. The high water captured many branches that normally hang over the river, and they threatened to upset us if we became entangled in them. We estimated the current at five to seven knots. This may not have been accurate, but it is safe to say that the Delaware, she was movin'.

To avoid brush on the eastern bank, we approached the Water Gap close to the western shore, at a bend in the river. We spotted a large, slow, lazy whirlpool about fifteen feet in diameter. A prudent sternman would have avoided it. But having seen whirlpools only at a distance below Niagara Falls, I exercised my prerogative as Fleet Admiral and pushed us into Scylla. My companion in the bow, Chuck Malme, glanced back at me. "Let's try it!" I yelled. And so we entered the pool, which was about as wide as our canoe was long, and did a slow, uncontrolled 360-degree turn. As we came around, I called "Forward!" and, with a few strokes, our canoe was out of the whirlpool and following the same course as before. To his credit, Chuck has never mentioned the incident. But after we stopped for lunch, he took the stern seat.

What about the fishing? Well, muddy water produces muddy fish. I was skunked, in part for lack of trying. The more experienced anglers among us caught only a few carps, two bullheads, and an embarrass-

ingly Lilliputian smallmouth bass. Fishing is generally best when the water is between flood and drought. We, unfortunately, were riding the flood. —R.S.

The Dingman's Falls Visitors' Center has free nature presentations, (717) 828-7802. Below Dingman's Falls, the fishing pier at Loch Lomond is accessible to the disabled.

Tackle

Whenever anglers, especially fly-fishers, are in this area of the nation, from Hancock to Stroudsburg (or from Bangor to Miami, for that matter), they should try to visit with Thom Rivell in Thom Rivell's Fly Fishing Tackle Shop, (717) 676-4446, now located in the Greentown Plaza, Greentown, PA 18426. It is on Route 507, two miles south of Lake Wallenpaupack and one-fourth mile north of Newfoundland. Although his new shop is no longer in Monroe County, Thom knows just about every stream in the Poconos. In his late seventies, Thom has been fishing the Poconos for more than sixty-five years and has forgotten more about fishing the area than most of us will know. However, this "Man Thinking" can help you with sound advice (about fishing and morality) and with the proper equipment. He will sell you what you need, and the emphasis is on "need." Thom will not try to sell you expensive stuff you don't need.

Rivell is a crusty regional treasure. The first time we stopped by in the mid-eighties, when his shop was close to Canadensis, we found an older man working at his bench on a custom-made fly rod. "I just stopped in to say 'Hello,'" I said. "Hello!" came a seemingly annoyed voice with frosty overtones. The surface prickliness is not matched by the texture of the man's heart. "Ask me anything you like," Rivell will say. "There's no dumb question. Dumb answers? Yes. But not dumb questions." When we asked him what about himself and his shop he would like us to emphasize here, he said simply, "Let your conscience be your guide." And so we suggest you go see Thom Rivell, call him, or send a fax to his telephone number.

In 1986 my wife and I took a belated honeymoon and stayed at the Pine Knob Inn in Canadensis, which is still operating as a fine place. We had read about the inn in the Philadelphia Magazine, *and after I saw that*

*the inn was on the Brodhead, I encouraged my wife's interest without
mentioning fly-fishing. At that time, I had not fished the Brodhead, and
my very own honeymoon would offer the opportunity.*

*We enjoyed the Pine Knob Inn, which in those days had a small art
gallery with several nice things. The food was good and the walks
around the grounds were a pleasure. I kept my fishing gear in the car
trunk until I couldn't stand it anymore. I do not enjoy swimming in
pools, and the inn had a little pool adjacent to the Brodhead.*

*"Look," I said to my wife, "you go swimming, and I'll fish by the
swimming pool and be next to you."*

"No!"

"Why not?"

"Just no!"

"You want to fish too?"

"No!"

"Am I learning something here about our possible futures?"

"No!"

"Want a drink?"

"Yes!"

*We went to the inn's tiny lounge, a "clean, well-lighted place," of
course. A couple of professors from Drexel University regaled us with fishing stories, and the bartender, who was the owner of the inn, introduced
us to the painter of a picture we had admired and regaled us with football
stories from his years playing ball at Temple University. I complained
pointedly about no fishing for me and, to cover myself, blamed it on my
ignorance of the creek. The painter said I could get educated by talking
to Thom Rivell, who had tied all the flies that decorated the walls of the
inn. I said I certainly would talk to him.*

"Shall we go up to the room now?"

"No!"

*"Look, I'll maybe go swimming tomorrow, but just go with me to
talk to this Rivell person."*

"O.K."

"O.K. which?"

"Talk to the Rivell person."

"Shall we go up now?"

"No!"

*Anyway, we drove the next day to Thom Rivell's shop, at that time
named the Royal Coachman and located a little south of Canadensis.*

After offering a gruff welcome, Thom stopped tying krill imitations, and I told him about the previous evening at Pine Knob. My wife, smilingly and innocently but with a touch of irony, asked if he really tied all those "just lovely flies" that decorated Pine Knob Inn.

"Well, hell, yes! No one else knows how to tie them like that. Those are historical flies like the ones used here fifty and a hundred years ago. Hell yes."

"They are very pretty," she said; "Could I buy some?"

"Young lady, I'd be pleased for you to buy some. Do you fish?"

"No."

"Why not? Don't you want to? Don't you know how? What's wrong with your husband? Get him to teach you."

"I guess I want to. I don't have a pole."

That last statement got me a fierce look from Thom, who stomped from behind his counter, almost snarling that he would make, build, construct her a darned "pole" and that her husband would pay for it.

I was secretly delighted, but said only that I'd pay. Thom led my wife back into his shop area, discussed the details of the rod he would build, and got together reel, line, leaders, and tippet material. When he came back with my wife in tow, he was chuckling. He winked at me and put a new baseball hat on my head. I think he had known what the score was before he ever mentioned the new fly rod. I laughed and fairly thanked him all to pieces. He said for us to pick up the rod in a couple of days, which we did. As I recall, Thom built that rod for less than $100, and he put my wife's name on it.

My wife was excited by anticipation, and she practiced casting with my stuff until we got her rod. I did not go swimming. And that's how Thom Rivell saved our honeymoon, if not our marriage.

And after I told the artist the whole story, we then bought his painting. My wife still fishes with that "pole"; we are still married; the painting is still on the wall; but I've had to go swimming a couple of times since then. —R.M.

Brodhead Creek and Poplar Run

"One cannot think well, love well, sleep well, if one has not dined well."

—VIRGINIA WOOLF (quoted on the menu at
Russells Restaurant in Bloomsburg, Pa.)

Brodhead Creek, which over the years has had trout fishing intermittently from above Canadensis all the way to the Delaware River at East Stroudsburg, is one of the great streams in the history of American fly-fishing. Historians of the sport rightly celebrate the famous waters of the Catskills and their early fishers, and in earlier pages of this book we took readers there when we wrote of the Beaverkill and the Willowemoc. Nevertheless, Brodhead Creek, which had fly-fishers as early as the eighteenth century, is where the sport began in America, although in the early years the fishing was more for food than for sport.

In the nineteenth century, fly-fishing emerged as a full-scale sport, and its development relied on fishing clubs with protected sections of the creek, most notably the private waters of Arthur Henry. Henry built an inn in the 1830s, Halfway House, which catered to mostly teamsters. In time, Halfway House became Henryville House, "the first trout fishing hotel in America," according to our source Mike Sajna in his *Pennsylvania Trout & Salmon Fishing Guide*, p. 133. Over the years and even after the Catskills emerged as the nation's fly-fishing center, many notable public figures stayed at Henryville House and fished the Brodhead. Among these were General Philip Sheridan, Buffalo Bill, Annie Oakley, Grover Cleveland, Benjamin Harrison, and Theodore Roosevelt. And, of course, many famous anglers fished the Brodhead, including James Leisenring, Ray Bergman, and Vince Marinaro.

To get to the Brodhead coming from the Lake Wallenpaupack-Promised Land area, take Route 390 past Mountain Lake and Skytop to the intersection with Route 447 just north of Canadensis. There are a couple of pitifully short access sections on the creek in Canadensis and south. If you were to stay at the Pine Knob Inn, you would have access on the inn's property. We caught several nice rainbows there during a honeymoon, but fish are rare nowadays. Route 447 follows the Brodhead south to Analomink, where it joins Route 191, which then leads into Stroudsburg as it roughly parallels the creek.

Because fishing on the upper Brodhead is now blocked by posted land, anglers should give little Poplar Run a shot. This brook is not stocked, but you can catch natives. And the scenery can be impressive, for the stream wanders through the Delaware State Forest before it empties into the Brodhead at a point close to Alpine Mountain. For precise locations, it is best to refer to the *Pennsylvania Atlas and Gazetteer* (DeLorme Mapping Co.) or to the map on page 36 of Dwight Landis's *Trout Streams of Pennsylvania*. Coming from Canadensis, follow 447 south for approximately six miles to Poplar Run. Three miles south of Canadensis, you should find Snow Hill Road on the left, and then after about three more miles you will come to Poplar

Run and the bridge on Route 447 that crosses over it. Just after the bridge
and on the left is Laurel Run Road; turn left onto Laurel Run Road and
continue to another bridge that crosses Poplar Run. From this bridge on
upstream, you can happily fish without tresspassing. It will be a well-spent
morning or afternoon.

Fishing the famous Brodhead Creek can be a pain. Typically, the creek
bed lies between one boulder after another; where boulders recede, big
rocks bite at your shins. Much worse than mere boulders are the numerous
"Posted" signs. From Canadensis to Analomink the creek is almost wholly
posted, although just north of Analomink, where SR 1002 crosses the creek,
is the beginning of the stocked section. The Brodhead is stocked from the
SR 1002 bridge to the Delaware River in East Stroudsburg, but getting to
the creek to fish can be very difficult in places. When you do get there, you
might find banks lined with heavy brush and the water swift and often too
deep to wade. Moreover, the lower section is cluttered with civilization, including factories, neighborhoods, Interstate 80, a sewage plant (not always
clean effluent), a paper mill, and East Stroudsburg State University.

In 1955, Hurricane Diane did severe damage to the creek and also
wiped out most of the prolific hatches. The Corps of Engineers channelized
the Brodhead for a little more than a mile south of Analomink to help
protect Stroudsburg from the kind of heavy flooding that Diane caused.
This stretch of the creek is stocked, and the Brodhead Chapter of Trout
Unlimited has been adding tons of boulders to provide the fish with some
cover. Nonetheless, recovery has been slow, if steady. The hatches, however,
are returning, especially in the spring, with Hendricksons followed by Blue-
winged Olives.

The Gorge, which is a section along the railroad tracks on the south
side of East Stroudsburg, gets the young, gutsy fishers who like to wade in
and compete with white-water canoeists. We don't fish there, but Dwight
Landis has fished there. In the detailed write-up of the Brodhead in his
Trout Streams of Pennsylvania, pp. 33–34, he tells you where to park and how
to descend into the Gorge, which passes between the sewage plant and the
paper mill. That water has a history of occasionally turning nasty, but it does
support a population of brown trout, so it can't be all bad. Every time we
visit this area, we stand around in wonderment. Here we are at the famed
Delaware Water Gap, and we simply cannot enjoy it to the hilt. It's our taste;
readers will make up their own minds.

If you drive south on Route 191 and into Stroudsburg, you will cross
over McMichaels Creek just after you pass the intersection with U.S. 209 and
before you get to I-80. In addition, if you turn right onto U.S. 209 (Main

Street), you would cross Pocono Creek. Both streams are stocked; both flow through urban areas; and, despite the stocked fish, both have discouraged us with the nearby traffic. However, Pocono Creek has its beginning near the ski resort on Camelback Mountain, and you can also fish it along I-80 near Tannersville where Pa. Routes 715 and 611 intersect.

Tackle

For fishing tackle, information, and conversation, we have visited Dunkelberger's Sport Outfitter, 585 Main St., Stroudsburg, PA 18360, (717) 421-7950. Other anglers have recommended Dunkelburger's to us.

Obviously, we are happiest fishing where the environment is reasonably natural, even when we are close to a road or houses, as in Allentown on the Little Lehigh or along Kelly Drive in Philadelphia on the Schuylkill. We would prefer fewer Pocono tourist attractions, and we think the Delaware Water Gap area has been too much exploited. Having written that, we will say again what the nation knows, that there are many inns, lodges, resorts, cabins, cottages, motels, hotels, and campgrounds in the Poconos and the Water Gap area, many of them of high quality. For more information, call the Pocono Mountains Vacation Bureau, (717) 421-5791; you can receive a variety of brochures, but be certain to ask for a copy of the *Poconos Vacation Guide*.

Other Attractions

Furthermore, there is plenty to do and see in the Stroudsburg area. Tourist havens for Pocono visitors abound, and there are many worthwhile restaurants. The Pocono Outlet Complex is at Ninth and Ann Street in Stroudsburg with some thirty shops. You'll find Odd-Lot Outlet on U.S. 209 in Marshalls Creek, which is north of East Stroudsburg, and the Pocono Bazaar Flea Market and the Christmas Factory are there, too.

Golf courses are in Analomink, Stroudsburg, Marshalls Creek, and Delaware Water Gap, and several of the resorts have their own courses. If you like Americana, visit the Quiet Valley Living Historical Farm, (717) 992-6161, 1000 Turkey Hill Road, Stroudsburg. Just for the fun of it, some folks would enjoy the Barley Creek Brewing Company, (717) 421-7470, in Tannersville. Head west out of Stroudsburg on I-80 and go to Tannersville. The brewery comes well equipped with restaurant, pub, nightclub, gift shop, and tours of the brewery itself. Call ahead for tour times and for specific directions.

Resorts

But for our visits to the Brodhead Creek and surroundings, we like to seek lodging and dining with fewer tourists and more of nature. If you have the wherewithall, Skytop Lodge, (800) 345-7759, an Orvis-endorsed facility, has it all for the angler and the family. Coming from the north, follow Route 390 into Skytop. From the south, take Route 447 into Canadensis. Just north of Canadensis, bear right onto 390 and follow it into Skytop.

Ed Mayotte, the president of Skytop Lodge, assures us that the fishing for trout in the lodge's own streams continues to be as good as it gets. The lodge's seventy-five-acre lake offers bass and panfish and provides rainbows for float-tube fishing. And if you are still holding out against float tubes, here is the place to get educated. We first tried a tube in a Montana lake a couple of years ago and, after a little practice, we were hooked (metaphorically). But all of that new additional gear can run up expenses. The instructors and guides at Skytop can advise you, for the lodge now has an Orvis Fly-fishing School that runs from May through October.

We have not attended this or any other school, so we cannot specifically recommend it, although Orvis schools tend to have good reputations. We learned as much from Joe Humphreys' *Trout Tactics* (Stackpole Books, 1981, 1993) as we did from about forty-five years of flailing away. Still, in retrospect, we recommend that novices, regardless of the gear one intends to use, get personal instruction. Learn the right way (or a "right" way) at the beginning to avoid bad habits and correct dumb mistakes. Assembling equipment is easy enough, and adequate casting (not truly skillful casting) is not very difficult to learn, but reading water and learning "bugs," baits, and fish habits require time and study. A good school will put it all together for you in one package; then subsequent practice and selected reading will encourage development. Mayotte tells us that Skytop Lodge is also scheduling women-only classes.

In any case, Skytop Lodge features a noted school, and there is an Orvis store to take your money for generally good angling equipment and nice clothing. What goes along are luxurious accommodations, excellent meals, tennis courts, and a golf course. We have not experienced it all, but there is a swimming pool (indoor), along with canoeing and kayaking and about thirty miles of hiking and mountain-bike trails. Children will love Skytop. It's pricey but awfully enticing.

Less expensive and with fewer luxuries is Pine Knob Inn, (717) 595-2532, which we have already mentioned. The inn, with twenty-five rooms, is located on Route 447 just south of Canadensis. Here you will discover a country decor and atmosphere in an 1840s building, but with upscale dining that includes five-course meals on a regularly changing menu. The chef is partial to Angus beef and to lobster, and the wine rack contains a small, but satisfactory selection of not-too-expensive wines. John and Cheryl Garman are the relatively new owners, and they are working to offer guests high quality at reasonable prices. We were sorry to learn that the art gallery is no longer in operation now that its building is a conference center, but the quiet walkways are still in place, and the Garmans have added a couple of gazebos. Youngsters will enjoy that swimming pool next to the Brodhead Creek that we have told you about.

Tobyhanna Creek

There are hundreds of miles of streams, not to mention lakes, in the Poconos, and we won't cover them all. In general, we have tended to stay fairly close to the Delaware River in this book, but we have so much enjoyed ourselves over the years on sections of Tobyhanna Creek that we must include it, even as we ignore its source, Tobyhanna Lake. The creek, notably the Delayed-Harvest, Artificial-Lures-Only section and the portion along Route 423 and despite the deep red color of the water from tannic acid, is one of the Poconos' better trout streams during the spring and early summer. We first learned of it from Owen "Truck" Roberts, a retired schoolteacher in Slatington, Pa.

I wish I had been in Truck's classroom before he retired from teaching. Truck is one of the best trout bums and fly tiers I know, and one afternoon I had the privilege of having him take me fishing on the Tobyhanna. In waders that chirped as we walked, Truck led me down a meadow path for about a mile to a spot that, he said, most anglers were too lazy to reach.

"Try right here," he said, indicating a spot on the creek with a lazy curve.

I stood in the middle of the stream, casting wet flies, dry flies, and nymphs—without success—as a very patient Truck Roberts watched. Finally he waded over to me. "Try some of these," he said, handing me several small, black, gnatlike wet flies.

*I tied one on and cast it out into the stream. "Bang!" a nice trout
hit it. I released the fish and tried again. "Bang!" another trout inhaled
my fly. This went on for at least twenty minutes, and it was one of the
most incredible fly-fishing experiences of my life.
Truck seemed proud of his pupil. —G.I.*

The Tobyhanna is stocked from its source in Tobyhanna Lake for seven
miles downstream through State Game Land 127 to a Pennsylvania Power
& Light Company (PP&L) service-road bridge that crosses the creek. The
bridge is not open to the public, and you will have to hike to it to fish the
lower end of the Delayed-Harvest section.

To get close to the PP&L bridge from the south, take the Northeast
Extension of the Pennsylvania Turnpike heading north and get off at
Exit 35. Go east about thirteen miles on Route 940, through Blakeslee, to
Route 423 at Pocono Lake (there's a stoplight). Turn left onto Route 423
and go 2.7 miles. When you see the sign, "Welcome to Coolbaugh Township," go three-tenths of a mile further and look to the right for two parking
areas, one after the other. Pull in at the second one, gear up, cross the
highway, and walk down the path beyond the long service gate (that's always
locked). When you gear up, you may not want to don your chest waders (we
recommend them, especially in early spring) for either the short or long
hike to the creek. It's better to wear hunting boots and carry your waders
around your neck until you arrive at the water.

It is best to make the decision in the parking lot whether you want to
take the short hike to the lower end of the Delayed-Harvest section beginning at the PP&L bridge or to take the long hike to the upper end, which is
a mile upstream and ends at Still Swamp Run. There is good fishing at both
ends, but the upper end is far less crowded at the season's beginning. To
get to the service bridge, follow the path from the gate until you shortly get
to a path with wheel ruts that branches to the left; follow it to the bridge,
where you can fish upstream in the Delayed-Harvest section or downstream
for open fishing.

To get to the upper end, you will have to walk about a mile. Don't take
the path that goes to the bridge, but keep walking straight ahead. Follow
the path, which has wheel ruts, sometimes faint and sometimes clear, to the
point where the wheel ruts (mostly from stocking trucks) turn left. You turn
left and walk about one hundred yards through a meadow and then some
trees to the creek. Once you are in the water, you can fish upstream or
down. Upstream leads past riffles and to a well-stocked pool, where you will

find chubs, too. Fish this pool on the bottom with #14 and #16 Gold-ribbed Hare's Ears and on the top with Black Midges and small Red Ants. If you see trout rising early in the season, you will do well with small Blue-winged Olives or Adams, but check the hatch to see whether you should switch to Quill Gordons or Red Quills. Later on, add Sulphurs and March Browns to your arsenal, but never forget those Red Ants. They keep on working until the trout are gone. And try this: cast in front of large rocks and obstructions; trout hang up in the easy water there.

You should know that you can wade downsteam all the way to the service bridge, if you can find someone to carry your boots and cooler back for you. If the water is not too high, it is a fine walk. If you are fishing by the bridge, the creek is fairly wide, maybe fifty feet; there are inviting pools, weed beds, and structures around boulders. Later in the spring, Sulphurs and Cream Midges work well, but the Adams is always a general purpose backup. However, on opening day and during the week after, we have seen this lower section packed. Most fishers are courteous enough, but we have witnessed those selfish acts, especially when anglers keep fish they take from the Delayed-Harvest section.

Dining and Lodging

If you take Route 940 from the Turnpike to Tobyhanna Creek, you will notice several restaurants. Among the places for substantial meals are the Edelweiss and Robert Christian's, the latter with good sandwiches and a horseshoe bar, from which tired fishers can watch sports events on the TV. Both are close to Pocono Lake between Blakeslee and Mt. Pocono. The Edelweiss is owned by the Augenstein family and features such German speciaties as schnitzels, sauerbraten, and great homemade spaetzle noodles. Each year the Edelweiss holds an old-fashioned pig roast.

If you come to the Tobyhanna Creek from the north, leave time for some enjoyment along your drive. Come down 191 after you visit with Thom Rivell and stop in South Sterling for good food. The French cuisine at the French Manor, (800) 523-8200, is excellent. The chef's choice is Supreme de Canard Grille, which is grilled smoked breast of duck with a sweet savory sauce with pecans and dried fruit. The building's architecture is engaging also, should you want to stay in one of the lovely rooms. The French Manor was built by Joseph Hirshhorn, the same art connoisseur after whom the Hirshhorn Museum in Washington, D.C., is named.

Perhaps you will want to dine at the 135-year-old Sterling Inn, (800) 523-8200, same number as the French Manor. The food here is also excellent, and you should try the breast of chicken sautéed with sun-dried toma-toes, mushrooms, and Marsala wine. The inn, with the same owners as the French Manor, is much larger than the manor. The rooms are Victorian, and there are suites with fireplaces. The inn has a pool, a spa, and tennis courts, among its various amenities.

By all means have a dinner at Hazzard's Raintree Restaurant, (717) 676-5090, also in South Sterling. Somewhat less formal than the other two es-tablishments, Hazzard's (with Laurie and David Hazzard as the genial hosts) has a pleasant lounge in the back that features Tom Preno as the fishing bartender. Tom Preno and Thom Rivell share knowledge and friendship, so be certain to bend an elbow while discussing Pocono fishing with the bartender. (If you prefer, have a glass of milk; it's okay.) But don't miss the food, and try for a table that overlooks the duck pond. Laurie suggests the popular shrimp, crab, and scallop cakes, which are sautéed and then baked. We have enjoyed an appetizer of roasted red peppers with anchovies and marinated cucumbers. The Friday night special is a lobster dinner.

If you continue south from South Sterling on Route 191, you will shortly come to Route 423, which will take you past Tobyhanna Lake and Tobyhanna State Park, which has extensive family campsites, to the parking lot for fishing Tobyhanna Creek. If, however, you stay on Route 191 and continue to La Anna, you will arrive at Holley Ross Pottery, (717) 676-3248, and its factory outlet. This extensive store can provide all sorts of pottery: ovenware, dinnerware, dolls, cranberry glass, birdbaths, and, as they say, a whole lot more. We have purchased gifts at the pottery for various holidays and are fond of Holley Ross.

LEHIGH AND NORTHAMPTON COUNTIES

"Fishing is a chance to wash one's soul with pure air, with the rush of the brook, or with the shimmer of the sun on the blue water."
—President **HERBERT HOOVER**,
Fishing for Fun and to Wash Your Soul.

THE LITTLE LEHIGH

The gem of Lehigh and Northampton County streams is the Little Le-high. It is so attractive and easy to access that it is remarkable it has survived in its present, nearly pristine, condition. Credit goes, in part, to the Little Lehigh Chapter of Trout Unlimited and the Little Lehigh Fish and Game

Protection Association. But much of the credit belongs to geology: small springs refresh and cool the stream after it is joined by Schaefer Spring Creek, south of Trexlertown.

The most accessible portion of the creek flows within part of the Allentown City Park System, and this is a good place to begin getting acquainted with it.

From Route 309, take Cedar Crest Boulevard south. Make a right on McUngie Road and, shortly, a left on Wild Cherry Lane. A fly-fishing only stretch runs downstream from Wild Cherry Lane to a dam about one mile below.

Another approach is to turn left off Cedar Crest Boulevard on Hatchery Road, which provides many access points to the Little Lehigh.

This portion of the stream maintains a good water level and cool temperature into the fall, and provides season-long angling. Keystone Road, also accessible from Cedar Crest Boulevard, follows the creek upstream to the Lehigh Valley Country Club.

Lower portions of the creek can be reached by following Hatchery Drive to Oxford Drive. A left on Oxford leads to the Lehigh Parkway and Lawrence Street, which parallels the creek. Sizable brown trout are said to be caught here, but the setting is less bucolic than upstream in the park.

If you want to explore the creek upstream, try beginning at the intersection of SR 3004 and Route 100. SR 3004 follows the creek, both upstream and downstream. A fly-fishing only stretch extends from just north of Metztown downstream to Laudenslager's Mill. This stretch suffers from siltation, low water, and higher temperatures in the summer. As a result, it is less crowded but less productive than the Allentown portion of the creek.

The Little Lehigh may be the only creek in the Northeast in which you can find limestone fed-spring waters, a grassy parkland setting, a fish hatchery, and a tackle shop providing sound advice and well-tied flies, all within the limits of a city park.

Other Attractions

Two local wineries are worth a visit. Clover Hill Vineyards & Winery, 9850 Newtown Road, Breinigsville, PA 18031, is owned by John and Pat Skrip, (610) 395-2468. It is beautifully situated on a hillside that brings to mind some of the little wineries of Temecula, outside San Diego. Winery hours are Monday through Saturday, 11:00 A.M. to 5:00 P.M., and Sunday, noon to 5:00 P.M. Try the Oak Vidal, the driest wine they offer, which is aged 7 months in French and American oak barrels ($9.95 a bottle). Also good is the Vidal Blanc ($7.25), a product of stainless steel tanks. Turtle Rock Red ($9.95) is better with a little chill. We have a problem with the tasting room because they don't change glasses, even when you're switching from reds to white.

Not far away is the Franklin Hill Vineyard, at 7833 Franklin Hill Road in Bangor, Pa., (610) 588-8708. Its first vines were planted in 1976, and its spare, almost mouth-puckering red is worth a try. (If you don't feel like driving to Northampton County, Franklin Hill's wines are available at The Grape Vine at the Manayunk Farmer's Market, 4120 Main Street, across from one of our favorite Manayunk restaurants, Vega Grill.)

The Little Lehigh is not only a gem in the eyes of anglers. It has the additional advantage of offering easy access to other points of interest. And at the center of many of these attractions is the City of Bethlehem.

History buffs should devote at least a half-day to the eighteenth-century Industrial Area located at South Main Street and Ohio Road. The Luckenback flour mill has been restored, and other trades, such as hide tanning, are demonstrated on weekends. A stairway leads up to Main Street and other points—the Moravian Museum (Gemein House), which dates from 1741; the antique and glass collection in the Annie S. Kemmerer Museum at 427 North New Street; and, at 501 Main Street, the John Sebastian Goundie House, which has a display of Early Empire and Federal furniture.

Each spring, Bethlehem holds an annual Shad festival, sponsored by the Delaware River Shad Fishermen's Association and Historic Bethlehem, Inc. Events include a shad dart tying contest, children's casting competition, a chefs' cook-off, and demonstrations on how to prepare a boat for a day of shad fishing and how to fillet your shad after catching it.

Next to the Shad Festival, the major attraction in Bethlehem is the annual Bach Festival. We have combined fishing with the festival and many other activities. For example, having released the trout you caught in the Little Lehigh, you may want to enjoy a trout raised in the spring ponds of the Spring Valley Inn at 1355 Station Avenue. After a trout dinner that followed a day of angling, we once listened to a classical guitar performance by John Wesley Dickinson. As they say, it doesn't get much better than that.

After dinner, stop for coffee and folk music at Godfrey Daniel's Coffee House at 7 East Fourth Street. It is the gathering spot for local folkies.

The interval between fishing in the morning and dining in the evening can be a time of great thirst. And thirst is not only a threat to health. It can lead to crotchety behavior, a general decrease in civility, and poor performance on the trout stream. A congenial, licensed hospitality parlor that treats thirst is the Brass Rail, 1137 Hamilton Boulevard at Twelfth Street in Allentown. If you're meeting there, take the Hamilton exit from Route 309. After fishing the Little Lehigh, take Hatchery Road to Hamilton.

A general observation: if you are thirsty in a strange town, consult other anglers. In the absence of a personal recommendation, consult the Yellow Pages under "Taverns," not "Restaurants." —R.S.

Easton

Easton is one of our favorite little cities in eastern Pennsylvania, and our opinion is shared by others. In his book, *The 100 Best Small Art Towns in America*, author John Villani rated Easton 93 because of its culture and vitality. According to a reporter for *The Express-Times*, Villani cited the State Theatre and the Morris R. Williams Center for the Arts at Lafayette College "as places that put Easton on the cultural map."

Shad fishing isn't part of the cultural scene at Easton, but as far as we're concerned, the opportunity to fish the Delaware surely adds additional luster to this town's ambience. During the spring, you'll find shad fishers lining the Delaware River banks near the Lehigh River, and many boats will be anchored out in the main current. Some of those fish will be trying to make it up the Lehigh. But according to the videocam set up at the Easton Dam fish ladders, only 33 American shad migrated up the Lehigh in 1994. The fascinating thing is the time of day when most of the shad moved up river. Shad fishers like to get out on the water at daybreak. But most of the Lehigh fish "posed" for the cameras between 5:00 P.M. and 10:00 P.M., according to outdoors writer Tom Fegely, of *The Morning Call* in Allentown.

Another interesting fact came from research on the Delaware: shad move later in the season than many fishers believe. According to an article in the April 1997 issue of *Field & Stream*, a study by New Jersey biologist Mark Boriek showed that the heaviest shad migrations around New Hope, Pa., in 1995 took place April 27 to 29, and that about 35 percent of the migration came after May 9—when many shad fishers have moved up river or are chasing striped bass at the shore. (Fishing earlier than usual also may pay off. Nuncio, of the Orvis Shop on Walnut Street in Philadelphia, caught a roe shad at Flat Rock Dam on the Schuylkill River in Gladwyne, Pa., on

March 15, 1997, when many shad fishers are just beginning to think about their upcoming season.)

A century ago, Easton became the juncture of three canals: the Delaware Canal, which ran from Easton to Bristol in Bucks County; the Lehigh Canal from Mauch Creek and White Haven to Easton; and the Morris Canal, which ran from Jersey City to Phillipsburg, across the Delaware River from Easton. Canal boats from the Lehigh were shuttled across the river using a cable guide system.

This system of canals, together with other canal and rail links, was part of a network constructed to compete with the commercially successful Erie Canal, which was completed in 1825. The intent was to move coal and goods from the west to New York City and Philadelphia. But the plan was too complex, and it called for too many transfers from rail to canal boat. Although some canals were in use for nearly a century, most of them saw little commercial traffic. Nevertheless, the potential profits, the cost and effort expended to build them, and the sheer wonder at the possibility of boarding a canal boat in White Haven and stepping off in Philadelphia or Jersey City, was a potent stimulus to the imaginations of many, then and now. Traces of the canals and locks remain, and with these vestiges of early capitalist expansion and canal folk songs lives the romance of that time.

The Canal Museum in Easton is the best place to get to know the canals. To reach it, take U.S. 22 from New Jersey or the west and exit at Route 611. Take 611 south and turn left into Hugh Moore Park. The 611–22 interchange is confusing because the signage is poor. Don't be surprised if you have to make more than one approach before touching down in the museum parking lot.

Inside, you'll find a well-produced video, "Pathways of Progress," models of canal boats, and a demonstration of a lock.

Walkers will enjoy the level towpaths. A six-mile path up the Lehigh Canal offers access to the river. Beyond this section, the path west is in poor condition in places.

To the south, the Delaware Canal towpath runs for sixty miles to Bristol. At the Easton end, the canal and towpath are protected as part of the Theodore Roosevelt State Park. South of New Hope, the towpath is clear as far as Washington Crossing Historical Park. From this point south to Bristol, the towpath's condition varies, and in places the path is difficult to follow.

One of us and his friend, Mike Kittross, walked the path from Easton to Bristol in four easy days. A hot summer sun can be onerous, but on overcast days or in cool weather, it's a pleasant walk. Along the way, many riverfront restaurants on Route 32 offer lunch and drinks.

Guides to both the Delaware and Lehigh Canals are available at the Canal Museum.

Dining

Try Cavallo's Country House, a BYOB establishment at 510 South Delaware Avenue on Route 611, especially on Sunday. (610) 252-2500.

Youell's Oyster House is another good spot that's favored by administrators (including several former Temple staffers) at Lafayette College.

If you are in the Bethlehem, Nazareth, or Lititz area, put your rod and wading boots aside for awhile to enjoy two unusual attractions in the area.

The first is the Sturgis Pretzel House at 219 East Main Street in Lititz. "Pretzels?" you might say, "Pretzels?" Yes, pretzels. Here's the story: In 1861, Julius Sturgis was given a recipe for pretzels by the baker for whom he had been an apprentice, Ambrose Rauch. It turns out that Rauch had acquired it from a homeless person in exchange for a meal. Julius Sturgis then opened the first bakery to sell pretzels commercially. It was an immediate success, and it is still producing pretzels in the shape of folded arms in prayer. While we were there, baker Gerald Phillips not only recounted the history of the business, but conveyed a sense of the dedication it takes to keep history alive.

By the way, Harley-Davidson produces a motorcycle model called the Sturgis. Some say it is named after a Midwest town where 200,000 bikers gather each year. In Lititz, however, they know the motorcycle is named after the pretzel.

The second visit you should make is to C.F. Martin & Company at 510 Sycamore Street in Nazareth. Although most public schools do not offer instruction in guitar playing, almost every member of at least two generations of Americans has managed to learn a few elementary strums. If you are one of them, you must make a pilgrimage to Martin. Tours of the factory are available every weekday at 1:15 P.M. Although they're in the business of making guitars and not entertaining tourists, their patience as they answer questions, the aroma of the wood, and the warm camaraderie of the staff are all memorable.

MONOCACY CREEK

The Monocacy is one of the limestone streams in eastern Pennsylvania that has, so far, withstood the rigors of urban pollution and still provides good fishing in the heart of the Moravian city of Bethlehem. For the survival of this freshwater gem, please give a round of applause (and contributions, if you are so inclined), to the good people at the Monocacy Watershed Association and the Monocacy Chapter of Trout Unlimited.

Although it flows through a city, the Monocacy is not easy to reach for fishing because homes and businesses occupy the banks at many places. To complicate matters, the principal access road runs some distance from the stream.

Begin by taking the Northeast Extension of the Pennsylvania Turnpike north to the Allentown-Bethlehem exit. Follow U.S. 22 east into Bethlehem, then turn north on Route 512. Continue to the town of Bath, and you are ready for a pilgrimage on the Monocacy.

Returning south on 512, access to the stream is easy for three miles to Locust Road, where the stream flows east, away from the road. This section has a combination of hatchery trout and hold-over browns that makes for interesting angling. But it may be low in late summer.

Continuing south on 512, cross U.S. 22 and turn east on Berry's Bridge Road. The regulated fishing area begins about one-half mile upstream. If you drive west on Berry's Bridge Road and then south on Center Street, you'll find the end of the regulated area just north of Illicks Mill Road. Macada Road and Bridle Path Road, which run west off Center Street, offer access and parking. This stretch is not stocked because the population of wild brown trout is sufficient to support fishing. It's a limited harvest area, and current regulations should be checked.

The stream is stocked south from Illicks Mill Road to its mouth at the entrance to the Lehigh River. The trophy stretch of the Monocacy is unique, and it will both try and reward any angler.

BUCKS COUNTY

Dining

The Cascades Restaurant in Kintnersville is situated on a gorgeous slope in Upper Bucks County. Often, when I fish the Upper Delaware, I like to follow the river home, and The Cascades is just a short detour off Route 611. Once, returning from a fishing trip up north, I stopped at the restaurant for lunch. As an excellent portion of grilled Norwegian salmon came to my table, I asked the waiter if there was a pay phone on the premises for me to call my office. A few minutes later he appeared with a cellular phone and invited me to make any call I needed—on the house.

—G.I.

The Apple Jack, "a rustic cellar bar," in Point Pleasant, is where 60's radical Abbie Hoffman spent his last days. With Harleys parked outside, it's not for everyone, but we've found some of the most knowledgeable Delaware fishers hanging out here.

The American Grill, at Routes 611 and 32 in Kintnersville, (215) 847-2033, is a great place for kids and adults. There are crayons on the tables, and patrons are invited to express themselves artistically on white sheets of paper that also serve as tablecloths. 1950s rock 'n roll plays constantly, and the food is very good.

The Cuttalosa Inn is one of our favorite places to dine, especially in the summer and early fall when you can eat outdoors, near a waterfall. Or, heading north on River Road, take the first left after the saw mill, travel through the woods, and emerge at the Carversville Inn in the tiny village of Carversville.

Black Bass Hotel, Route 32, Lumberville, celebrated its 250th anniversary in 1995, (215) 297-5770. The hotel has two suites and seven rooms. Rates: $55 to $175 per night, higher on weekends. This famous inn has played host to Angela Lansbury, Moss Hart, Ann-Margret, and many others. It looks out on the foot bridge that takes pedestrians across the Delaware to Bulls Island State Park in New Jersey. (The stone footings of the bridge are good places to find walleyes.)

Other attractions

Bucks County River Country, Point Pleasant, offers family tubing trips down the Delaware River. While these folks may sometimes annoy bank fishermen, they are not as disruptive as the jet ski nuts. Open daily during the tubing season, Bucks County River Country is on Route 32 (River Road). Kayaks are also available for rent. Call (215) 297-8823.

Dilly's Corner, on Route 32 across from the venerable Centre Bridge Inn, is the place where local families have flocked for ice cream for years.

LUMBERVILLE

Bob Smith, Bob Marler, and I were shad fishing one morning on the Delaware in Bucks County, just north of the Black Bass Hotel in Lumberville. We were among a group of about a dozen shad fishermen, all clad in waders and standing elbow to elbow at a narrow spot where the river is constricted.

No one was catching anything, and everyone was losing shad darts on the rocks and river debris. After an hour of futility, I headed back to the shoreline to take a break, leaving an opening in the line of fishermen. Two bearded locals, who looked like they could have been extras for a remake of the movie "Deliverance," were sprawled on the beach. They eyed me walking out of the river, and one of them said to the other, "You go out there and take that guy's spot, and you'll get yourself a shad."

I heard them, and as the newcomer passed me, I said, "Go get 'em, tiger."

He reached my spot, made one cast, and hooked into a battling shad. His friend on shore roared with jeering laughter that was not soon forgotten by me, even in the solace of the Apple Jack bar up River Road in Point Pleasant. —G.I.

LAKE GALENA

Lake Galena, at Peace Valley Park in New Britain Township, is west of Doylestown. Once again, rapacious developers and foolish local officials have helped destroy a beautiful lake. Bucks County lost control of the lake in 1994 when it sold the infamous Point Pleasant pumping station on the Delaware River. Because of an interim agreement, the North Penn and North Wales water authorities can drain water from the lake to provide for their customers. Everybody wins—except the birds, the fish, and serious anglers. To reach Lake Galena, take Route 152, Limekiln Pike, north from its intersection with U.S. 202. If the wind is from the southwest, or you wish to reach the boat livery, turn right on Creek Road. The lake is reached in slightly less than a mile. If the wind is from the north, or you wish to reach the fish pier, pass Creek Road and turn right onto New Galena Road. The lake is one mile east.

A bonus: each month, when there's a full moon, the Peace Valley Nature Center offers a free "Full Moon Walk" to explore nature by night. For information, (215) 345-7860.

I happily recall bobbing idly in a rented canoe on a foggy summer afternoon. The shores of Lake Galena were reduced to soft, gray contours, and the conversation my wife and I enjoyed had the same soft outlines. I fished lazily, with no results. There had been more productive days, including one in which two of us spent a pleasant afternoon catching and

releasing more than two dozen bluegills. (This may not be demanding fishing, but early in the season when the timing of cast and strike are a bit rusty after a long winter, it is enormously satisfying.) On this day, however, the fishing was wrapped in the sybaritic pleasures of the fog, the gentle motion of the canoe, the conversation, and the awareness that a fish, more energetic than I, might somehow impale itself on my hook. None did. It didn't matter. Sometimes, as they say, the fishing is more important than the fish. —R.S.

LAKE NOCKAMIXON

Lake Nockamixon was created by the Department of Environmental Resources in 1974 as part of Nockamixon State Park. The lake fell on hard times because of pollution runoff, much of it from local farms and septic systems; algae took over and pesticides and PCBs were found in the sediment. The Federal EPA helped out in 1983, and Quakertown built a sewage treatment plant. Bob Staub, a retired park ranger at Nockamixon, says the stone fishing pier is good for youngsters and novices.

To reach Lake Nockamixon, take Route 611 north to Route 412 and, almost immediately, southwest on Route 563. The experience of approaching Nockamixon is an end in itself. The eastern end of the lake is watched by a slender-spired church that looks as though it were transported from the Rhine country. The sight of a fleet of Sunfish or other day sailors can gladden the heart. This lake has an ambience that lingers in the memory long after a day of fishing, sailing, hunting, or hiking. It is what all lakes should be. For dining, try J.B.'s Lake House Inn, 1100 Old Bethlehem Road, Perkasie, or Cappie's on Route 563. For tackle, Bucks County Outfitters, Route 313 and Fifth St., Perkasie, (215) 257-9536.

SOME OTHER BUCKS FISHING SPOTS

Pine Run

If you are in the New Britain area, west of Doylestown on U.S. 202, turn north opposite Delaware Valley College, park near the site of the covered bridge, and wade east. You will find interesting angling for smallmouth bass, perch, and sunfish in this section. If you go west, turn north on Route 152, and turn east after a mile on Newville Road, you will encounter the North Branch. We have had little success here, but friends report that, in the spring, it is a productive stretch.

Pidcock Creek

This small but attractive stream can be reached from Route 32 at Washington Crossing State Park. Turn west on SR 1003 just north of the park, go left at the Y-intersection, and park near the covered bridge. This is a picturesque spot. Half of the fun is being there, 40 percent is the access to New Hope, and the remainder is the fishing. Have fun and don't take it seriously!

Neshaminy Creek

This creek runs through heavily developed parts of Bucks County, but nevertheless offers a few opportunities for the angler. Our favorite access is easy to find. Turn off Route 611 two miles south of Doylestown onto Almshouse Road heading east. The creek can be seen on your left a few hundred yards down the road. If you can find a spot for your car, you can wade to the creek. Alternately, continue east and turn left on Valley Road. This road parallels the creek for a half-mile or so.

Another approach is to take Route 463 to the Tyler State Park turn (west on State Road 2036). Some anglers consider this the most productive section of the creek.

Tohickon Creek

If it's too warm to fish Lake Nockamixon, try Tohickon Creek just below the dam at the southeast corner of the Nockamixon State Park. This stream carries cool water into summer and often provides good angling when other streams are lethargic. It can also be reached from Route 32 by turning north on SR 1009 and entering Ralph Stover State Park. We prefer the stretch nearer the lake, but the park provides shade, opportunities for picnics, and pleasant walking and birding.

Cabin Run Creek

Assume it's a pleasant summer day. You and a friend are to celebrate a birthday, anniversary, or windfall with dinner in Stockton or Lambertville, N.J., or in New Hope on the Pennsylvania side. In the subtle, manipulative way of an angler, you plot some fishing in the afternoon before dinner. But where? And what would attract a nonangling companion? Cabin Run Creek was designed by a thoughtful deity for such occasions. It offers angling, birding, and short walks.

The best place to begin is Ralph Stover State Park. See Tohickon Creek above. Cabin Run joins Tohickon at the western end of the park. It is slightly more private, less frequented, and more productive of good before-dinner conversation. It is difficult fishing, but a light fly rod and patience will do well here.

Doylestown

The Mercer Museum, 84 South Pine Street, (215) 345-0210, contains more than 50,000 tools and artifacts, the oldest dating from the Native Americans of from 6,000 to 8,000 B.C. The building itself dates to about 1916. Monday through Saturday, 10:00 A.M. to 5:00 P.M. Sunday, noon to 5:00 P.M. Open to 9:00 P.M. on Tuesday.

The James A. Michener Art Museum, 138 South Pine Street, (215) 340-9800. A permanent collection of nineteenth- and twentieth-century American art, plus new exhibitions, Michener's own legacy, and the Nakashima Reading Room, featuring furniture of the great Langhorne woodworker who died in 1990. Tuesday through Friday, 10:00 A.M. to 4:30 P.M. Saturday and Sunday, 10:00 A.M. to 5:00 P.M. Closed Mondays.

The Moravian Pottery and Tiles Works, 130 Swamp Road (Route 313), (215) 345-6722. This Henry Mercer facility was completed in 1913 and produces tiles and mosaics for buildings throughout the world. Self-guided and guided tours available. Monday through Sunday, 10:00 A.M. to 5:00 P.M., with last tour at 4:00 P.M.

Fonthill Museum, East Court Street and Route 313, (215) 348-9461. Henry Mercer's castle built of hand-mixed concrete. There are 44 rooms, 18 fireplaces, 32 stairwells, and more than 200 windows. Reservations required for the guided tour. Admission is $5 for adults, and children under six are free.

Don't forget to stop at Bucks County's first microbrewery. It's McGowan's Buckingham Mountain Brewing Company & Restaurant at 5775 U.S. 202 in Lahaska, Pa., (215) 794-7302. This emporium, which was rebuilt after a disastrous fire in early 1997, is open seven days a week for lunch and dinner. Pints usually go for $3.75, but they'll only charge you $2 during Happy Hour from 4:30 to 6:30 P.M., Monday through Thursday, and from 9 to midnight Monday through Thursday and from 10:00 P.M. to 1:00 A.M. Friday and Saturday, but by then the ice in your cooler will have melted and the fish you were planning to take home will have lost your interest as tablefare. Buckingham Mountain offers such alcoholic delights as Hermit Albert's Pale Ale, Desperation Ale, Liam's Lager, Ed's Double Red Eye, Pighouse Porter, and (our favorite, based on nothing more than an appreciation for Kurt Vonnegut) Slaughterhouse Stout.

PHILADELPHIA

Tackle

Hands down, the best bait and tackle shop in Philadelphia is Brinkman's at State Road and Linden Avenue, which moved into larger quarters in 1996. Bruce Brinkman and his family know just about everything there is to know about freshwater and saltwater fishing, and they readily share their knowledge. Novices need not fear that basic questions they ask will be greeted with rolling eyes and thinly disguised ridicule. Brinkman's also sells hunting and fishing licenses. This place has our top recommendation.

Across the street on State Road, Vinnie's offers cold beer and decent roast pork sandwiches. Down at the river, try Mimi's for dinner.

Heading south on State Road, look for Pennypack Street and a sign for the Fire Academy. Turn left and go all the way to the river. This spot is where sharpies catch stripers.

PENNYPACK CREEK

In the spring, when the water is high and cool, Pennypack Creek offers angling opportunities in and just outside the City of Philadelphia. The most rustic area of the creek is found in the stretch between Bryn Athyn and Huntingdon Valley. To reach it, take Route 63 east from Willow Grove or west from U.S. 1. Route 63 crosses the creek just west of the intersection with Route 232. One can enter here and wade north.

The easiest access to a good angling area is from the Pennypack Creek Wilderness. It can be reached by taking Edge Hill Road east from Route 611. The winding road follows the contours of the land. The entrance to the Wilderness is on the right at 2955 Edge Hill Road. In the late spring Pennypack offers both angling and birding opportunities. We have seen orioles, both Baltimore and orchard, in numbers. The typical woodland birds, such as tufted titmouse, varieties of sparrows, red-winged blackbirds, and smaller hawks such as the American kestrel, can be found near the creek. The staff of the Pennypack Wilderness, maintained by the Pennypack Watershed Association, is knowledgeable and offers an education program. If you have scruples about carrying fishing gear through a sanctuary, take the road to the west of the park and leave your car near the bridge. Fishing here, on light tackle, for smallmouth bass, perch, and sunfish, is best in the early summer.

One of the charms of the creek is that it flows through Pennypack Park in Philadelphia. Bustleton Avenue and Verree Road intersect the park and provide access to the creek. The park has the rhythm and the people—children playing, families enjoying picnics—of any urban park. There is something particularly satisfying about angling in the city. It is a remembered pleasure, a reminder of what life in the area was like before we all arrived. Don't expect large fish, but you can be certain of catching something. As we said, it is a good place for children and families.

The Sportmaster on Robbins Avenue, on the way to the Tacony-Palmyra Bridge, has a selection of hunting and fishing gear.

In the shadow of the Tacony-Palmyra Bridge, just off State Road, there's a popular pier used by fishers.

The Philadelphia Airport Area

One of the most characteristically urban places, both to fish and bird, lies behind Philadelphia International Airport. Drive south on Island Avenue, cross Interstate 95, past what Philadelphians remember as the old International Terminal, and follow the signs for Old Fort Mifflin. When those signs indicate a left turn, continue straight toward the ARCO oil tank area and the river.

Here is a place you can fish successfully for carp, largemouth bass, perch, and other species that can survive in an urbanized riverway. Turning skyward, in the winter you can find many smaller hawks such as the northern harrier and American kestrel. In the summer, goldfinch, blue grosbeaks, and swamp sparrows nest in this area.

One morning in May I arose in a foul mood. Work and other obligations had kept me from fishing for longer than I felt I could tolerate. The day ahead looked like the previous weeks: meetings and desk work until an hour or so after the usual quitting time. And then a drive to Philadelphia International Airport for the one bright spot in the day: my wife's arrival on a 9:30 P.M. flight from Boston.

Then I had an idea. Why not put binoculars and a fishing rod in the car and try the area along the Delaware behind the airport? That's exactly what I did, but finding a suitable site wasn't easy. A traffic cop, probably feeling much as I did, waved me past the turn I wanted to make, and it took me 10 minutes to find my way back. A red-winged blackbird welcomed me when I finally arrived at the river near the ARCO tank farm. A charm of goldfinches was busily feeding on a bush I couldn't identify. I spotted several sparrows and, to my surprise, an Indigo bunting. As the sun settled in the west, the birds were reduced to silhouettes. That "common grayness" was settling in. It was time to turn from birding to fishing.

I assembled my travel fly rod and cast a fly upon the water. Nothing happened. Anxious to extend my range and get away from a bush threatening my back cast, I moved farther and farther out on the marshy, muddy border of the river. After several minutes I had a strike. A small bluegill took my fly and gave me a splashy little fight. As I brought him in and took a step farther out to reach him, I was aware for the first time that my feet were not only very damp but covered with mud.

The 9:30 flight was on time. When Suzanne came down the ramp I welcomed her with a hug and a big "Hello, darling." A nonfisher, she looked at me warily and asked, "What did you do to your shoes?"

—R.S.

John Heinz Tinicum Preserve

Although Darby Creek is not prime fishing water, it runs alongside one of the better birding spots in Philadelphia. The John Heinz Tinicum National Environmental Center can be reached by following signs toward Philadelphia International Airport. From the Schuylkill Expressway (I-76), take Exit 5 toward the Airport and Twenty-sixth Street. At the second light, turn right and cross the Penrose Avenue Bridge. Turn right at the sign for Interstate 95 and Island Avenue. At the next light, turn right onto Eighty-fourth Street. At the second light, turn right to the entrance. If you have a road map, simply head for Eighty-sixth Street and Lindbergh Boulevard.

The variety of bird life in this area is astonishing. Palm, mourning, and Wilson's warblers are here, as well as both fish and common crows—it's worth a visit just to hear the dry, un-crow-like call of the former. Everyone—except us—has apparently spotted the Traill's flycatcher, which nests here. During the summer months you can find green and great blue herons, Louisiana herons, cattle egret, and glossy ibis.

THE SCHUYLKILL RIVER

"If the angler happens to catch a fish, then surely no man is gladder in spirit than he."

—DAME JULIANA BERNERS, in her 1496 book,
A Treatise on Fishing with a Hook

To many people, the Schuylkill is a river of athletes, young and old, who look like modern-day descendants of Thomas Eakins's scullers. They glide with apparent ease past Philadelphia's boathouses on the north bank of the river, turning shortly before reaching the Greek Revival Philadelphia Museum of Art. In fact, two members of the famous Kelly family trained on the Schuylkill and went on to become Olympic Gold Medalists.

Morning commuters, driving east into the city of Philadelphia on Kelly Drive, are often treated to a watercolorist's delight: the morning sun glowing through the river mist. For anyone who has lived in and loved Philadelphia, the Schuylkill is forever locked in memory.

Many anglers, however, find little to entice them in the lower portion of the river, from Norristown to the confluence with the Delaware. Yet this portion of the Schuylkill is alive with all kinds of fish—not all of them worthy of the table.

One of the best access areas in the lower Schuylkill is Flat Rock Park, off the Schuylkill Expressway (I-76) at Gladwyne in Montgomery County. Dave Plasket, a glassblower in Temple University's Chemistry Department, heads for Flat Rock whenever he has a yen to fly-fish for feisty small-mouth bass.

Catfish thrive in this stretch of the river, and bass are taken from small outboard-powered boats from Conshohocken west to Norristown.

Fishing on the Schuylkill, however, is best from Valley Forge National Historical Park west to the river's source 110 miles upstream.

For those who long for "river fishing from banks, the way we did it when we were kids," the Schuylkill frontage in and north of Pottstown offers bass, sunfish, and occasional pickerel. This is water fished best with spinning gear that's capable of long casts.

From U.S. 422, take Route 662 south. It will provide access from the north side of the river. A right turn just before the bridge across the river will take you to unnumbered town roads that approach the Schuylkill. On the south bank, Route 724 parallels the river from Pottstown northwest to Reading. From Gibraltar northwest, the river suffers from the impact of the small city.

In Reading, the wonderful Tulpehocken Creek, which we discuss later, joins the Schuylkill. Continuing north from Reading on Route 61, you can take side roads to Leesport or Mohrsville, where access to the river is easy. But from this point north, the Schuylkill responds to weather: it's high after rain and low during a drought.

During the regular fishing season, the stretch of water abutting Auburn can be rewarding. To reach it from Route 61, take Route 895 west.

But Schuylkill Haven and Pottsville have not been kind to the river. If you plan to follow the river north, skip these towns and try the Schuylkill at Saint Clair, which can be reached off Route 61.

WISSAHICKON CREEK

"For peace and quiet, the Wissahickon might not be the best trout stream in the state, but it is located in a beautiful setting and you certainly won't be disappointed with the amount of fish it contains."
—Vic Attardo, in *Pennsylvania Afield*

This creek is near and dear to the hearts of people who live in the northwestern section of Philadelphia. It is the stream along which they walk or jog, ride their horses, feed ducks, stroll with lovers, people-watch—and catch stocked trout.

Where did we get the name of this creek (there's a Wissahickon Avenue, too)? According to Robert Alotta, author of the Temple University Press book, *Street Names of Philadelphia,* Wissahickon is "a corruption of the Indian name *wisameckham,* meaning 'catfish stream.' For a brief period, the stream was called Whitpaine's Creek, after an early settler, Richard Whitpaine."

In City limits, fishing action on the Wissahickon is concentrated within Fairmount Park south, from Northwestern Avenue to a half-mile south of Valley Green Inn. Access is convenient from Northwestern Avenue, Springfield Avenue in Chestnut Hill, or Ridge Avenue in Roxborough. Parking is available at all these locations.

In season, trout can be found in pools off the path that is east of Northwestern Avenue. A pool just upstream of the covered bridge can be productive. Within two miles below Valley Green Inn, there are three good pools which hold trout.

For many, the best fishing on the creek is just north of the City limits. Morris Arboretum and Chestnut Hill College abut the stream and make access difficult. North of them, however, there is easy access from Flourtown Road in Whitemarsh. Stay on the road for a half-mile and park in an overflow lot for a country club. Walk along a grassy path for a half-mile upstream and, just south of the riffle under a high railroad bridge, you'll find some of the best fishing on the creek. Our occasional fishing companion, Lloyd Sturgeon, conducted an informal census of the stream using, to our delight, worms. He assures us there is an ample supply of bluegills. You will seldom be skunked. There's a popular area a half-mile further south, but it is frequented by ducks, people who feed ducks, and people who come to watch people feed ducks. To the north, there is access from the Route 73 bridge and, further still, in the borough of Ambler. The best fishing, however, is from Valley Green Road south to the City line.

For a meal or dust-cutter after fishing, one can hardly go wrong at the Valley Green Inn, one of Philadelphia's most historic and charming dining spots. East of the stream, on Germantown Avenue in Chestnut Hill, is McNally's bar, home of Guinness on tap and the Schmitter, a sandwich that former *Philadelphia Inquirer* columnist Steve Lopez called "a heart attack on a bun." Those fishing farther north will find Cisco's Bar on Bethlehem Pike, where sportsmen raise mugs of beer under the watchful gaze of moose and elk heads. Note: Valley Green Inn is in the City, off Springfield Avenue, while Valley Green Road is five miles north, off Bethlehem Pike.

The Wissahickon isn't a wilderness stream, but it provides urban angling that's hard to match in other cities.

Birding the Fishing Spots of the Wissahickon

Although the best birding in the Wissahickon Valley is in Carpenter's Woods at the intersection of Sedgewick and Wayne avenues in the Mount Airy section of the city, there is rewarding birding near some of the better fishing areas. Passerines will be found in large numbers during the migrations near the intersection of Route 73 and the Wissahickon Creek and, in lesser numbers, along Hidden Drive west of Valley Green. Warblers are usually present in early May and, in September, the "confusing fall warblers" can be found in sufficient variety to frustrate even an experienced birder.

MONTGOMERY COUNTY

PERKIOMEN CREEK AND GREEN LANE RESERVOIR

Perkiomen Creek rises near the triangle formed by the boundaries of Montgomery, Berks, and Lehigh Counties. The angler is likely to first notice it, however, a few miles southeast, where Perry Road and Fruitville Road cross the creek. Both roads run south from SR 1042, which parallels the creek's north bank. SR 1042 intersects Route 29 in the village of Palm. Head southeast on SR 1042, toward East Greenville. The roads are easy to identify and provide good access to a Perkiomen that is narrow here but cool and pleasant to fish.

Just west of the town of Red Hill, the Perkiomen enters Green Lane Reservoir, a popular fishing, picnicking, and birding area. Boats are available for rent here. Stories are told locally of large bass taken from shore, but your chances are best if you fish deep from a boat.

To reach Green Lane Reservoir, take Walt Road to the southeast off Route 29, just north of Red Hill. South of Red Hill, the reservoir can be reached by taking Market Road, Red Hill Road, or Knight Road to the south off Route 29. Knight Road intersects Route 663, which offers access to the reservoir's western side.

From the reservoir south to Collegeville, Route 29 parallels the Perkiomen Creek and offers numerous access points. Some favorites include SR 1037, where it intersects Route 29 at the village of Green Lane; south of the bridge which can be found by taking Spring Mount Road east from Route 29; and the pool south of the intersections of Routes 113 and 29.

South of Collegeville, SR 4008, running east from Route 29, provides access to a pleasant area in Central Perkiomen Valley Park. The intersection of Sunnyside Road and SR 4002 in the town of Audubon is near another area which has produced bass. Having said all this, we must add that most anglers will find that the most pleasant and productive fishing occurs upstream of Route 113.

SKIPPACK CREEK

Generations interact in unpredictable ways. My father taught me to fish with bait and colorful plugs. But it was our son, Eric, who taught me how to fly fish. He was ten, and he did it on a stream not unlike the Skippack. —R.S.

If the old real estate saw about value—"location, location, location"— were applied to fishing, Skippack would be a prized creek. Located in burgeoning Montgomery County, not far from Philadelphia, the stream flows through farmland and enters Evansburg State Park, where several roads cross it on picturesque stone bridges. Stands of mature trees provide shade on sunny summer afternoons.

In the early season, when the Commonwealth stocks Skippack with rainbows and browns, wading is recommended to escape the overhanging trees. The water is high then, and the hatchery trout can provide anglers with good sport. Depending upon the weather, Skippack's water quality may be good into late June. After summer takes its toll, however, the stream becomes logy, with stagnant backwater. Unlike the Perkiomen, into which it flows just south of Collegeville, the Skippack does not have a reservoir or spring to help maintain its level.

Although anglers from further off may not find the creek worth a special trip, those in the area should not miss it. The mature forest, varied bird life, easy access, and a pervading sense that it has not changed much in the last century make it a refreshing half-day venture. The park contains picnic areas, a model eighteenth-century garden, splendid birding in season, and other attractions for nonfishing members of a family. Warblers can be found here in abundance in the spring, an occasional red-tailed hawk in the summer, and woodpeckers—mostly downies among the aging trees, and there is always the cool relief from summer's heat along the banks.

To reach Skippack Creek, drive east on Route 73 from the town of Skippack and turn south on SR 3001 about one-half mile after crossing the creek. Take the first right to the bridge. If you do not catch your personal limit at this location, continue and take a left on Mayhall Road. This road will take you to the center of the park and a designated fishing area.

The Skippack is a minor stream, but it is out of the way and quiet, even during the crowded early weeks of the season. And a stop at the Village of Skippack, with its antique shops, restaurants, galleries, and gift shops is mandatory for nonangling companions of fishers.

The creek can also be reached from Route 73 between Center Point and the town of Evansburg or, from the south, off U.S. 422. Parking is available, and the Skippack Trail, which runs along the south and east banks of the stream, allows anglers to get away from congested areas near the roads. A map of the forest is available from the park office.

Dining

Food and drink can be found at Champs Sports Bar in the Center Point Golf Club on Route 73 and in a number of restaurants in the tourist mecca of the Village of Skippack.

VALLEY CREEK

Russell Conwell, the founder of Temple University, is famous for his observation that one need not search the world for riches; one may find a diamond in one's own backyard. Valley Creek is a diamond—a rough diamond—in Philadelphia's backyard.

The lower portion of this creek meanders through Valley Forge National Park, just before it enters the Schuylkill River. A short creek, it nevertheless offers a dozen miles of fishing.

Valley Creek is spring-fed, rising from the limestone aquifer that keeps its temperature in the 70s on even the hottest of summer days. Like similar streams, Valley Creek's flow is maintained during the summer, and it offers anglers opportunities when other creeks become mere trickles because of low water.

In recent years the creek has suffered from pollution, and it has not received the protection it deserves. Despite the neglect, there's a healthy population of brown trout for spin anglers, bait fishers, and fly fishers. The Valley Forge Chapter of Trout Unlimited has made practical and political efforts to save the stream. Their members deserve everyone's support. The creek is designated as a "no-kill" stream.

A tributary, Little Valley Creek, is somewhat more secluded, and happens to be our favorite. Fly fishers will find that the brown trout respond to a variety of flies, and that "matching the hatch," although possibly more productive, is not necessary on either stream.

Valley Creek is a diamond in the rough, but the ambience of Valley Forge—and the knowledge that George Washington's troops used this stream during their difficult winter—gives the angler a sense of being part of our nation's history.

Valley Creek is easily reached from Exit 24 of the Pennsylvania Turnpike, from U.S. 422 and Route 23, just across the Schuylkill River from Conshohocken. Roads to the national park are well-marked. Route 252 parallels the creek. There is convenient parking near a covered bridge where Route 252 intersects Yellow Springs Road. From there south, past an iron bridge and the Turnpike bridge, wading is recommended. Upstream, the creek enters residential areas, and is less than secluded.

Little Valley Creek can be entered from Swedesford Road, just west of U.S. 202.

Delaware County

RIDLEY CREEK

"I'll tell you, what I want is that they'll find me dead here someday, with a fly rod in my hand and a 27-inch fish dragging me around the crick. For me, that would be the perfect death."
—a grizzled Ridley Creek fisherman, quoted in the
Philadelphia Inquirer (April 2, 1995)

Ridley Creek is the graduate school for anyone interested in fly-fishing near a large city. Although some consider it "pleasant"—a back-handed compliment—we think it's a model of successful trout stream management in an urban/suburban environment.

The fish are of average size, smaller than those in nearby Valley Creek, but the ambience of this stream is unbeatable. It supports varied and strong hatches; the wading is secure; the access is simple with adequate parking.

You can approach the creek from Route 3, west of Newtown Square. Turn north on Plumsock Road and left on SR 2010 (Goshen Road), which crosses the stream and provides access to its less-fished stretch.

The best fishing, however, is found by back-tracking east on Route 3 and turning south on Sandy Flash Drive into Ridley Creek State Park. Parking at the historic Colonial Mansion will give you access to the stream. Or you may continue east on Route 3 and turn south on Providence Road. Then turn right at the second intersection, Bishop Hollow Road, and continue to the three-way intersection with Ridley Creek Road. This will place you in the middle of the Fly-Fishing-Only section of the stream.

From the parking at Colonial Mansion on Sandy Flash Drive, you can walk to the upstream section of the creek, where it is roughly thirty feet wide and easy to wade. Here there are numerous pools that hold trout into midsummer. Access to the lower section is easy if you park near the dam and walk upstream along the bicycle path.

The best part of the creek is the Fly-Fishing-Only section which begins at the dam and extends downstream six-tenths of a mile to Dismal Run, a private stretch of water. It is this section of the creek that is worthy of the "graduate school" designation. It is heavily fished, and the trout are not forgiving of splashy casts, drifts that drag, or clumsily handled nymphs. Anglers with a light touch can harvest a double reward: a fish and the satisfaction of knowing they caught it in difficult conditions.

Take a look at the fishers, too. They are usually appropriately clad and outfitted, often with the best equipment. When you fish this stretch of Ridley Creek, you are a member of a stylish and skilled fellowship!

Members of the Delco Anglers and Trout Unlimited have worked with the Commonwealth to preserve and improve the stream. Ridley is a good example of what can be done when conservationists and government agencies join hands.

Birding

According to Harding and Harding, one of the best places for birding in Ridley Creek State Park is the short stretch of the creek along Sycamore Mills Road. This is a varied habitat that attracts many migrants. The Hardings report seeing up to 25 species here during the spring and fall migrations. We have seen 12 species in late June. In truth, we have been far more successful in birding than in fishing this demanding "graduate school."

Tackle

Eyler's Fly & Tackle, 895 Penn Street, Bryn Mawr, PA 19010, (610) 527-3388, is owned by Tom and Alice Forwood. Eyler's is an Orvis dealer and Cortland Pro-Shop. It's open Tuesday through Friday, 10:00 A.M. to 5:30 P.M.; Wednesday and Friday evenings, 6:30 P.M. to 9:00 P.M.; Saturday, 9:00 A.M. to 5:00 P.M. Closed Sunday and Monday.

CHESTER COUNTY

"One frequently overlooked option open to local fishermen is angling for the elusive wild trout of Chester County . . . Like most anglers, I'm not inclined to give away the locations of my own Chester County wild trout hotspots."

—TOM TATUM in the *Daily Local News* of West Chester

(July 5, 1994)

FRENCH CREEK

A friend and I were out hiking. Shortly after the trail we were following entered French Creek State Park, we heard the soft, bittersweet sound of mountain dulcimers.

With some serendipity, we had stumbled upon the annual French Creek Dulcimer Retreat of the Greater Pinelands (New Jersey) Dulcimer Society. It was a memorable introduction to French Creek, and a week later I returned to try the fishing. It was as good and unusual as the music. —R.S.

The Valley Greens Association has petitioned the Commonwealth of Pennsylvania to upgrade French Creek from a stream of "high quality" to one of "exceptional value." The change would ban any discharges into French Creek, unless they were as pure as the creek.

If you fish French Creek, by all means take other members of your family with you. They will enjoy the picnic grounds, the hiking, and, most of all, the historic iron works. In the eighteenth century, an entrepreneur named Mark Bird established Hopewell Furnace alongside French Creek.

Bird's prosperity was tempered by his patriotism, because he went into debt to supply General Washington at Valley Forge and the fledgling nation kept telling him the 1770's equivalent of "the check is in the mail."

As a result, Bird suffered financially, and the iron works fell into disrepair for some 150 years. In the 1930s, Civilian Conservation Corps members restored the furnace and created a small town next to it to demonstrate life in the nineteenth century. Hopewell Village is now a National Historic Site. It deserves a few hours of any angler's time between casting and hatches. And speaking of fishing. . . .

It's easy to get within a mile or two of French Creek, but difficult to find the best fishing spots. From the south, Route 100 crosses the creek below Pughtown. Beaver Run enters French Creek, and if conditions are not promising in the main channel, try this tributary.

Upstream, Route 23 crosses the creek near St. Peters. The creek is stocked with trout from St. Peters downstream, and 1.5 miles of it—from north of Sheeder Mill Road—are designated as Fly-Fishing Only. Hollow Road and Sheeder Road flank opposite banks of another tributary, Birch Run, which enters the creek near the end of the Fly-Fishing-Only section.

Downstream, SR 1045 runs north from the town of Kimberton and crosses French Creek, providing good access. Farther down, Routes 23 and 113 cross the creek, with access to the lower section, which holds smallmouth bass.

French Creek is a surprisingly clean stream, cleansed by the rocks and gravel through which it flows. It does not have a reliable source of cool water, however, and usually warms above the comfortable temperature for trout by mid-June. The creek supports a wide variety of hatches, which allow for angling action most mornings and evenings. Caddis hatches are the most common.

This is a popular stream, partly because of the fishing, partly because of its proximity to Philadelphia, and to some extent because of the crowds attracted by French Creek Park and the Valley Forge National Historical Site. It is most pleasant on weekday mornings, particularly if a light breeze is moving the air.

BRANDYWINE CREEK

"A man would look very foolish if he simply stood in the water without a rod and contemplated those sights and sounds known only to anglers."

—A. J. McClane, *The Practical Fly Fisherman*

Each spring the Wilmington Trail Club sponsors a thirty-five-mile, one-day hike of this creek. It's a marvelous way to get to know this stretch of water and to discover meanders and pools that cannot be seen from any road. For less intrepid anglers, the following directions may help:

There are two Brandywine Creeks—East Branch and West Branch. The East Branch is easy to reach from SR 282 between the villages of Lyndell and Glenmore. This stretch is stocked with trout and provides good early season angling.

The West Branch can be reached both upstream and down from the village of Honey Brook. SR 4012, north, crosses the stream. The difficulty of reaching the West Branch keeps the number of anglers down, and the difficulty of fishing some of the narrower stretches also discourages those unwilling to lose terminal tackle.

Despite the drawbacks, one can easily imagine that Izaak Walton would have enjoyed this modest stream.

Tackle

Brandywine Outfitters, 200 West Lincoln Highway, Exton, PA 19341, (610) 594-8008.

Chip's Bait & Tackle, Sharpless Square, 325 E. Gay Street, West Chester, PA 19380, (610) 696-FISH.

I.L.A. Guns & Ammo, 739 Downingtown Pike, West Chester, PA 19380, (610) 692-4110.

Gordon's Sports Supply, 129 Pottstown Pike, Eagle, PA 19480, (610) 458-5153.

Dining and Other Attractions

Stop at the Chadds Ford Inn for great crab cakes; the Mendenhall Inn, Route 52, in Mendenhall, (610) 388-1181; or visit the Chaddsford Winery, Route 1, Chadds Ford, (215) 388-6221. Hours: Tuesday through Saturday, 10:00 A.M.-5:30 P.M. Sunday, noon to 5:00 P.M. Open for tasting and wine sales. Special events are held throughout the year. This winery is gaining more than a regional reputation for quality. The February 28, 1995, issue of *Wine Spectator* gave 88 points out of 100 to Chadds Ford's Chardonnay Pennsylvania Stargazers Vineyard 1991. In the same edition, the winery's Chardonnay Pennsylvania Philip Roth Vineyard 1991 received a score of 87.

Dilworthtown Inn, which has been reconstructed since a fire destroyed most of the historic property, is a dining treasure. Other worthy places of interest include the Brandywine River Museum, with N. C. Wyeth, Andrew, and Jamie Wyeth artworks, at U.S. 1 and Pa. Route 100, Chadds Ford, (610) 388-2700; Winterthur, the du Pont family home, draws 175,000 visitors a year to its 1,000 acres of gardens; Longwood Gardens, with spectacular displays of flowers, trees, and shrubs; and Phillips Mushrooms and Mushroom Museum on U.S. 1 in Kennett Square, just south of Longwood Gardens, where you may buy fresh crimini mushrooms, as well as portabellas, oyster mushrooms, shitakes, and the exotic "hen of the woods."

Berks County

TULPEHOCKEN CREEK

The best trout stream in southeastern Pennsylvania? In the opinion of many, the Tulpy is just that. Running over a limestone bed, the creek benefits from the dam at Blue Marsh Lake managed by the U.S. Army Corps of Engineers. The dam sustains water levels in late summer and also keeps the water temperature low enough to encourage the sizable trout that inhabit the stream.

On your way to the creek, it's easy to get lost in Reading—not a bad thing in itself. Take the Paper Mill Road exit from U.S. 422 and proceed north to a tee junction. Paper Mill Road continues to the left. To the right is Tulpehocken Road. Let's begin by turning left and following Paper Mill Road to its junction with Rebers Bridge Road. Take a right and park your car on the left, just before the bridge. A path leads down to the stream, which is wide, shallow, and easy to wade. There are several pools in this stretch upstream to the beginning of the Delayed Harvest area just below the dam on Blue Marsh Lake. A wide meander in the stream allows the angler to find a good casting place in virtually any wind. You can drive to the meander by crossing the bridge at Rebers Bridge Road, turning left on Palisades Drive, and then taking the first left.

Just below the Rebers Bridge Road bridge, Plum Creek enters the Tulpehocken and provides excellent trout fishing at the confluence. This is, in fact, a good place to test your skills.

The Delayed Harvest area, which begins just below the dam, continues downstream to a covered bridge. To fish this downstream water, return to Paper Mill Road and keep to the left at the intersection with Tulpehocken Road. A parking area at the Van Reed Road bridge, and another at the covered bridge, offer access to the stream.

Much of the credit for the quality of fishing in the Tulpy must go to the Corps of Engineers and the Tulpehocken Chapter of Trout Unlimited.

Above the dam, Blue Marsh Lake provides good bass fishing and rewards those who can cast long lines. According to a 1995 Pennsylvania Fish and Boat Commission survey, the number of "keeper-size" bass was at a record level. And in the same year, an angler from Reading caught a twenty-eight-pound muskie from the spillway at Blue Marsh.

It had been a hot, humid afternoon on the Tulpehocken, so we were glad to meet in the parking lot near the Rebers Bridge Road to compare notes, open the car's trunk, and slake our thirst with something cold, wet, and corny—a moist and cool Coors Lite, to be exact.

No sooner had we popped the caps than a perky, uniformed employee of the U.S. Army Corps of Engineers sauntered up.

"Good afternoon, gentlemen," he said. We responded with a hearty greeting.

"I see you're enjoying a beverage," he observed.

"That's right," one of us responded. "Care to have one?"

"Thank you, no. You gentlemen should know that this is a Federal reservation. Alcoholic beverages are prohibited."

There was a pause while we considered the matter.

"I have to write a citation for anyone possessing alcohol."

The brightest among us, grasping the point that had eluded me, said: "But if we empty them we won't be violating the rule?"

So we fertilized the ground with that cool, refreshing liquid.

But this act was insufficient for a young man in pursuit of justice.

"Possession includes those," he said, glancing at our backup emergency six-pack in the trunk.

And so, in the hot, muggy afternoon of a summer's day, we committed the contents of those six bottles to the earth from which it had come.

"Thank you, gentlemen," said the alert young man. "Have a good day." —R.S.

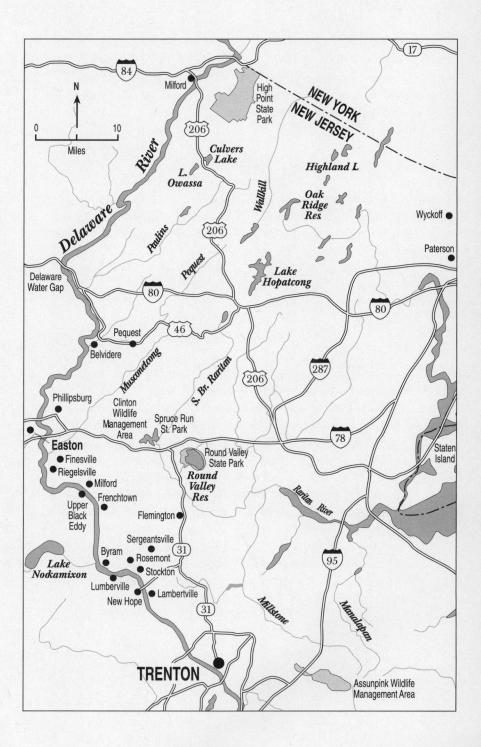

Freshwater Fishing
in Northern New Jersey

SUSSEX AND WARREN COUNTIES

"Personally, I find fishing intensely boring, a degrading occupation in which a supposedly intelligent human being matches wits with what is said to be a lower species."
  —HAIM SHAPIRO, *The Jerusalem Post* (December 20, 1996)

"In my experience, it seems that pessimists don't take up fishing in a serious way because they see the water as an empty vessel and their beliefs are confirmed each time they get skunked. Optimists, however, go out with the 'feeling' that the next cast will connect with the fish of a lifetime."
  —BILL STAMATIS, *The Fisherman* (January 16, 1997)

"Everyone who fly fishes for trout ought to have a home stream. Big Flat Brook in the mountains of Sussex County, in New Jersey's northwestern corner, fills the bill for me."
  —*New York Times* reporter WILLIAM K. STEVENS

The northwest New Jersey counties of Sussex and Warren offer visitors some of the state's most beautiful scenery and some of the best trout and river fishing in the entire Delaware Valley region.

It is also a part of the Garden State that is not well-known to those who think of Secaucus, Camden, Newark, and Atlantic City when they conjure up New Jersey. "Lightly populated, with farms, hills and tree-covered ridges, the state's northern area looks much like northern Pennsylvania," commented a travel writer for *The Washington Post*. "And it has large and diverse parks and forests, offering natural and historic attractions."

These parts are so un-Jersey-like that it was surprising to many people that the State's Division of Fish, Game and Wildlife issued a 1996 press release urging local citizens not to feed black bears and to "bear proof" their residences. The Division warned that "New Jersey has a growing black bear population," primarily in Sussex, Warren, western Morris, and Passaic counties. (Just in case you come across a bruin in New Jersey, call the Division's Wildlife Research Section at (908) 735-7040. Be reasonably assured that the bear won't wait around for the state folks to arrive.)

SUSSEX COUNTY

In Sussex County, one place you may see a black bear and, as a bonus, witness a classic New Jersey sunrise—an experience rivaled only by a trip to Corsons Inlet in Ocean City to watch the orb that sustains life emerge like a blood orange from the ocean—is High Point Monument in High Point State Park.

Sussex also offers access to Delaware River fishing off U.S. 206, just before the road crosses the river and enters Pennsylvania's Pike County and its seat of Milford. Before heading over the Delaware, make a right on River Road and then a left at a dirt lane. Park and walk down a long, abandoned roadway, then scramble down to the river. This is a popular springtime gathering spot for shad fishers, but it's not for the out-of-shape angler.

One problem here is that the river across from Milford Beach is narrow, and the channel current, in which the shad like to swim, is usually close to the Jersey side. As a result, those of us who don't have boats and who must cast for fish from the bank often find ourselves competing from the shoreline with inconsiderate boat anglers who have the *chutzpah* to anchor directly in front of us.

In addition to the Delaware, Sussex has some of the Garden State's premier trout streams. At the top of the list is the long Big Flat Brook, which flows through the Kittatiny Mountains, almost parallel with the Delaware, from High Point State Park until it merges with the river near Flatbrookville, just north of neighboring Warren County. It is said that Babe Ruth fished for trout in the Big Flat Brook, which has hatchery-raised brooks, rainbows and browns.

A delightful area is the 20-acre Saw Mill Lake (some call it Saw Mill *Pond*) in the middle of High Point State Park. In addition to trout, the lake has largemouth bass, panfish, and catfish.

One of the most popular stretches is in the lower portion of the stream, between the Delaware River and the bridge at U.S. 206. A third of this area is Fly-fishing-Only, except for the winter and early spring. The so-called Blewett Tract is open year-round to fly-rodders. Take N.J. Route 521 off U.S. 206 to Three Bridges, where there is parking, and the "no-kill" Blewett Tract upstream to Junction Pool, where the Little Flat Brook meets its big brother.

For access to the lower Big Flat, drive to Walpack Center near the 400-acre Walpack Wildlife Management Area and park. Other Sussex angling areas worthy of attention include Lake Aeroflex, which was first stocked with trout in 1996, and Cranberry Lake, which received a stocking of 2,000 northern pike in the same year.

Tackle and Food

If you're on upper U.S. 206, you might as well cross to Milford and visit the Sportman's Rendezvous, which is conveniently located across from a Pennsylvania State Store. Back in New Jersey on 206, we like the Flat Brook Tap House for pizza, sandwiches, and cold beer. It's a friendly spot, too. Farther south, on the left, is the eponymous Pub 'n Grub.

WARREN COUNTY

The western edge of Warren County is prime river-fishing country, with a wide assortment of opportunities to catch shad, stripers, muskies, largemouth and smallmouth bass, walleye, panfish, and trout that find their way into the Delaware. In Belvidere there is a state boat ramp off Front Street. but local folk did not react kindly to its installation. In August 1994, the Town Council, reacting to residents' complaints about twenty-four-hour activity at the ramp, closed off access to the street from 9:00 P.M. to 5:00 A.M.

There is no boat ramp at the Ratzman Access, but it is one of the newest shoreline fishing locations in Warren County, just south of Belvidere in White Township. Opened in 1997, Ratzman Access is nine-tenths of a mile down Foul Rift Road, off N.J. Route 620. Look for it west of the railroad tracks.

Hot Dog Johnny's, on U.S. 46, is one of those legendary places you and the kids return to every time you're this far north. Old-timers may aver that the dogs aren't as good since the death of the founder, but don't tell that to his family members who continue a brisk business as purveyors of the humble hot dog, with or without kraut.

> *"I've been fishing since childhood. My father was an accomplished fisherman who loved the outdoors, and it was quite natural that he taught me how to fish."*
> —New Jersey Governor CHRISTIE WHITMAN, at the Pequest River in Warren County on Opening Day of trout season
> (April 9, 1994)

Van Campens Brook, which flows into the Delaware, has wild rainbow, brook, and brown trout. This beautiful, ten-mile stretch of clear, clean water in the Delaware Water Gap National Recreation Area is best fished with ultra-light spinning gear and relatively short, light fly-fishing leaders. Take Old Mine Road off Interstate 80 after crossing the Delaware Water Gap. Go to Millbrook and follow Old Mine Road (Route 606), which runs along the brook. Be forewarned that Van Campens is an increasingly popular site for anglers.

The Pequest River

For many families, a visit each spring to the Pequest Trout Hatchery and Natural Resource Education Center is a "must" event. The New Jersey Division of Fish, Game and Wildlife holds an annual Open House at the hatchery on Route 46 in Oxford, N.J. Pequest is the nursery for some 600,000 brook, brown, and rainbow trout a year, and it offers the excitement of seeing the trout that will be stocked, plus exhibits, Living History events, and the opportunity to hike through the 1,612-acre Pequest Wildlife Management Area, (908) 637-4125.

The Pequest River flows through the Pequest Wildlife Management Area, with a width of about sixty feet in places, and its swath through this public area provides ready access.

What kind of denizens lurk in the Pequest River? In October 1993 Myron Korinok of Trenton fished the Pequest and landed a six-pound, ten-ounce rainbow that was twenty-four inches long. It took first place for the rainbow trout category that year in the New Jersey Angler Sportsmen's Association competition.

In 1997, three new access sites, totaling twenty-one acres, were added along the south bank of the Pequest River in White Township. The sites are not contiguous, but they begin at Pequest Drive and Route 519 and run downstream.

The Musconetcong

The Musconetcong is New Jersey's largest Piedmont tributary of the Delaware River.

Russ Wilson, who writes for the *Fisherman* magazine, pointed out that "from its rather obscure origin in Sussex County near the town of Stanhope to its confluence with the Delaware River . . . some thirty miles distant, [the Musconetcong] is a stream that is made to order for the dedicated trout fisher."

An easy spot to reach isn't far upstream from where the "Muskie" enters the Delaware. Take N.J. Route 627 through Mount Joy, New Jersey's Riegelsville, and Finesville. There are places along the south side of the road to park, and anglers can walk downhill through some woods and marshy areas to the stream.

A bonus in fishing this lower section of the Musconetcong River is Abba Vineyards, which is conveniently located on a hill overlooking a small parking area along Route 627. Abba's tasting room is open on the weekends to thirsty anglers.

New public access stretches that have been added recently to the "Muskie" include Butler Park, with 2,500 feet of streamside fishing, and Shurts Road in Franklin Township.

HUNTERDON COUNTY

"Cast and swat. Cast and swat. Fly fishing may be a sport invented by insects with fly fishermen as bait."
—P. J. O'ROURKE, "A Fly-Fishing Primer"

Hunterdon offers excellent river fishing, petite trout streams which are best fished early in the season, and two major reservoirs with some of the finest angling in New Jersey. The county has also has an abundance of fine restaurants and one of the premier wine shops in the Delaware Valley.

Four riverfront towns are worthy of your time for fishing, exploring, and just plain "hanging out": Milford, Frenchtown, Stockton, and Lambertville.

Milford, the northernmost of this quartet, is across the Delaware from Upper Black Eddy, Pa., at the intersection of N.J. Route 619 (which springs north out of Frenchtown) and N.J. Route 519. There is fishing access to the river down by the bridge, and above the town there's a municipal fishing area and a small dam.

Aside from fishing the Delaware, one of the reasons for visiting Milford is the Ship's Inn, (908) 995-7007, an English pub that offers British ales and stouts on tap, as well as good pub food.

FRENCHTOWN

If you follow Route 619 south, you will come to Frenchtown, the second of our interesting river towns.

There is access to the river from the parking area just off to the right after you cross the bridge from Uhlerstown, Pa. (During the summer, the farm market on the Pennsylvania side of the bridge has excellent corn for sale.) You'll need a pair of waders to get serious about fishing for the small-mouth bass that can be found just below the bridge. The river here also holds trout, and in the springtime it's a favorite location for shad fishermen, as long as the water isn't high and dangerous.

The town itself is well worth exploring, beginning with the ice cream shop near the bridge. For lunch or dinner, the Frenchtown Inn, across from the ice cream emporium, serves some of the region's finest cuisine in a lovely setting. After dinner, retire to the rustic bar on the inn's east side and mingle with local anglers.

Frenchtown also has interesting antique stores, a bicycle shop, a fabulous store for waterfowl decoys and prints, Ron Kobli's Decoys & Wildlife Gallery at 55 Bridge Street, (609) 996-0807, and the National Hotel (with a fine old bar), all within short walking distance.

When you leave Frenchtown by turning south on Route 29, be sure to obey the posted 25 m.p.h. speed limit until you see the sign signalling an increase to 55 m.p.h. The local gendarmes make a habit of hiding out in a parking lot on the right, waiting to snare unsuspecting drivers entering and leaving the town.

Just south of Frenchtown is the Delaware River's Kingwood access for boat fishermen. Route 29 also offers a number of places where you can pull off the road, walk across a bike path, and scramble down to the river for fishing. They include Frenchman's Hole and Byram, north of Raven Rock, where the remains of an old bridge can be seen and fished. Located 1.7 miles south of the town of Byram is Bulls Island State Park, where there is a old iron bridge that takes you across to Lumberville, Pennsylvania, the Black Bass Hotel, and an excellent site for shad fishing.

In springtime, of course, it is the shad that's the major attraction in these parts. The American shad has a history as rich as its flesh. In fact, the story is told that, during the difficult winter at Valley Forge in 1776, our patriots survived by eating salted-down shad. (It is undocumented, of course, but we may surmise that the bony shad contributed to the misery endured by General Washington's brave troops.)

I had been fishing for shad for three or four years, and all I had to show for it was a second mortgage to pay for the shad darts I'd lost to rocks and tree limbs submerged in the Delaware. Then, one day, lightning struck, and all the "dues" and frustration were forgotten.

It happened at Byram, a famous shad "hot spot" on the New Jersey side of the river, north of Stockton. It was 5 o'clock in the morning but the riverbank already was crowded with fishermen; more were arriving every minute. Three boats were anchored out in the water in front of us, within easy casting distance. I had been fishing for only a few minutes, using a quarter-ounce, red-and-white shad dart that was tied to eight-pound test line on a Pfleuger spincasting rod and a Daiwa reel.

Suddenly something powerful struck my line. Just for an instant, I thought my dart had snagged something again on the river bottom— until the "snag" began fighting for its life.

Fearful of tearing the dart from the shad's soft mouth, I carefully played the fish onto the beach. As usual, I had forgotten to bring along a large net, which is part of the dedicated shad fisher's required gear. After a fight that lasted about five minutes, I had a four-pound buck shad flopping at my feet.

Out on the water, more boats were converging on the hot spot, and shore-bound fishermen around me were starting to hook into shad, and it was obvious that a large pod of the migrating fish were moving upriver right past us. I looked down at my catch with a sense of guilt. Sheer, dumb luck had helped me accomplish what natural predators, pollution, and netters to the south had failed to do: halt a noble fish on its long and difficult journey for the survival of its species.

But this was not the time or place for such meditation. The fish were on the move, and I was in the grip of shad fever. —G.I.

One of the intriguing aspects of shad fishing is that techniques, rods, lures, and lines are always changing. For many years, the required shad lure was the lead dart of varying size, depending upon water conditions and how far up the river one was situated. First it was the traditional red and white dart, followed later by silver, yellow, red, and even fluorescent green and orange darts. Then we were instructed to buy a nail-painting kit in order to quickly rig up darts in the prevailing "hot" color that was turning on the fish on any particular day and place. Now the hot lure is the shad flutter spoon, and braided line is "in." What will the well-equipped angler of the year 2000 use to pursue shad? It's anyone's guess.

The cliché about real estate—the three most important things are "location, location, and location"—is also true for shad fishing. Where you position yourself makes all the difference. Several years ago, George Leber and I were fishing from his boat off Byram. We were anchored up just at the river's bend, smack in the middle of the channel. There were dozens of shad fishermen in boats nearby, but they weren't catching anything. Suddenly George and I began hauling in shad. It was nonstop action, and we only halted when our arms got tired of pulling the fish aboard. The other anglers must have been cursing us, because they watched enviously at our success. By sheer accident, we had found the shad "honey hole" on the river. —G.I.

After the shad run is over, there is great springtime sport as the herring, following in the wake of their larger cousins, head up the Delaware to spawn. One afternoon George Leber and I put his outboard in at Bulls Island, motored up the river a few miles, anchored, and rigged up with ultralight fishing rods and reels. Our terminal tackle was nothing more

than a small gold hook with a small split shot on the line ahead of the
hook. We cast out from the boat, and on virtually every retrieve we had
a feisty little herring at the end of the line. George salted some of them to
eat later, while most of my catch was headed for the freezer to use as striper
bait. —G.I.

STOCKTON

"My wife and I, we take day trips, but the nicest part is coming
home."
      —a senior resident of Stockton, explaining to a *New York*
      ***Times* writer why he loves the river town**

We can understand the man's sentiments because Stockton is one of
the nicest little towns on the river. So far—knock on wood—it hasn't been
spoiled by rapacious developers and hordes of tourists: it still has the oldest
existing school in the Garden State.

The town is laid out like a large "T." At the western end of the letter's
main stem (Bridge Street) is the bridge that will take you over the Delaware
to Pennsylvania and the Centre Bridge Inn and Dilly's Ice Cream place. At
the top of the "T," on the north-south Main Street (Route 29) is the Stockton Inn, (609) 397-1250. The main part of the inn dates to 1710, while the
Federal House is a restored home, circa 1850. One claim to the Stockton
Inn's fame is that it inspired the Rodgers and Hart song, "There's A Small
Hotel With a Wishing Well," from the Broadway musical "On Your Toes."
In cooler months you can dine next to large fireplaces in rooms with murals
of eighteenth-century Hunterdon County scenes around you. When the
weather turns up the thermometer, try the Glass Room overlooking the garden, or opt for the garden with a trout pond and water fall. Following a late
afternoon shad-fishing expedition one spring, we once had an excellent
lobster dinner at the inn. It is open for lunch and dinner, and the small bar
off to the left is a cozy respite after a hard day's fishing.

The Stockton Inn looks west toward Bridge Street, and halfway between
the inn and the bridge is one of the best-stocked wine shops in the region,
Phillips' Fine Wines & Liquors. The store, which celebrated its fiftieth anniversary in 1996, is operated by the knowledgeable and friendly Dick Phillips, scion of the original owner. This place has a great selection of Califor-

nia wines, and Dick, who lives in nearby Kingwood, and his staff can be counted on for honest, reliable advice on purchasing wine. Phone: (609) 397-0587 or 0589. One of the best places for dining is Meil's Restaurant, Bridge Street and Route 29 (Main Street), (609) 397-8033.

LAMBERTVILLE

Lambertville is the next town going south on the river. Larger than Stockton, it has more than its share of traffic problems, especially each spring during the annual Lambertville Shad Festival sponsored by the local Chamber of Commerce.

The shad festival is a hectic nightmare, with up to 20,000 people cramming into the tiny borough—but don't miss it. Held each year in late April, the festival challenges area chefs to create innovative dishes to glorify shad and shad roe.

For youngsters and adults, the major event takes place on the river, where shad are netted, as they have been for 100 years. Fred Lewis had the only commercial shad netting operation on the Delaware, although shad are caught in pound nets placed in Delaware Bay—a practice that has led to complaints of over-fishing in recent years from upriver anglers who have been catching fewer and fewer fish.

Lewis, who tagged and released half his catch, has turned the operation over to his grandson, Steve Meserve. We once purchased an eight-pound roe shad from Lewis at day's end after the individual who had ordered it was a no-show. We rushed home, slit the belly open, extracted two bright reddish-orange sacs of roe, and placed them carefully in a sauté pan. The rest of the fish was split and roasted the next day, while our dinner guests cursed the bones.

Shad nettings can be seen in Lambertville most Saturdays from late March through early May. Youngsters take great delight in watching what is hauled in from the river depths. In Lewis's operation, boatmen row a large net out into the river and bring one end back to the bank, where workers pull the net to the beach. An incredible array of creatures end up flopping out of the net onto the shore—smallmouth and largemouth bass, catfish, and, if they happen to be running, shad. Everything else is returned to the green-dark waters of the Delaware.

During the spring shad run, anglers park along the outskirts of town, off Route 29, and walk down to the wing dam at Lambertville. There is also a boat launch in mid-town at the Lambertville Station.

Lambertville has a microbrewery that produces a malt elixir called River Horse Ale. Remember the ancient Greek name for hippopotamus? *Ippopotamus,* literally "horse of the river." A huge hippo graces the logo of this microbrewery, which opened in 1995 under the direction of Jim and Jack Bryan.

Open to the public, the River Horse Brewery is located at 80 Lambert Lane, Suite 120, Lambertville, N.J. 08530, (609) 397-7776. Internet: http:// www.riverhorse.com. (Those who don't get to New Jersey can sample the beer on tap at the Cock 'n Bull Restaurant in Peddler's Village, Lahaska.)

Cooking Shad

What follows are some of our favorite shad recipes. Elsewhere in this book are other time-tested ways to cook the fish one catches. In preparing any fish, follow the sage advice of chef Terry Laybourne, who worked in a restaurant at Newcastle, England, and who told the *Financial Times*: "The more simply fish is treated, the better it eats." The chef's recommendation belongs with the admonition of *New York Times* outdoor writer Nelson Bryant, whose words should be stamped on every fishing and hunting license sold in America: "Ideally, skilled hunters and anglers should be equally expert in cooking whatever was harvested, for it is at the table that reverence is paid to the creatures that have been slain."

Cooking Shad Roe

In preparing shad roe, a major hurdle to overcome is preventing the twin sacs from exploding and expelling the tiny eggs all over your kitchen. A method we use is to sauté them very, very slowly in clarified butter, carefully turning the roe often. A Bucks County chef, Skip Trimble, uses this technique: each roe sac is pierced with a fork or sharp knife every three inches, then the roe is covered with cold water, which is brought to a boil. Take the roe off the heat, dry it, and cook it in a frying pan with bacon. When shad is in season, one of our obligatory stops is Fuji's, a Japanese restaurant on Route 130 in Cinnaminson, N.J., where the chef broils and slices the roe in a way we have been unable to duplicate at home.

The *Intelligencer/Record* published this shad roe recipe from then-Chef Chuck DeLargy of the Black Bass Hotel, on April 26, 1995:

Braised roe with leeks, tarragon, and capers in white wine

2 shad roe sets
Flour for dredging
8 slices bacon
Juice of 1 lemon
1/2 cup julienned leeks (white part)
Salt and freshly ground pepper

2/3 cup fish or chicken stock
2/3 cup dry white wine
2/3 cup dry vermouth
1 tablespoon capers
1 bunch fresh tarragon

Rinse the roe and pat dry. Dredge in flour. Cook bacon strips in a large oven-proof skillet, set aside and reserve a small amount of the fat. (If you wish to discard the bacon fat, add some butter to the frying pan.) Brown roe for two minutes on one side, then turn over and add leeks, lemon juice, stock, white wine, and vermouth.

Add salt and pepper to taste, cover skillet, and place in a preheated oven at 400 degrees. Bake for 10 minutes. Remove from oven, uncover pan, and gently remove roe to a heated platter. Reduce liquid by half, then add chopped tarragon and capers to sauce. Adjust seasoning. Top roe with the sauce and garnish with chopped bacon. Makes 2 servings.

Peppered shad filet (Dave Butz, *Philadelphia Inquirer,* May 5, 1991)

1/4 cup olive oil
2 boneless shad filets
1/4 cup coarsely ground green peppercorns
1/4 cup coarsely ground black peppercorns
1 cup flour

1/2 cup vodka
1 whole lime
1/4 pound (1 stick) butter
2 tablespoons Dijon mustard

Heat olive oil in a large skillet until it begins to smoke. Coat filets with green and black peppercorns. Sprinkle with flour and sauté in oil until golden brown. Flip the filets and brown on the other side.

Pour 1/4 cup vodka and lime juice over filets.

Reduce heat and simmer ten minutes.

Remove cooked filets and arrange on a serving tray. Add remaining vodka to skillet with butter and mustard. Bring sauce to a boil and pour over shad filets. Makes two servings.

Shad or Trout?

During the early spring, it's a difficult decision whether to fish for shad on the Delaware or for trout in the nearby streams. (For fishers of salt and freshwater, the dilemma is even more difficult, because mackerel are running off the coast and striped bass are cruising at Gravelling Point near Tuckerton.) On New Jersey's trout opener, we often try to do both by fishing the river very early in the morning and then heading to some of the local streams for the 8:00 A.M. Opener. On the first weekend of trout season, one of the most popular spots is the Delaware-Raritan Canal at Bulls Island. Here anglers switch from shad darts and light-to-medium rods to ultra-light spinning gear with Rooster Tails, meal worms, salmon eggs, and other assorted baits fished deep in the cold water. (Thanks to a reciprocal agreement, New Jersey trout anglers with a valid license can now walk across the metal bridge at Bulls Island and legally fish for shad on the Pennsylvania side of the Delaware at Lumberville without having a Keystone fishing license.)

THE LOCKATONG

The Lockatong is a stocked trout stream with limited access, but its proximity to the river in Hunterdon makes it convenient for both shad and trout anglers. It is not worth much attention after the first several weeks of the season.

To reach the most accessible part from Stockton, proceed north on Route 29. Just after Hidden Valley Nursery, turn right onto Federal Twist Road, then right again on Rosemont Raven Rock Road and follow it 3.2 miles to an iron bridge.

Immediately after crossing the bridge, there is space on the left for two or three cars. It's posted everywhere else. Try drifting a worm or a Muddler Minnow along the creek's northwestern bank.

Dining

One of our favorite places for a good sandwich, cold beverage, and conversation with other outdoors people is the Forge and Anvil, at Route 519 and Barbertown Point Breeze Road in Barbertown, (908) 996-4271. The Cafe at Rosemont, on Route 519 and Rosemont-Ringoes Road in Rosemont, serves breakfast, lunch, and dinner, (609) 397-4097. The Cafe's 1997 Valentine's Day dinner was a steal—four courses with such individual choices as lobster cream soup, spiced shrimp with chipotle sour cream, grilled quail with barley risotto and pomegranate baby carrots, dessert, a complimentary champagne toast, and coffee and tea—all for $80 per couple.

For a bed and breakfast, try Rosemont's Victoria, 823 Rosemont-Ringoes Road (Route 604), Rosemont, NJ 08556, (609) 397-3804.

THE WICKECHEOKE

In the spring, the Wickecheoke is one of New Jersey's smallest and prettiest trout streams. Follow Route 29 through Stockton. Right after the Prallsville Mill Historic Village, bear right onto Route 523. Then make a right onto Lower Creek Road. About five-tenths of a mile down the road on the right is the loveliest pool on the Wichecheoke as it wends its way past a rock cliff.

From Route 29, Route 523 follows the creek about 2.6 miles to a covered bridge. Although much of the area is private property, there are a number of places you can pull off the road and fish. The creek gets most of its pressure during the first weeks of the season. By early June, the water is often too low for decent fishing. We have been successful here with small Mickey Finn streamers fished just north of the quaint covered bridge. Within one hundred yards south of the bridge, there are some decent pools that hold trout.

Dining

A good reason for fishing the Wichecheoke is the excuse it provides to visit the old stone Sergeantsville Inn (pronounce it SIR-gentsville), part of which was built in 1763. "We don't know if George Washington slept here," they admit. In cold weather huddle close to the fireplace because the wind easily finds its way through the cracks. But the food is first-rate, and the bar offers comforting Cognac, which is especially good after you've spent a chilly spring day down below on the river in pursuit of the elusive shad, or on the Wichecheoke for trout.

The inn is located at the intersection of Routes 523 and 604 in Sergeantsville, 11 minutes from Flemington. Phone: (609) 397-3700.

Tackle

Sportsman's Rendezvous, 174 Route 31, Flemington, NJ 08822, (908) 788-5828. They open at 5:00 A.M. on weekends and 6:00 A.M. on weekdays when trout season begins.

Not far away . . .

Nearby opportunities for fishing include the South Branch of the Raritan River, especially the famous Ken Lockwood Gorge, north of the town of High Bridge. The gorge is open to fly-fishing only from April to November, and closed during stocking. Brown, brook, and rainbow trout are here, plus sunfish, smallmouth bass, and rock bass. A small dirt road takes you into the heart of the gorge, and it can get very crowded in the early part of trout season. If float tubers splash through, don't try to snag them.

Tackle
Dan's Sport Shop, 1738 Route 31, Clinton, NJ 08809, (908) 735-7909, is the place to go for bait, tackle, and local information. Oliver's, 44 Main St., Clinton, NJ 08809, (908) 735-5959, specializes in fly-fishing, including Orvis flies.

Closer to the river, try the Capoolong Creek Wildlife Management Area, which covers 61 acres in Hunterdon County. It can be reached from Route 579 in Pittstown or from Hogback-Landsdown Road in Landsdown. You'll find trout (browns and rainbows), plus smallmouths, rock bass, and sunfish.

SPRUCE RUN RESERVOIR

Spruce Run Reservoir is part of the Clinton Wildlife Management Area, and offers opportunities for largemouth bass, northern pike, and brook, brown, and rainbow trout. Try where Spruce Run Creek enters the reservoir. Get there by heading north on Route 31 and, north of Clinton, turn left on Van Syckel's Road.

In 1996, New Jersey's Division of Fish, Game and Wildlife stocked Spruce Run with 13,400 six-inch northern pike fingerlings. "Anglers can expect these fish to reach trophy size [more than twenty-four inches] in just a few years," said Bob McDowell, director of the division. Be prepared for these miniature "alligators."

ROUND VALLEY RESERVOIR

The reservoir is part of the Round Valley Wildlife Management Area, and it is designated as a Trophy Trout Area. According to State officials, Round Valley is considered "New Jersey's finest trout lake."

Big lake trout and largemouth bass also prowl these waters. Try the boat launch by the campers' section. The ramp is free to anyone with a valid New Jersey hunting or fishing license. Access is from Routes 31 and 78 or U.S. 22. In June 1994, Carl Bird of the town of Alpha in Hunterdon County caught a New Jersey State record lake trout—24.86 pounds and 40.5 inches long—from Round Valley. We have fished from the shore at Round Valley, but those with boats clearly have the advantage.

Heading south again . . .

From Lambertville, continue south on Route 29, toward Trenton, and you will find plenty of opportunities for fishing along the Delaware and Raritan Canal, including the banks at Titusville and at Washington Crossing State Park. Anglers with fly rods and waders can have a lot of fun casting for hefty bluegills down on the river.

My daughter Pam was about three years old and we were picnicking on a summer's day along the Delaware and Raritan Canal, just north of Titusville.

"I want to fish," she said, looking down at the bluegills cruising around the edge of the canal.

"I'm sorry, but we didn't bring any fishing rods, Pam. Next time we'll have to remember to take along some gear," I tried to explain.

"I want to fish."

"We can't."

"I want to fish."

"Forget it. Now eat your sandwich."

Undaunted, Pam began foraging for gear. She found a piece of twine, then a safety pin. She tied the string to the pin. Looking around for bait, she spotted an evil Japanese beetle munching its way through a leaf on a nearby bush. Seeing her diligence, I relented and impaled the hapless beetle on the pin.

My daughter tossed her bait into the canal. Within seconds, she was triumphantly hauling a nice-sized bluegill onto the ground.

"See?" she said with the confidence that only a three-year-old pos-sesses. "I told you we could fish." —G.I.

Before we leave this part of the Garden State, let's go back to Titusville, above Trenton. During January and February, when much of the area is in the grip of hard ice, take the kids for a ride to the 126-acre Howell Living History Farm and see a recreated ice harvest. Ice is cut from a shallow pond, covered with sawdust, and stored in an icehouse until the summer, just as it was done in our great-grandfather's day.

Call first to find out if they're cutting ice: (609) 737-3299. The Living History Farm is on Valley Road, off Route 29, south of Lambertville.

MERCER-MONMOUTH COUNTIES

Pity poor Trenton. The capital of New Jersey has garnered a bad reputation for poverty and crime (which is declining), but the old town has much going for it: excellent Italian restaurants, friendly tavern/restaurants like the Lorenzo's, across from the train station (alas, the legendary Tony Kall's is only a dim memory), jazz bars like H&H, the Trenton Thunder that plays in a popular minor-league ballpark, two competing newspapers—the solid *Trenton Times* and a feisty tabloid, the *Trentonian*—and lots of American history.

One of the most interesting historical sites is the Trenton Barracks, which dates to 1758 when it was erected as a haven for British soldiers during the French and Indian War. In our American War of Revolution, it served as a hospital and barracks for the Brits. Each year on the weekend after Christmas, the Old Barracks Museum sponsors a reenactment of the Battle of Trenton, with several hundred volunteers serving as Redcoats, Hessians, and George Washington's troops.

The Old Barracks is located on Barrack Street, which used to be known as South Willow Street. It is near the War Memorial and the state Capitol Building. Its museum is open seven days a week, 10:00 A.M. to 5:00 P.M. And, yes, there is a gift shop. Admission to the museum: adults, $2; senior citizens, $1; children under 12, fifty cents.

The Mercer-Monmouth County area offers anglers many fishing opportunities, not only along the Delaware in Trenton at the Marine Terminal but at a number of nearby lakes. One of the best is the 5,500-acre Assunpink Wildlife Management Area. Its largest impoundment is Lake Assunpink, covering 225 acres. It offers largemouth bass and channel catfish, while the pickerel and crappie fishing is described by the state as "excellent." Only electric motors are allowed, but there is plenty of shoreline fishing.

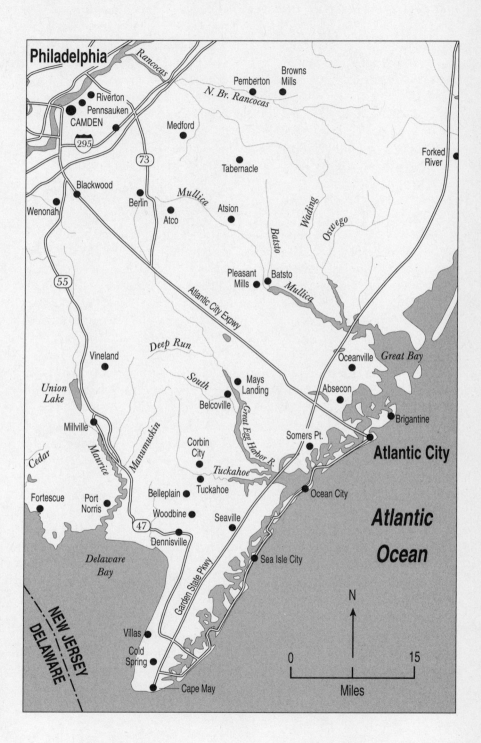

Freshwater Fishing in South Jersey

"It is not possible to introduce pesticides to water anywhere without threatening the purity of water everywhere."
—**CHARLES K. FOX,** *Rising Trout*

It has been suggested that one reason for the decline of Rome was the pernicious effect on the Romans of lead in pipes used to supply water for the imperial capital. Now there is environmental concern over another toxic metal—mercury—in our food chain.

According to the Environmental Protection Agency, about 250 tons of mercury are dispatched into the nation's air every year from such sources as incinerators, coal-fired power plants, and companies that use mercury compounds in manufacturing. Methylmercury, which has been found in fish, can damage a person's central nervous system.

In 1993, The Academy of Natural Sciences in Philadelphia, working under contract with the State's Department of Environmental Protection and Energy, surveyed 56 New Jersey lakes and tested 313 fish. The findings: high levels of mercury in some freshwater fish, including chain pickerel, yellow bullhead catfish, and largemouth bass.

Waters where elevated levels of mercury were found have been posted. These findings were not expected to have much effect on recreational fishing in the Garden State. For one thing, the overwhelming majority of bass fishermen practice "catch and release" as their guiding philosophy. Chain pickerel are eaten only by someone who has absolutely nothing else for dinner because their bony structure make them virtually uneatable. (A

State survey found that only 5 percent of these terribly bony fish are taken home for the table.)

According to the FDA, the safe threshold level for mercury is 1.0 parts per million. At the Atlantic City Reservoir, fish with mercury contamination from 3 to 8.9 ppm were found. (Fishing is not allowed at the Reservoir.)

In 1994, the Garden State warned pregnant women to cut back on eating largemouth bass, pickerel, and catfish from freshwater streams and lakes.

Among the waters in which certain fish had high levels of mercury are these: Batsto Lake and the Mullica River, Atlantic County; Harrisville Lake, Wilson Lake, and New Brooklyn Lake, Gloucester County; Wading River, Atlantic and Burlington Counties; East Creek Lake and Lake Nummy, Cape May County; Union Lake, Cumberland County; and the Cooper River, Big Timber Creek, and Newtown Lake, Camden County.

There are 1,200 lakes in the Garden State, and the New Jersey Department of Environmental Protection declared all of them "threatened" because of pollution.

The Delaware Riverkeeper Network publishes a Toxic Fish Alert, which provides the latest information on Delaware River advisories for areas below Trenton, as well as tributary streams in Pennsylvania, New Jersey, and Delaware. For a copy, send a self-addressed, stamped envelope to Delaware Riverkeeper Network, P.O. Box 753, Lambertville, NJ 08530. Mark the envelope flap "Toxic Fish."

BURLINGTON COUNTY

Burlington is one of New Jersey's largest and most historic counties, extending like a giant tapered stripe from the Delaware River eastward through the vast Pine Barrens to a narrow strip of saltwater at Great Bay. Brothers of French emperors and great writers have resided in Burlington County, and anglers who aren't familiar with its fishing opportunities should waste no time discovering them.

This is an appropriate place to mention a letter published September 2, 1996, in the *Burlington County Times*. It was in response to an earlier article about the replacement of a traffic circle at Routes 70 and 541 in Medford Township. The article mentioned that, as part of the reconstruction, a bridge would be built over "a small stream."

Mark S. Thomas, president of the Rancocas Watershed Conservancy in Mount Holly, had to respond. His letter, headlined "Every stream counts," is an eloquent statement about streams everywhere. It surely has a place in any book about fishing:

"This stream," said Thomas, "is known as 'Sharp's Run', named perhaps after A. Sharp, whose name was listed next to this run on an 1849 map of the area. It takes its origin from springs in northeastern-most Evesham Township and runs due east, under Route 541, and empties into the southwest branch of the Rancocas Creek.

"This creek has suffered for decades from highway runoff, especially at the Medford traffic circle. In more recent years, runoff from suburban development, especially sediment from construction and fertilizer from lawns, has altered the ecology of the stream and made it inhospitable to aquatic life.

"These changes in the Sharp's Run basin are left downstream at places such as Camp Dark Waters, where Sharp's Run empties into the southwest branch. The recent highway construction, with its attendant earth-moving activities on its banks, has turned the stream into a soupy, soil-laden water course.

"It may seem like a small matter that a relatively little-known creek suffers the indignities of our car-oriented culture. However, thousands of similar insults are delivered to the Rancocas Creek and its tributaries throughout the watershed on a regular basis. The sum of these injuries is a serious decline in the health of the Rancocas stream system that many of us have come to know and love. We must improve the attention we pay to this watery resource, from the smallest backyard ditches to the wide tidal stretches of the Rancocas at its confluence with the Delaware.

"The activities of our society, from the state level down to the individual landowner, must reflect an increased knowledge of and respect for the health requirements of the waterway that has shaped the subtle beauty of the landscape we call home."

Thomas concluded his letter with the phone number of the Rancocas Watershed Conservancy, (609) 265-1401.

BURLINGTON CITY

Burlington City is a town rich in history. For starters, there is an abode named for one of our favorite American authors, the James Fenimore Cooper House, at 457 High Street, which dates to about 1780. Nine years later, the author of *The Leatherstocking Tales* was born here. Cooper's five novels of the American frontier can still speak to us today, if we listen. In 1923, the Burlington County Historical Society took over the Cooper House. Among the site's artifacts are those once owned by Napoleon's brother, Joseph Bonaparte.

Walk along the city's riverfront promenade and then head to nearby Sylvan Lake to fish for stocked trout or dine at Cafe Gallery, 219 High Street, (609) 386-6150.

The road south out of Burlington City will take you to a number of interesting river towns, some with fishing access to the Delaware. For example, in Delran Township below Riverside, a right turn off River Road onto American Legion Drive, will put you along a long stretch of the river.

Tackle

Jim's Outdoor Sportsman, East Broad St. at Cinnaminson Ave., Palmyra, NJ 08065, (609) 303-1103.

Cap's Bait & Tackle, 16 Norman Ave., Delran, NJ 08075, (609) 461-4952.

Dining

The White Eagle at River Road and Chester Avenue is one of those places where the "locals" hang out. It serves decent bar food, and there is ample parking out back.

Royal Delaware River Yacht Club and Marina, 447 North Randolph Street, Cinnaminson, (609) 829-5050, has a boat ramp, and a road next to it offers good access to the river. But a sign put up by the Cinnaminson Sewerage Authority warns that the area will be closed if "littering and vandalism don't stop." Walk the lily pads at the mouth of Pompeson Creek to the south.

RIVERTON

Riverton is a wonderful Delaware River town, with nineteenth-century homes, the earliest yacht club in America, and gas lamps on Bank Avenue, a narrow road that runs south along the river to Palmyra.

For fishing, there is very limited access at Bank Avenue and Linden Avenue. In 1996, the borough of Riverton made a grassy plot out of a former dirt parking area, which means that anglers must now park east on Linden Avenue and walk to the river. But this area has largemouth bass, carp, catfish, stripers, and tiger muskies. On any weekend morning in the late spring and summer, you'll see bass fishers out in their boats, casting around the structure surrounding the historic Riverton Yacht Club.

PENNSAUKEN CREEK

If you head east on Route 73 from the Tacony-Palmyra Bridge, take the jug handle at Remington Avenue, across from the Woodbine Inn, head back west on 73 and, just past the inn and before a gasoline station, pull off into a large dirt tract along the Pennsauken Creek. Here your best bet is largemouth bass that grow to good size in this part of the creek. Spinner baits can be very productive; we've had good luck with chartreuse and a spinner we call the "Hallowe'en Lure," with a black and burnt-orange skirt. Nearby is Savona Foods Inc., 8500 Remington Avenue, Pennsauken, NJ 08110, across from the high school. This warehouse for Italian foods is open to the public and deserves a visit, (609) 662-8880, fax (609) 662-7773.

THE RANCOCAS CREEK

The Rancocas has largemouth bass and hybrid tiger muskies. For muskies, try using big plugs, especially yellow ones that imitate gold shiners. Access is a problem for the bank angler on the Rancocas. There is a small access area, including a concrete ramp, on the Marne Highway, Route 537, just past the Fisherman's Inn Restaurant. For a sandwich and a beer, you can't go wrong at Eddie's, an excellent bar and restaurant on the Marne Highway. There's also Flo's, and limited bank fishing at the nearby Rancocas State Park.

PINE BARRENS FISHING IN BURLINGTON COUNTY

We knew a fellow from Cape May County who spent almost all of his free time "boondoggling." That's the word he used to describe the practice of loading up his pick-em-up truck with several fishing rods, a well-stocked tackle box, and a cooler of ice-cold beer, and driving around looking for new places to fish.

With its sandy roads, few people, and cedar lakes and ponds, the Pine Barrens of Burlington County is a boondoggler's dream.

Let's look at a few places.

Pemberton Lake

Pemberton Lake is part of a Wildlife Management Area. Its 44 acres are located off Route 644, south of Pemberton, N.J. There are several access areas for fishing at the north end of the lake. You could also go to the end of the lake on Route 644 and turn left onto a dirt road, Coleman's Bridge

Road. It will take you to the south end, where several sandy paths lead to the water. There is also a broad access area further down the road, and many anglers launch canoes from this location.

A bonus: keep Pemberton in mind the next time Thanksgiving comes around. Bush's Turkey Farm on Route 644 offers the best fresh-killed domestic gobblers anywhere. To order a turkey, call (609) 894-8287. But beware—these birds are habit-forming.

TABERNACLE

The Girl Scout's Camp Inawendiwin, at Powell Place Road and Oak Lane in Tabernacle Township, is private land. But when camp is not in session, it's accessible to the public, thanks to funding from the New Jersey Green Acres program.

To reach the camp, head north on Route 70 after the Red Lion Circle. Go to Powell Place Road and turn right. Park along Powell Place and take a short walk along a sandy path, lined by pine trees, to two cedar lakes. The large one on your left is home to monster pickerel. We have taken them on purple plastic worms, on spinner baits, and on just about any other freshwater lure. A local Tabernacle resident, James Reilley, hauls good-sized largemouth bass from the lake on the right, below the spillway but this section was drained for dam repairs in summer 1997.

Dining
The Tabernacle Inn on U.S. 206 at Medford-Tabernacle Road is where you can get anything from a sandwich to a prime rib dinner.

For a decent sandwich and imported beers on tap, try the Village Tavern at the intersection of Medford-Tabernacle Road and New Road. Across the street is Nixon's General Store, a local landmark. For fresh vegetables in season, go to Conte's Market on Flyatt Street.

For those who want a nonfishing challenge, head down the dirt road known as Carranza Road to the Emilio Carranza Memorial, an obelisk set down incongruously in the Pine Barrens. The marker commemorates the death of a famous Mexican pilot, Carranza, whose plane crashed here in 1928. According to local lore, no one has had the courage to spend the night alone at the memorial on the anniversary of Carranza's death. We've never tested the legend, and have no wish to do so.

By now, if you haven't been scared out of your wits at the Carranza Memorial or eaten yet at the Village Tavern or the Tabernacle Inn, head south on Route 206, past Indian Mills Lake (good spot for largemouth, bluegills and pickerel), and stop for a sandwich and cup of clam chowder at the Pic-a-lilli Inn. Here is one of the main gathering spots for the boys who live in the Pine Barrens, and it's a place you can play pool and drink a cold one while picking up a lot of good local information about hunting and fishing in the area.

Lake Atsion

Just a few miles south, on U.S. 206, is Lake Atsion, where there's public swimming, fishing, and camping. Atsion has plenty of pickerel, but the spot we like is on the other side of 206, below the spillway that runs under the highway. Here big pickerel lurk in the grass along the small pond. A few years ago, we watched as an angler pulled out the biggest pickerel we've ever seen. He caught it on a live minnow cast from the concrete abutment just below the road.

We generally use small spinning lures, such as Rooster Tails, tied directly onto six-pound test monofilament. Some pickerel fishers rely on steel leaders, much like anglers who use leaders as insurance policies when fishing for sharp-toothed blues. But we've never lost a pickerel, and until we do we'll eschew the leaders, which make casting more difficult.

No matter if we're pickerel fishing in isolated Pineland cedar creeks, "stump-jumping" deer with shotguns, or gunning for fast-flying wood ducks in reed-camoflaged blinds, we always try to stop at the New Hedger House on Route 563, a few miles north of Chatsworth, the "capital" of the New Jersey Pine Barrens.

"You shoulda seen it!" exclaimed the barmaid at the New Hedger House one Saturday morning when we sat down after an unsuccessful duck hunt. "The bikers had a convention here, and they lined up along the road outside, and the biker girls got on the back of the bikes, and the guys tied their hands behind 'em, and then the guys tied hot dogs on strings hangin' from the trees, and they rode by, with the girls on the back of the bikes, and each girl had to try to bite the hot dogs as they passed by. You shoulda seen it!" —G.I.

My brother-in-law George Stroup, a "trouble" man for Atlantic Electric, tells the story about the Green Bank Inn during the 1973 Arab oil embargo. New Jersey Governor Brendan Byrne had ordered all commercial establishments to conserve fuel by maintaining a temperature of not more than 62 degrees. State troopers, armed with thermometers, were assigned to enforce the ukase by making unannounced visits to restaurants, taverns, and stores. Those places that did not comply would be forced to close. But when the police got to the Green Bank Inn, they found the temperature to be in the high 70s. "Turn it down or close!" the owner was told. "We can't," he said. "Our heat is from that wood-burning stove." That didn't matter, the cops said. An order is an order. So the Green Bank Inn had to put less wood into its stove. —G.I.

There has been a crackdown on boozy canoe trips down the Pine Barrens rivers. In the 1970s, the English Department at Temple University may have set a Guinness Book record for the most cases of beer transported down the Oswego River, but those days are gone. Eagle-eyed State rangers now pay special attention to coolers and their contents.

It was one of those combination trips—fishing the Pine Barrens streams for pickerel while canoeing and picnicking along the way. My friend Bob Elwell, a Philadelphia police officer, and his wife, Dot, had never canoed before. But they wanted to join our group, even though Bob had his leg in a cast from an on-duty accident. My son, George, and I led off the flotilla of four canoes from Mick's Canoe Rental, with Bob and Dot in the middle and George and Joan Leber riding backup.

Off we went, dodging downed trees and brush, until George and I reached a clear spot where we could put in to fish, eat lunch and await the rest of the contingent. They never arrived. Soon after we launched, Bob and Dot went head first into the stream. His cast was waterlogged, the beer in his cooler spilled into the water, and the two of them crawled to the bank and asked the rangers for help. So much for canoeing the Pine Barrens. —G.I.

Tackle

Sportsmen's Center, U.S. 130, Bordentown, NJ 08505, (609) 298-5300, is one of the best gear-up places for experts and novices alike.

Harry's Army and Navy, 691 Route 130, Yardville, NJ 08620, (609) 585-5450, is a close second to the Sportsmen's Center.

Mike's Sportsmen's Den, Holly Plaza Shopping Center, Skeet Road, Medford, NJ 08055, (609) 654-0131, is owned by Jim and Doug Welsher.

Kings Bait, Tackle & Accessories, 379 Lakehurst Road, Browns Mills, NJ 08015, (609) 735-1866.

Ricky's Army and Navy Store, 2925 U.S. 130, Delran, NJ 08075, (609) 461-6666.

BATSTO

Historic Batsto Village is a "must" family stop. Located in the Wharton Tract of the Pinelands, this village with more than 33 buildings is off Route 542, east of Hammonton. Batsto's bog iron furnace was founded in 1766, and it supplied musket balls for the Continental Army. In recent years there has been a dispute over whether to emphasize Batsto's eighteenth-century or Victorian heritage. In 1996, the State and preservationists reached a compromise—Batsto will be a haven for both historic periods.

A worthwhile organization is the Batsto Citizens Committee, whose members assist in the development of the village. An active membership costs only $5, and you can be a patron for the mere sum of $25. Write to William J. Rafferty, 1353 S. Myrtle Street, Vineland, NJ 08360.

Nearby, take the kids over to the Atlantic County side of Route 542 and fish the Batsto River, which has pickerel and suckers.

CAMDEN COUNTY

The Cooper River Park, off U.S. 130 in lower Pennsauken Township, is a good place to take the family for panfish, bass, and fun. There's plenty of parking, as well as swings and sliding boards.

Take 130 south past the former Airport Circle. At the first light before the circle, make a right and then a left to get onto North Park Road on the west side of 130. One of the spots we like is a parking area on the right, about 1.1 miles from Route 130 and next to a Christopher Columbus pointing to the northeast. (It was erected by the Sons of Italy Grand Lodge of America.) Your fishing here is usually accompanied by a serenade of cawing crows, honking geese, and crying sea gulls. Our friend Dave Plasket caught a huge bass here several years ago.

Dining and Wining

Nearby is the Balconic Cafe. When you come into the North Park Road you'll see a sign for The Deli. We don't know how they treat anglers, but their sign announces that "joggers are welcome."

Fishers who are also serious wine drinkers must visit Moore Brothers when fishing this section of Cooper River. Just after you make the turn and cross U.S. 130, look for a little sign in the industrial park to your left. Turn here and go to the last building to enter a veritable Mecca for wine enthusiasts, a place where you'll find wines from small French vineyards you've never heard of—all shipped and stored under strict temperature-controlled conditions. (Brother Gregory Moore is the consulting sommelier for Georges Perrier's extraordinary Le Bec-Fin restaurant on Walnut Street in Philadelphia.) Open Saturdays, 9:00 A.M. to 6:00 P.M. and Sundays, 11:00 A.M. to 5:00 P.M. Closed Mondays. Moore Brothers Wine Company, 7180 North Park Drive, Pennsauken, NJ 08110, (609) 317-1177; fax: (609) 317-0055; e-mail: info@moorebros.com; web site: www.moorebros.com.

OAK POND

Oak Pond is a former gravel pit in the 6,566-acre Winslow Wildlife Management Area, which straddles Camden and Gloucester Counties. From the pond, you can hear the "whoosh" of the Atlantic City Expressway. This is a good site for youngsters, because along part of the pond there is a sandy ledge before deep water begins.

Park at the lot and walk through scrub oaks and pines to a path that winds around the 12-acre pond. It holds stocked trout, many hungry bluegills, and largemouth bass. During a fishing trip here in the summer of 1996, we saw families with kids fishing from the bank as well as a few boats out in the water. No alcohol is permitted, and they mean it.

From Central Philadelphia, get off the Atlantic City Expressway at Winslow-Blue Anchor (Route 73). Head north on 73 to the light at Davis Avenue. Turn left, and go as far as you can. When the road ends, make a right turn and you'll see the entrance on the left.

From the Tacony-Palmyra Bridge, come south on Route 73 to Davis Avenue and turn right.

Dining
We fish Oak Pond as an excuse to visit Francesco's on Route 73, north of Beebetown Road. This restaurant is one of Camden County's best-kept secrets. For starters, it serves South Jersey's most addictive roasted red peppers with anchovies and sliced fresh garlic—perhaps the most glorious culinary combination ever created by the human mind. The pasta is home-

made, the scungilli first-rate, and there are daily specials that merit your attention. Francesco's has a good bar that complements an excellent, informal restaurant. Service is usually sterling.

Tackle
Fish & Fur Sporting Goods, 1000 N. Black Horse Pike, Blackwood, NJ 08012, (609) 228-4340.

Sportsman's Paradise, 471 White Horse Pike, Atco, NJ 08004, (609) 768-0003, on the right side of the highway heading toward Atlantic City.

Howard's Sporting Goods, Berlin Farmers Market, Berlin, NJ 08009, (609) 767-1119.

GLOUCESTER COUNTY

Alcyon Lake in Pitman, N.J., was once a fine fishing area. But the seventeen-acre lake was fouled by pollution seeping from Lipari Landfill, which has been called the worst Superfund site in the nation. Two decades ago, Lipari was the reservoir for 2.9 million gallons of toxic wastes, including chromium, mercury, arsenic, and lead. Some of the pollutants came from the Philadelphia-based Rohm & Haas Company, which is footing a large part of the clean-up bill.

Lake Alcyon was drained and its bottom scraped clean of toxic mud. Although work continues, Alcyon was opened for boating and fishing in 1996.

Mullica Hill Pond, off Route 77, and Harrisonville Lake, on the Gloucester County-Salem County border south of Harrisonville, are popular with anglers during the opening of trout season. In 1996, the State added another bonus at Harrisonville Lake—stocked channel catfish that averaged three pounds in weight.

Tackle
The Reel Doctor, owned by outdoors writer Ralph Knisell, 100 W. Mantua Ave., Wenonah, NJ 08090, (609) 468-6731.

Larry's Fisherman's Cove, 570 Bridgeton Pike, Mantua, NJ 08051, (609) 464-0052.

Hook-Line & Sinker, Inc., CVS Shopping Center, Route 45, West Deptford, NJ 08096, (609) 468-7744.

ATLANTIC COUNTY

In recent years, Atlantic County has been subjected to the greed of developers who transmogrified unspoiled land west of Atlantic City's casinos into apartments, townhouses, and single homes for people who work in, but who don't want to live in, the World's Greatest Playground. In spite of the regrettable and continuing loss of open spaces, the county has a decent system of parks, which one day may be all that's left of what was once a relatively rural area.

Heading down the White Horse Pike from Philadelphia, the first major opportunity for freshwater angling is Hammonton Lake. This tract is actually in Mullica Township, east of Hammonton, and it's a popular venue for families on opening day of trout season. Access has become more difficult in recent years because of the opening of an office complex on one side of the lake and Kessler Memorial Hospital on the other.

In early spring, a good spot for white perch is at the Lower Bank Bridge which crosses the Mullica River from Route 652, north of the city of Egg Harbor. There is limited parking on either side of the bridge entrance. This is also a location for stripers, but we've found the bridge fishers to be secretive when asked for advice about what the fish are biting on.

Farther south, Egg Harbor Lake, off Route 50, has some small pickerel that are easily gulled by youngsters fishing with spinner baits like white Rooster Tails.

Dining

Try the Forks Inn, 4500 Pleasant Mills Road, near the confluence of the Batsto and Mullica Rivers ("call for directions," they advise), (609) 567-8889.

The venerable Sweetwater Casino seems to have made a comeback under new owners Steve Vann, Cliff Shute, and Randy Fitkin after being unrecommendable for years except for its view of the Mullica River. The Casino is located on Seventh Street in Mullica Township, (609) 965-3285. (According to the *Press* of Atlantic City, the Sweetwater actually has a patent on its cheese spread, and the restaurant goes through almost 14 tons of the stuff annually.)

The Inn at Egg Harbor, 446 St. Louis Avenue, Egg Harbor City, (609) 965-7878, owned by Bob and Sue Miller, has a small bar and a good country music singer on Friday nights.

Then there is the Renault Winery at 72 North Bremen Avenue in Egg

Harbor City, (609) 965-2111. It is open from 10:00 A.M. to 4:30 P.M. Monday through Saturday, and from noon to 4:30 P.M. on Sunday. The winery has plans to build an eighteen-hole golf course and two hotels, including one with 100 rooms.

And speaking of wineries, Tomasello's at 225 S. White Horse Pike in Hammonton took the 1997 Governor's Cup for the best New Jersey wine. It's the largest winery in the state, (609) 561-0567.

One of the newer establishments is the Cedar Creek Brewery & Restaurant, 236 Philadelphia Avenue, Egg Harbor City, near the intersection of the White Horse Pike (U.S. 30) and Route 50, (609) 965-6367. This brew pub—the first in Atlantic County—features lunch and dinner specials, seven days a week. Cedar Creek makes at least 10 beers on the premises, including Lark Light Ale, Amintonck Ale, Privateer Pale Ale, and Little Giant Chocolate Porter. Brewmaster is Scott Hansen, a local South Jersey guy from Lindenwold, and the chef is Frank Luisi.

The finest dining establishment in this area is the Ram's Head Inn at 9 West White Horse Pike, Absecon Highlands, (609) 652-8576. We'd make only one suggestion: get rid of the pretentious valet parking.

BIRCH GROVE PARK

Birch Grove is a delightful place for youngsters and adults to fish. It has stocked trout during the spring; some big bass that get hungry for spinner baits and "Rat-L-Traps" in the summer months; and nature trails, a zoo, birding, campsites, picnic area, and a food stand—all for the mere sum of $1 to park. (Birch Grove has about 250 parking spaces. In 1996, plans to expand parking ran into opposition from neighbors who did not want two acres of park trees sawed down.)

It was opening day of New Jersey's trout season, and I was at Birch Grove Park, sporting a brand-new Kunnan fiberglass ultra-light spinning rod. After several hours of unsuccessful angling, I temporarily deserted the horde of anglers along the park's ponds, and headed to the men's room, proudly carrying my new rod like a fly-fisher, with the handle pointed straight in front of me and the tip of the pole sticking horizontally behind.

I opened the lavatory door without realizing that it closed quickly.

*Crunch! I heard a sickening sound as the door sliced off the tip of my
Kunnan. I can still hear that sound today. —G.I.*

Another part of the Atlantic County Park System is Estell Manor, south
of Mays Landing, off Route 50. This park has picnic areas, nature trails, and
the ruins of the Estell Glass Works, built in 1834 by John Estell and David
Estell, Jr. The glass works is being restored under the Historic Preservation
Bond Program.

There is also a Veterans Cemetery and a floating dock. Five youngsters
were fishing with bobbers one summer's day when we approached.

"What are you fishin' for?" we asked.

"Anything that's bitin'," came the obvious reply.

On the trail leading from the floating dock there was the unmistakable,
dual-colored "J" of a turkey spore—a sign that wild turkeys are thriving in
the southern forests of New Jersey and that the stocking program has been
a success.

Traveling by car through the sandy roads of the park, you'll pass the
Bethlehem Loading Co.'s World War I foundation of smokeless powder
magazine.

The park rangers are ensconced in a white-painted house built by
Aaron Shaw in 1824.

You can also borrow a bike and ride through the park. Annual events
include a "Biking for Bugs" outing, with bike trips to special areas for interesting insects.

Maple Lake, or Crescent Lake, was added to the state park at Estell
Manor in 1995.

The park is open 7:30 A.M. to dusk. For information, call (609)
645-5960.

Another Atlantic County Park is at Weymouth, where the remnants of
an iron works can be seen. The Weymouth River runs through this popular
site, and although it is said that pickerel lurk in the waters, we have yet to
catch our first Weymouth River fish at this site. It's more fun to barbecue in
the cool, leafy glen.

The Weymouth River is part of the Great Egg Harbor River system, one
of two New Jersey rivers protected under the federal Wild and Scenic Act.
The fishing dock along the river at Mays Landing is a popular spot for adults
and youngsters with life jackets. This area has pickerel and yellow perch.
Use minnows or grass shrimp on float rigs, or spinners.

Dining

Hallowich Log Cabin, 7318 Black Horse Pike, Weymouth, serves Polish-Ukrainian food, (609) 625-2714. Kielbasa, stuffed cabbage, and other delicacies are offered.

The Inn at Sugar Hill, U.S. 40 and Route 559, Mays Landing, (609) 625-2226.

Old River Tavern, 5341 Somers Point-Mays Landing Road (Route 559), one mile east of the Atlantic County Court House, (609) 625-9805.

Crabby's, a good seafood place one mile south of Mays Landing on Route 50 at Belcoville, (609) 625-2722.

Chet's, an award-winning restaurant at 5401 U.S. 40, between the Hamilton Mall and Mays Landing, (609) 625-1234.

The Great American Pub & Grille, across from Hamilton Mall, (609) 625-9500.

Other attractions

Balic Winery, 6623 U.S. 40, Mays Landing, NJ 08330, is open from 9:30 A.M. to 5:30 P.M., every day except Sunday, (609) 625-2166.

Lester G. MacNamara Wildlife Management Area (WMA): One of the largest wildlife management areas in New Jersey is the 12,438-acre Lester G. MacNamara WMA in Atlantic and Cape May Counties. This huge tract offers good freshwater and saltwater fishing, a boat launch, birding, trapping, and hunting for deer, upland game, and ducks. Access to the office is from Tuckahoe-Marmora Road on Route 631. Look for the sign and turn onto a dirt road. Follow the main stem 2.3 miles to the Tuckahoe River. There is a boat ramp and bank fishing at the water's edge. To the left, you can see the boats east of the Tuckahoe River Bridge at John Yank's Marine boat yard, where a 130-foot tour boat is being rebuilt to become a venue for dinner cruises past the Statue of Liberty.

In the WMA's freshwater sections, you'll find largemouth bass, yellow perch, sunfish, pickerel, and eels. (In the saltwater of the Tuckahoe River and Great Egg Harbor River, there are white perch, striped bass, fluke, flounder, and eels.

Dining

The area has a number of interesting restaurants and taverns. The Tuckahoe River divides the Atlantic County portion of Lester G. Mac-Namara WMA, on the north, from the Cape May County side on the south. In Atlantic County, try The Buck on Route 50 in Corbin City. Here's how the restaurant critic for the *Press* of Atlantic City set the culinary stage in a December 1, 1996, review of the restaurant: "When the first cold snap hits, there's something that makes man (and woman) want to eat in wood-paneled places, far from the city, with crackling fires and animal heads on the wall." You may choose the bar area on the north end of the building or the dining room with a working fireplace. The early bird specials are especially good bargains. We like The Buck, (609) 628-3117.

Other spots in Corbin City are The Corbin House, 119 Route 50, which has excellent Italian food, served by the owners of Mama Mia's in Williamstown, N.J., (609) 628-4415; the Corbin Cafe, 405 Route 50, (609) 628-2100; and the Corbin Manor Inn also on Route 50.

Corbin City, incidentally, is where Temple University's WRTI-FM translator is located, broadcasting jazz to South Jersey.

On the other side of the Tuckahoe River, in Cape May County, there's a colorful bar called the Triton, at the intersection of Routes 616 and 50. This can be a salty place, frequented by bearded men who speak of tog fishing, boats, hunting dogs, and catfish. If you understand this language, give it a try. You'll also get a very good sandwich at the Triton.

If you have a sweet tooth, you must stop at the Tuckahoe Cheese Factory, 2117 Route 50, Tuckahoe, NJ 08250, (609) 628-2154. A whole cheesecake is $24. Try Joan's Sampler, which includes cherry, Amaretto, and chocolate cheesecake plus carrot cake and triple chocolate cake. There are no artificial colorings, flavorings or preservatives. "If we seem a little fussy," says their brochure, "it's because we are." Open Monday, Wednesday, Thursday, Friday, and Saturday 9–6; Sunday, 2–5. Closed Tuesday.

Kupetz Bar at the intersection of Routes 557 and 552 is a small and friendly place that's good for a cold beer and a sandwich on the way home from a freshwater or saltwater fishing trip.

Good Italian food can be had at DeThomasi's 5 Points Inn, at the intersection of Routes 540 and 557, near the border of Atlantic and Cumberland counties.

CUMBERLAND COUNTY

Shaws Mill Pond is tucked in the southwest corner of the huge Edward G. Bevan Wildlife Management Area, which covers more than 12,000 acres. Located near the town of Newport, the pond can be reached by taking Route 553 south, past the Newport-Centre Grove Road, to Shaws Mill Road.

The Division of Fish, Game and Wildlife calls Shaws Mill Pond "one of the best largemouth bass waters in the area." It is also stocked with trout in the spring, and the first entry in the 1997 *The Press* (Atlantic City) Fishing Contest was a three-pound, twelve-ounce chain pickerel caught on March 5 at Shaw Mills Pond by one Mike Wydra of Millville.

Cedar Lake Park, off Route 553 in Lawrence Township, has a small boat ramp, swings for kids, and lots of local geese. Another freshwater site is the Clarks Pond Wildlife Area, with 78 acres, just above Fairton and south of Route 553.

UNION LAKE

"Bass anglers seeking a change of scenery which offers some of the Garden State's hottest fishing action should take a look at Cumberland County's Union Lake."

—BOB BRUNISHOLZ, *The Trentonian.*

Hugh Carberry, a State Senior Fisheries Biologist, agrees with Mr. Brunisholz. Union Lake is, he wrote, "a multi-faceted gem," with largemouth, smallmouth, and striped bass, which are growing larger thanks to a fish ladder that opened a "door" to the Maurice River to such tasty morsels as herring and gizzard shad.

Many serious bass fishermen are concerned because the State has released almost 3,000 tiger muskellunge into Union Lake. These hybrid muskies cannot reproduce, but they are the freshwater equivalent of hungry bluefish.

Giampietro Lake Pond in Vineland is good for bank fishing for bass. Ron Cheruka, former bass fishing columnist for *The Press* of Atlantic City, once caught an eight-pound largemouth from this shallow lake.

Also in Giampietro Park is Ellis Pond, which is stocked with trout. On opening day, young and old anglers line the banks while those in canoes and small bass boats with electric motors cruise in search of fish. You'll see young men with their baseball caps on backwards, middle-aged men in camo clothes, and old-timers in cowboy hats.

Route 655 (Lincoln Avenue) runs right past the lake.

CUMBERLAND POND

Cumberland Pond, which is part of the 14,000-acre Peaslee Wildlife Management Area, is a good spot for chain pickerel. From Philadelphia, take the North-South Freeway to Route 55 south. Get off at the Millville exit and head east on Route 49 until you see the pond on the left. The best time to fish for big pickerel is in the autumn months, when the critters are fattening up for the winter. You can fish the shore along Route 49.

MAURICE RIVER

Vice President Al Gore was one of many assembled dignitaries on October 26, 1994, for a celebration of the Maurice River's designation as protected water under the umbrella of the Federal Wild and Scenic Rivers Act. (Locals pronounce the river as in "Morris.") The law, which had been signed earlier in the year by President Clinton, protects about thirty-seven miles of the Maurice and two tributaries, Manumuskin and Menantico. No other river system in private ownership in the United States has such protection.

Writer Pete Dunne was right on target when he said in the *New York Times*: "Happily, the Maurice River is . . . a gem. In a state that has sullied most of its rivers with industrial, agricultural, or municipal waste, the Maurice and its tributaries remain almost pure."

The Maurice runs forty-two miles through Gloucester, Salem, and Cumberland counties. More than 50 percent of endangered animal species in New Jersey live in the area. There are bald eagles and ospreys here.

Manumuskin Preserve is nearly 3,300 acres and owned now by the Nature Conservancy, which purchased part of it and received part of it as a gift from Waste Management, Inc.

"As a river," wrote *New York Times* reporter Iver Peterson in 1994, "the Maurice doesn't look like much at first—broad and flat, snaking in lazy oxbows through the tidal marshlands and sandy uplands of southern New Jersey to the shallow, shimmering Delaware Bay."

One of our favorite family fishing spots—mainly because its accessibility—is Mauricetown Park just south of the drawbridge in Mauricetown. Here is a wonderful old municipality that has an annual seafood festival, antiques, and other events, including a muskrat dinner. The park has a pier, boat ramp, and free parking. Youngsters who fish this spot will usually find plenty of feisty catfish and carp to whet their interest for action. White perch, stripers, weakies, and blues sometimes prowl the river here at certain times of the year.

Wheaton Village

Want to make your own paperweight under the supervision of a master glass artist? Or visit a museum of American glass? Or watch Sue Gogin and

Terry Plasket turn on their potter's wheel and spin lead-free clay into bowls, cups, vases, and other ornaments? Then you should take the family to Wheaton Village in Millville. Other features include a half-scale model of an 1863 train, the 1876 Centre Grove Schoolhouse, and the Stained Glass Studio, plus many annual events like car shows, doll shows, and a Grand Christmas Exhibition.

Wheaton Village is located at 1501 Glasstown Road in Millville, about halfway between Philadelphia and Atlantic City. From Philadelphia, take the Walt Whitman Bridge to Route 42 and then to Route 55 South (a road along which you should observe the speed limit!). Get off at Exit 26 and follow the Wheaton Village signs. Phone: (800) 998-4552 or (609) 825-6800. The Village is open seven days a week, April through December, from 10: 00 A.M. to 5:00 P.M. During January, February, and March, it is only open Wednesday through Sunday. Admission is $6.50 for adults, $5.50 for senior citizens, and $3.50 for students. Children 5 and under are free.

The Bridgeton Zoo

It's official name is the Cohanzick Zoo, it's the oldest one in the Garden State (established in 1934), it's *free*, and in recent years it has been undergoing some changes with help from a Green Acres grant. Two white tigers were scheduled to arrive from Bridgeton's sister city in Sweden in September 1997, and a new education center should be ready by 1998. This is well worth a family visit, and with some planning, a smart fisher can wet a line in the Maurice River as it flows through the city and then take the kids to the zoo. Trenchermen and women won't want to miss another popular event each year in Bridgeton—the seafood festival.

Tackle

Blackwater Sports Center, 2228 N. Delsea Drive, Vineland, NJ 08360, (609) 691-1571, open daily year-round and Friday evenings.

CAPE MAY COUNTY

Dennisville Lake is one of the most popular places for trout in the early season. It is northwest of the town of Dennisville, near the intersection of the Delsea Drive (Route 47) and Route 611.

But those who want to avoid the crowds on opening day head for West Pond. "The extreme south is a good place to fish [on the first day of trout season]," conservation officer Mark Stullenburger told the *Press* of Atlantic City in 1994.

Officer Stullenburger's observation was right on target when we visited West Pond on opening day, April 12, 1997. It was a gray day with rain showers, but it still was the first day of trout season. We saw only a dozen or so anglers, including a salty-looking veteran with a nice string of trout and two youngsters whose father had taken refuge in his recreational vehicle while they fished happily in the drizzle.

West Pond is located just north of Cape May Court House off U.S. 9. If you're traveling south, make a right at the sign for the Cape May County Park & Zoo, then another right to the parking area for the pond. You can also make a right at Exit 11 of the Garden State Parkway and drive straight to the county park.

There is another option for anglers who want to avoid all the crowds. Bauer's Fishing Pond, 3025 South Shore Road, Seaville, N.J., near Parkway Exit 25, a quarter-mile south of Route 50, is a pay-to-fish proposition. Owned and operated by Joe Bauer, the lake has shoreline and pier fishing for trout, catfish, largemouth bass, and hybrid stripers. It costs $10 for eight hours of fishing by adults, $5 for children, plus an extra fee per pound of fish kept for table fare or those injured that cannot be returned. Live bait and lures may be used. Call (609) 624-1304.

BELLEPLAIN

Belleplain State Forest, in Cape May and Cumberland Counties, was established in 1928, and today has more than 12,000 acres of oak, pine, white cedar, holly, and laurel woodlands. Old-timers will recall that the Depression-era Civilian Conservation Corps was responsible for building much of Belleplain.

Truthfully, serious fishing is not the major enticement to visit this State Forest, but it is one of South Jersey's finest facilities for camping, swimming, walking nature trails, horseback riding, hunting, picnicking, and family fishing (compared to the aforementioned *serious* fishing). It is also the place to pick up permits for beach buggies on Corsons Inlet State Park.

The kids will enjoy the twenty-six-acre Lake Nummy, the first water recreation area you pass after entering the park. Named in honor of the last Lenni Lenape Native American chief of Cape May County, Nummy holds panfish and a few pickerel and bass, if you can find them. During the summer, there's a canoe concession. Two other popular spots are the 65-acre East Creek Pond and Pickle Factory Pond.

To reach Belleplain, take south Exit 17 of the Garden State Parkway and head west on County Route 550, through the town of Woodbine. It is also accessible off Route 47, the Delsea Drive, on the way to Cape May. Belleplain State Forest has friendly personnel to help you. Call 609) 861-2404.

Dining

A decent place to chow down, either before entering Belleplain or after leaving the park, is the Dionysus Restaurant, Washington Avenue in Woodbine (609) 861-5803. It's open seven days a week for breakfast, lunch, and dinner, and Evangelos Kossyvakis can serve up a tasty gyro with tzatziki sauce ($5.50), in addition to such standard fare as a tuna club, a reuben 'n rye, and good French fries. For your trip into the woods of Belleplain, take-out is available.

Dionysus is an interesting place that may find you eavesdropping one moment on a pair of college students sharing academic war stories and, at the next table, on a group of hungry, orange-capped rabbit hunters making excuses why they missed shooting the little bunnies. Adjacent to Dionysus is a store that sells some sporting goods.

The Delaware Bay

"No angler worthy of the name particularly cares whether people think him lazy or not, but he is likely to be somewhat more sensitive to the equally common charge of dishonesty."
—ODELL SHEPARD, *Thy Rod and Thy Creel*

New Jersey's Delaware Bay is one of the finest fishing areas of the East Coast, bar none. It is productive, seductive, and fecund. But there are some who misuse this great Garden State "fish factory."

In 1996, in what *The Press* of Atlantic City called "a 'fish bust' of unprecedented proportions," two Millville, N.J., men were arrested for having 515 weakfish more than their daily bag limit and 87 undersized weakies. The poachers reportedly caught the weakfish at night near Miah Maull Light in the Delaware Bay, using an old—but not illegal, in New Jersey—tactic of shining lights into the water to attract baitfish, which attract the bigger game. They later paid fines totalling $3,000.

The crime of these two hapless individuals pales when one considers the murder that happens legally in Delaware Bay. In 1994, the New Jersey Department of Environmental Protection granted Public Service Electric and Gas, operator of the Salem nuclear power plants on Alloways Creek, a permit to continue killing billions of fish with its water intake procedures. The *quid pro quo* was that the PSEG is supposed to restore some 20,000 acres of wetlands in New Jersey and Delaware as nurseries to create new fish for the company to destroy.

To cool the reactors, the Salem plant must suck in three billion gallons of water a day. That H_2O comes from the Delaware, and in the process, millions of fish eggs and small fish get sucked up too. After the Salem I and Salem II reactors were shut down in 1995, fish populations in Delaware Bay seemed to improve. Salem II was given the green light to restart in 1997.

In 1996, a proposal by Public Service Electric and Gas Co. to spray a herbicide on nearly 3,000 acres of Delaware Bay wetlands generated more controversy. The objective was to destroy a plant pest—phragmites—which has taken over the Bay's marshes. The utility wanted to use glyphosate to get at the roots of the tenacious reed. This undertaking would help PSE&G restore the native plants like foxtail that were there before the phragmites took over.

The Nature Conservancy has a contract to manage some 16,000 acres of prime Delaware Bay wetlands for Public Service, in addition to the 5,000 acres it owns. The area covers land in Cape May, Cumberland, and Salem Counties.

GREENWICH

Greenwich was founded in 1622 as a port city. Its streets were planned by William Penn, and years later it was the site of the "Greenwich Tea Burning Party," which took place after the local Colonists learned that a captain had sailed up the Cohansey and unloaded a cache of tea in a Tory's home on Market Street. Dressed as Native Americans, the patriots raided the house, took boxes of tea, and put the torch to them in a field.

Dining

For lunch or dinner, stop in at the Ship John Inn, with a dining room that overlooks the Cohansey River. The inn is operated by Elaine Raynes, and the chef is Fredrick Belfaus, formerly of the Ram's Head Inn near Absecon in Atlantic County. Recommended dishes include the crab cakes and flounder stuffed with crab meat. For reservations: (609) 451-1444 or (800) 829-7447. The inn also offers sunset cruises.

The Fairfield Inn on Route 553 has good sandwiches, but it's closed Sundays, when many people are heading back, hungry, from a day's fishing on Delaware Bay.

Other Attractions

Each December, the Cumberland County Historical Society sponsors a Christmas House Tour, when residents of Greenwich's private homes welcome visitors. There are also Christmas exhibits, a live nativity, carollers, and other seasonal attractions. In 1996, the tour cost $8. For information, contact the Historical Society at (609) 455-4055 or (609) 451-8454.

Tackle
Barton's Bait Shop on Route 553 in Fairton.

Dining
FORTESCUE

Going south on Route 553, turn right at Route 656, proceed to the blinking light (just past Wild Bill's Bait and Tackle) and turn left onto Fortescue Road. You are about to arrive at the fishing capital of Delaware Bay— at least on the New Jersey side.

There are many good party boats here. One of our favorites is the *Miss Fortescue,* which sails daily during the season from 7:00 A.M. until 1:00 P.M., and then from 3:00 P.M. to 9:00 P.M. Call Higbee's Marina at (609) 447-4157.

The old man had a single thought in mind when he boarded the Miss Fortescue for a day of fishing on Delaware Bay. "I don't want no bluefish and I don't want no weakfish," he announced to the other hopeful fishermen, including me and my then 15-year-old son, George. "All I want is one flounder—just one—so I can take it home for my wife. She loves flounder," he said.

But, nearing day's end, it was obvious that the sea gods had frowned on the old man. The captain of the 48-foot "Miss Fortescue" headed back to port, and the old man was empty-handed.

Thanks to my son, I was more fortunate. As usual, he had outfished me, enriching our cooler with two nice bluefish and a medium-sized fluke. In my mind, I was already devouring the tasty fillets with a properly chilled bottle of Puligny Montrachet.

The culinary fantasy evaporated when my son sidled up to me.

"Dad," he said, "do you mind if I give the old man my flounder? He didn't catch anything, and he said his wife likes flounder."

What could any father—even a hungry one—say to such a display of selfless generosity?

"It's your fish," I responded. "It's up to you. But it would be a nice thing to do."

He plucked the flounder from the cooler, carried it with both hands to the port side of the boat, and offered it to the old man. The donee accepted the gift with gratefulness and uncommon alacrity.

But a few minutes later, George learned that unselfish behavior sometimes brings immediate rewards. For the first time in his young angling career, he won the party boat's pool for the largest fish. One of his blues earned him $24 and a "Pool Winner" button that he proudly wore on his fishing cap. —G.I.

Higbee's Marina and Restaurant serves up breakfast and lunch. An example of a breakfast special is creamed chipped beef on toast with home fried potatoes. And if there's more "cream" than beef, who cares, for $3.50?

Other good party boats include the *Fortescue Queen,* captained by Don Pike (609-447-4667), and *Bonanza II,* which usually sails at 7:30 A.M. (609-447-4490).

If you don't want to get on a party boat, consider beach fishing and boat rentals: proceed past Higbee's Marina, along Downe Avenue, for four-tenths of a mile until the road dead-ends. Turn left, past the Charlesworth Hotel (which serves dinner, Wednesday through Sunday, from 4:00 to 9:00 P.M. and on Sunday from noon to 8:00 P.M.), and drive to a long stretch of beach and bulkhead facing Delaware Bay. Many people park their cars and fish here for weakfish and blues during the summer. For a nice family outing, bring along surf poles, bait, sand spikes, portable chairs, beach umbrella, and a cooler filled with sandwiches and cold beverages.

This roadway also has a number of boat rental places. On a good, calm day, it is fun to take out a small boat and fish for blues and weakies right off the beach. (Make sure you remember a landmark, because it's easy to forget the dock you left hours earlier.)

Poor Charlie McCloskey never had a chance. My friend Charlie, a well-known expert on labor relations, fancied himself, for some inscrutable reason, as an authority on angling as well. One day this poor misguided individual had the temerity to challenge me to a "fish-off."

I suggested a simple test: we would each rent outboard boats at Fortescue, anchor next to each other, and see who caught the most fish. To make sure that Charlie played by the same rules—a formidable task, given his record of dissembling at sea—I asked "honest" Bob Marler to fish from McCloskey's boat.

What Charlie didn't know was that I had no intention of playing by the rules. I knew his reputation. Here is a man who once tried to bribe a young kid aboard the "Applejack" out of Atlantic City to give him his brother's monster sea bass so Charlie could claim it for the pool; the same individual once pirated a frozen fluke aboard a friend's boat and, after an unsuccessful day of fishing, slipped it over the rail on his hook and pretended he had caught it.

Such a man deserves no mercy. On the evening before our trip, I went to Brinkman's Bait and Tackle in Northeast Philadelphia, bought some thick squid, cut it into tantalizing tapered strips, and marinated it overnight in shedder crab oil—an irresistible meal for the weakfish we'd be after.

The next morning we were out on the water by 8:00 A.M. with a good incoming tide. Within three hours, my ice chest was full, but Charlie had managed to trick only a handful of the most obtuse weakfish in all of Delaware Bay. Charlie did have one last desperate trick up his sleeve. During the fishing, my line got hung up on something, and I had to break it and tie on a new rig. Hours later, when we pulled up our anchors to head for shore, Charlie discovered that my line had become entangled on his anchor line—with my weakfish still attached to my hook. Despite this evidence, Charlie still claimed the fish as his. —G.I.

Retrace the road you took to the beach area but continue straight past Downe Avenue and you'll see Myers Marina. Restaurant critic Ed Hitzel recommends the crabcakes cooked at Myers by Mary Johnson. (Long-time Fortescue fishers will remember the Garrison House, which Johnson owned.) Hitzel calls the Johnson crabcakes "among the best we've tried in 20 years."

Coming around again to the party-boat docks, try Al's Bait House, a well-stocked fishing emporium. And if you don't get any fish, Al's Fresh Seafood is conveniently located right next door.

Coming out of Fortescue, make a left at the blinking light and go to the Newport Landing Marina, which rents out boats for crabbing. Patricia's Waterfront Cafe is here, too.

PORT NORRIS

Turn right at the Longreach Marina and go four-tenths of a mile down a stone road. Park and walk along mounds of crushed clam and oyster shells to a spot along the Maurice River. Watch out for cables in the water, which can snag your lines. On weekends, another problem is boat traffic. But this spot will give up good-sized catfish, weakfish, and stripers. Cast out into the river and take a good hard seat on some discarded concrete.

Tackle
Longreach Marina, High & Broad, Port Norris, NJ 08349, (609) 785-1818.

The Shellpile Restaurant and Raw Bar looked good after a morning of fishing the Maurice River—until we discovered that, in order to get a cold beer with lunch in "dry" Commercial Township, one had to join a private club.

"How much does a membership cost?" I asked the young blonde barmaid as my son and I settled into two comfortable stools.

"Ten dollars."

"That's pretty stiff," I observed.

She smiled a smile that said she'd been through this drill many times before.

"There's also a seventy-two-hour waiting period until your membership is approved," she explained.

"You mean," my son ventured, not quite comprehending the situation we faced, "that even if we paid the ten dollars we still wouldn't be able to have a beer here until seventy-two hours had passed?"

"That's right," she confirmed.

"Thank you," I said. "We'll leave."

They obviously don't want riff-raff like us contaminating the Shellpile Restaurant and Raw Bar. —G.I.

In addition to the dirt road that provides access to the river, there is a small public wharf owned by Commercial Township at Hands Landing Road, just past Miller Road, from which you can fish.

For those looking to take live hardshell crabs home during the season, try Reeves Brothers (dockside phone 609-785-9610) or Bateman's Live Crabs (609) 785-0109.

This is a story about the good old days. In the mid-1970s, my friends and I would take our sons to Matts Landing for night weakfishing aboard the Miss Diane, captained by a young man from Ocean City named Mark Christianson.

During the summer months, we would leave our homes in Burlington County after work and drive to the Delaware Bay dock. Captain Mark would ease the Miss Diane into the Maurice River around 8:00 P.M. and head for Forty Foot Lighthouse. Once there, at dusk, he'd anchor up and turn on large generator-powered lights that shown down into the water.

The lights would attract baitfish which, in turn, attracted big tide runner weakies, monster weakfish—the kind rarely seen today because of the Salem Nuclear Power Plant. It was wonderful to sit out there in the lights within the darkness, with the moan of the lighthouse, the gentle rocking of the boat, and the minnows swimming toward the light, followed by the frenzy of weakfish breaking the water to gorge themselves on the smaller prey. The best way to catch the big fish was to imitate the baitfish by dropping lines that had little shad darts at the terminal. The action was unbelievable, with virtually every cast producing hits. We'd return to the dock very late in the night, our burlap sacks bulging with the beautiful fish, many of them plump with roe.

In retrospect, we helped ruin the weakfish run in Delaware Bay, too, but it was only a small part of the reason compared to the destruction caused by other more catastrophic environmental factors like the nuclear generating plant. —G.I.

Coastal Saltwater

"My granddaughter, Sierra, wasn't having any luck one day. I told her
to try spitting over the side. She did—and bang! We had one."
                    —JOHN HERSEY, *Blues*

"When good friend and expert saltwater fisherman Mel Kemp asks me
to fish the shore with him, I hesitate for only one reason. You get up at
four in the morning, drive an hour and a half to the beach, race
through breakfast, get to the boat, go out for the day.
    "You get back to the dock in mid-afternoon, clean and fillet your
catch, pack your gear in the car and drive back home around 5 : 00 or
6 : 00 P.M.
    "Brother, that's at least a fourteen-hour day. That ain't fishing,
it's WORK! Who needs it?
    "I'll stick with a little lake, pond or river close to home.
    "Maybe no fish, but also no surf. And no sweat."
—ARNOLD C. ROPEIK, in the *Trenton Times* (February 14, 1997)

🐟 At this writing, New Jersey—thankfully—still has no saltwater fishing
license, along its 127 miles of coastline, except for an $18 "permit" re-
quired by the bureaucratic bunglers of the National Marine Fisheries Service (NMFS) of boaters who fish offshore for tuna. Despite the need for the
equivalent of a freshwater license in the brine, those who pursue saltwater
fish in New Jersey (and, according to the NMFS, our numbers grew from
654,000 in 1982 to 927,000 in 1995) still must pay as much attention to size
and bag limits in the salt as they do in freshwater.

This fact was driven home on a party boat one summer's day when we hauled in one of our favorite table fish, tautog or blackfish. "You'll have to throw that one back," said the mate. The tog was an inch shy of the 12-inch size limit, and we watched hungrily as it was tossed back into the wine-dark sea.

"Fishing isn't what it used to be," wrote *Atlantic City Press* reporter G. Patrick Pawling in 1996. "It's a lot more regulated, and complicated. With more limits on the size and number of fish, and with more regulations coming, a day of fishing at the New Jersey shore takes a little more thinking."

Commercial fishermen are crying the blues, too. In 1995, they brought in almost 180 million pounds of fish and shellfish, with a total value of more than $95 million. Atlantic mackerel topped the list for pounds of fish— 4.8 million—but in dollar value to the fishermen, the king was the surf clam, which netted them more than $27 million. Yet although the catches were at their highest levels in more than two generations, the high-quality species had declined.

Even NASA is lending a hand to commercial fishermen. The agency shelled out half of a $2.4 million bill for a three-year study of the waters off the northeastern United States. The research, gleaned from satellite images, will be used to predict the location of fish, the temperature of water, currents, and levels of plankton, according to the Associated Press (July 25, 1996). Commercial fishermen contend that there was poor data that led to limits on haddock, cod, and yellowtail flounder.

Others are looking closer to earth for answers. New Jersey's Division of Fish, Game and Wildlife has an Adopt-A-Wreck program. With this effort, tax-deductible funds are donated to help prepare, clean and tow old vessels (even barges and Army tanks!) out to sea to provide a home for many species of fish. For information, (609) 748-2020.

PRACTICAL TIPS FOR SALTWATER FISHING

For newcomers to the boundless pleasures of saltwater angling, here are a few tips gleaned from years of knocking around the surf and sea:

1. Practice catch and release. It's fun to tag your fish, and tags are available from the American Littoral Society, Sandy Hook, Highlands, NJ 07732, (908) 291-0055.

2. Fish for the table should be respected. The tastiest fish is that which is cleaned and iced as soon as it comes out of the water.

3. Consider renting a boat for fishing and crabbing. The cost varies, but it averages between $40 and $45 a day. For newcomers, here is a checklist of things to take with you in your boat, and some advice on what to do:

—Sunglasses, sun screen, and a hat are essential.

—A long-sleeved shirt is good to have for protection from the sun or to ward off a chilly wind.

—Take aboard tackle that's appropriate for the prey you seek. For example: a light rod is good when drifting for fluke, but stiffer gear is needed when big blues are prowling the bays and inlets.

—Wear appropriate shoes that won't slip when they get wet.

—Insect repellant can be a Godsend, especially when you're in the back bays.

—Pay attention to the weather. Get off the water if it looks like a storm is coming up or if the wind starts kicking up the waves.

—Take a cooler with block ice if possible because it lasts longer than cubes. Wrap food and beverages in plastic—there's nothing less appetizing than a ham-on-rye sandwich seasoned with fish blood and scales.

—It's best to hold the beer until you are back at the dock. In recent years, the Marine Police and Coast Guard have really cracked down on people who drink on the water.

—Turn the boat head-on to take wakes from passing boats.

—Rent the boat as early as possible to get on the water before the jet ski yahoos start ruining the fishing.

—To avoid the crowds, fish on weekdays.

—If you are fishing an area for the first time, make a mental note of landmarks. It's surprisingly easy to get disoriented once you are away from the dock.

—Ask the people at the boat rental for their suggestions on hot fishing spots. They want you to be successful, because they thrive on repeat customers.

—Basic equipment includes a knife in a sheath, pliers (especially for removing hooks from the mouths of nasty bluefish), a rag for wiping your hands, and Band-aids for the inevitable fish-hook injury.

4. A good alternative to renting your own small boat is the party or "head" boat, under the control of a knowledgeable captain.

There are hundreds of party boats from Sandy Hook in North Jersey to Cape May and the Delaware Bay. They vary in quality, depending upon many variables. Here are signs to look for in finding good party boats:

—Are the "heads" clean? A restaurant consultant observed once that one of the first things he inspects in a restaurant is the lavatories. "It shows that management cares," he said. The same may be said of bathrooms aboard charter and party boats.

—Is the boat clean outside and inside? Are strips of clam and squid still sticking to the boat rails from yesterday's trip?

—Are children welcome? Smart party boat captains recognize that kids are the paying customers of tomorrow. They work hard to insure a positive experience for them. (By the same token, don't go out on a boat in sloppy weather with youngsters. Also, choose a boat that is not headed far off shore when you have children with you. The experience may sour your kids on saltwater fishing for good.)

—Are rowdies unwelcome? Some boats go too far by banning alcohol, despite the fact that one of life's great pleasures is an ice-cold beer on the rail of a party boat on a tranquil sea under a bright sun. Other boats may go the other way. One of the most unpleasant experiences we ever had was aboard a night head boat out of a Delaware Bay port. A large group of people showed up drunk at the dock. They continued to consume a lethal combination of beer, wine, and hard liquor while fishing, and almost lost one of their members overboard. They returned to the dock drunker than they had left. Although they abused only themselves that evening, the captain should have "streeted" them before they boarded. Apparently, he was more interested in fares than in safety.

—Does the captain care if you catch fish? Some captains head out to sea, drop the anchor, and leave you to the vagaries of Poseidon. Good captains move around when the fishing drops off. They work hard for their customers because they value your business and want you back again.

—Are the mates helpful? Good mates have a knack for helping without making you feel like a fool. They offer advice, untangle lines, unhook fish, cut up and distribute bait, and make your party boat or charter trip an enjoyable experience. If they do all this, they deserve a generous tip when you disembark.

—Does the captain communicate with his fares? We prefer the captain who tells you why he's moving, what's going on, and what's happening beneath the sea.

—Does the boat practice safety first?

—Are there repeat customers aboard? A sure sign of satisfied customers is the guy at the boat rail who turns to you and says, "I was out with this captain a week ago, and we did real good."

—Are you treated fairly? If there's a particularly rough trip, good captains will distribute free or discount tickets for another trip in the future.

—Take seriously your responsibilities as a party boat fare. Be considerate of your fishing companions by watching your line and trying to avoid tangles. With children aboard, try to set a good example. If the captain has tried hard and the boat still has little fish to show for it, assume a philosophical approach and enjoy the boat ride.

—Listen to the advice of the captain. Repeat: listen to the advice of the captain.

A group of Temple administrators and faculty gathered in Cape May early one evening with predetermined plans to fish for monster black drum. We had "psyched" each other out about heading into Delaware Bay for these huge creatures. But when we got to the dock, the captain suggested we turn our attention instead to weakfish.

"The drum fishing hasn't been all that good," he advised. "I'd recommend you go out for weakies near the mouth of the bay instead."

But hard-headed and stubborn anglers were we.

"We drove all the way down here for drum," we argued, "and it's drum we want to fish for."

The captain shrugged. We loaded our gear aboard the boat, and headed up the dark bay for drum.

Eight hours later, in the wee hours of the morning, we returned to the dock with no drum, no drum bites, and only a few bluefish to show for our efforts. But fishermen from other boats that went out for weakies were cleaning their fish—lots of big tiderunners. We had skunked ourselves because we refused to take the advice of someone who knew much more about the local fishing scene than we did. —G.I.

—Plan to arrive at least an hour before the boat is scheduled to leave. Your best bet is to find a spot on the stern of the party boat,

and, if this location is already taken, try to pick a place on the
starboard or port sides as close to the stern as possible. Why? We
don't really know, except that in our experience more fish are
caught from the stern, and party boat regulars treasure this spot.

5. Hiring a charter. Unlike a party boat, which is mostly a random collection of strangers who show up to go fishing on any given day, a charter
gives you the fun of going fishing with your own group—relatives, friends,
workplace colleagues, or, if you have the money, just yourself. Charters can
provide some of the most memorable fishing you've ever had. Once in a
while, they might be memorable for other reasons.

Here is a horror story that, fortunately, is an anomaly among charters.
It was written by a Harrisburg angler, and published as a letter to the editor
in the *Fisherman* on October 31, 1996:

> I recently went canyon fishing with five other fishermen who all have
> more than twenty-five years fishing experience. After paying $1,800 for
> the charter all we were able to do was ride and sleep for thirty hours,
> except when the mate caught a fish (and) we could reel it in like I do
> with my five-year-old grandson.
>
> We chunked at night and we wanted to fish, but the mate was the
> only one allowed to fish, even when there were fish boiling behind the
> boat. We told the mate we wanted to fish but his reply was to give us
> one pole with a two-ounce jig to share.
>
> It's a fact that there is little difference fishing in a chum slick for
> bluefish than fishing in a chunk slick for tuna, except for the size
> of the fish and the pole. . . . You can bet we will never charter this boat
> again or any other that thinks this is fishing.

When chartering a boat, be prepared to alter your plans in response to
changing weather conditions. A few years ago, a group of Temple administrators chartered a half-day afternoon trip aboard the sixty-two-foot *Jersey
Devil*, captained by an experienced young man named Eric Lundvall out of
Barnegat Light, (609) 495-0022. We arrived at Long Beach Island in a tor-
rential rain. Eric was ready to cancel, but left the ultimate decision to us.
While we debated our predicament in a nearby watering hole, the rain
seemed to ease a little. We decided to try it, but Eric advised us to shelve our
plans for offshore bluefishing because of an uncomfortably stiff wind.

We went fishing and had a wonderful time drifting close to the beach
for fluke. By the time we returned to the dock, the bad weather had disappeared, and we had made a trip that many of us still talk about years later.

Here are some things to consider when you hire a charter:

—Call well in advance to reserve the date you want. Some anglers book for next year's charter before they step off the boat *this* year.

—Ask questions—size of the boat; where the captain will take you and the likely conditions you'll meet; the total price structure; who keeps the catch; is beer allowed on board.

—Find out how much of a deposit is required, and the captain's policy on refunds for bad weather or last-minute cancellations.

—Tip the mates who help you.

—Avoid Captain Ahabs. A few charter captains—like one we encountered some years back when we were fishing for King salmon on Lake Ontario—treat their customers no better than prisoners of war or Parris Island recruits. "Sit down!" "Get that rod up!" "Reel!" "Throw up *overboard*, goddamit!"—These are some of the commands you may hear, laced with appropriate expletives. As a paying customer, you do not have to subject yourself to this kind of cruel and unusual punishment.

7. Respect your catch I: practice catch and release.

8. Respect your catch II: if you are keeping fish for the table—and don't be defensive about it—put them on ice immediately, and clean them as soon as possible. Or have the mate fillet them on the way back to the dock. It usually costs pennies a fish.

9. In most instances, the fish you catch belongs to you—except for certain species like big tuna. "All fish belong to the people who charter the boat," advises *New York Post* outdoors writer Ken Moran, "but when it comes to tuna there is usually a split required with the boat. Always ask ahead for the captain's policy," Moran sagely advises.

New Jersey has a 16-page directory of charter and party boats, along with sound advice and a list of state records for fish. Write to Marine Fisheries Administration, Division of Fish, Game, and Wildlife, CN400, Trenton, NJ 08625. Enclose a self-addressed, stamped envelope (SASE).

There is also Angler's Choice, a sport fishing charter service that represents captains from Long Beach Island to Cape May. Founded by Jeff Cohn, Angler's Choice will put callers in touch with all kinds of charter opportunities. The number is (609) 272-2244. It's done on a commission basis by the boat captains. The only thing anglers pay for is the call.

Another source of information is the Atlantic County Party and Charter Boat Association. From April 1 to December 15 of each year, you can get information about boats and rates by calling (609) 653-9164.

THE JOY OF SURF FISHING

Few angling experiences can match the aesthetic pleasure of casting lures or bait into a foaming surf at the New Jersey shore. This is the saltwater equivalent of trout fishing; in one endeavor, you have to match the hatch; in the other, you must have the good fortune to be on the beach at the right place at the right time for a "blitz." Otherwise, you will probably have little to show for the time, energy, and expenditures involved. But who cares?

It is 10 o'clock at night on an early October evening in Ocean City, N.J. An awesome full moon is coming up over the ocean as the tide is rising, and I'm standing in chest waders, waist deep, listening to the gentle surf, inhaling the fresh salt perfume, contemplating the soft Sodom-and-Gomorrah glow of Atlantic City to the north, feeling the powerful 13-foot surf rod in my hand, tasting the spray of an occasional wave that slaps against my Neoprenes, and playing a game with my mind as I try to dredge up fragments of great watery prose and poetry, like "The sea is high again, with a thrilling flush of wind," and "The ridged lip set upstream, you flail/Inland again, your exile in the sea/Unconditionally cancelled by the pull/Of your home water's gravity." This is happiness, no matter how many fish I'll fool in the surf tonight! —G.I.

Many municipalities permit cars on the beach, a practice that makes fishing the surf a lot easier. If you take your vehicle onto the sand, the New Jersey Beach Buggy Association (NJBBA) says you should carry such items as a tow rope, tire jack, wooden board, air gauge, and shovel.

The March 20, 1997, edition of the *Fisherman* published the full NJBBA report on access to the beach for surf fishing. Here is part of the association's review, starting with Wildwood and going as far north as Brigantine. Just remember that all of this information is subject to change. (See appendix for how to join the New Jersey Beach Buggy Association.)

Wildwood: $15 fee. Access on Cresse Avenue. Must have required equipment. Obtained at City Clerk's Office.

North Wildwood: $5 permit for North Wildwood residents, $15 for non-residents. Permit obtained at North Wildwood Police Station with inspection of the vehicle. Permit is from September 15 to May 15. Entrance at Fifteenth Street and the beach.

Stone Harbor: A $10 permit required from September 15 to June 15. Permit obtained from the Borough Clerk between August 15 and September 30, from 9:00 A.M. to 4:00 P.M. weekdays, or by writing for an application and enclosing a stamped, self-addressed envelope. Inspection of vehicle and proper equipment is required. Beach entrance at 122nd Street. No vehicles allowed northeast of 122nd.

Avalon: Permit is $10, from September 15 to May 15. Obtained from the Police Department at City Hall during the week from 9:00 A.M. to 4:30 P.M. or by writing for an application and enclosing a self-addressed, stamped envelope. Inspection of vehicle and proper equipment is required at the Police Station between 9:00 A.M. and 4:00 P.M.

Sea Isle City: $15 permit from September 15 to May 15. Permit obtained from Police Department at City Hall during the week from 9:00 A.M. to 4:30 P.M. or by writing for an application and enclosing a stamped, self-addressed envelope. For fishing north of Thirty-first Street, enter at Twenty-second Street. For fishing south of Fifty-seventh Street, enter at Seventy-fifth or Eighty-fifth Streets.

Ocean City: $75 permit, limited to 300 people. Waiting list in effect for permits. Four-wheel drive vehicles only. Open from September 15. Permit obtained at Police Department. No buggy operation between North Street and Twenty-third Street.

Longport: During Striper Derby only. Permit obtained free from Police Department. Access at Eleventh Street and the jetty north to the sea wall.

Margate: During Striper Derby only. Permit is free from Police Department. Access roads at Delevan, Grandville, and Washington Avenues.

Ventnor: During Striper Derby only. Permit is free from the Police Department. Access roads at Suffolk and Newport Avenues.

Atlantic City: During Striper Derby only. Permit to cross the boardwalk is free at the Office of the City Engineer. Access roads at New Hampshire, Delaware, and Albany Avenues.

Brigantine: $75 permit obtained at City Hall or Lifeguard Headquarters at Seventeenth Street and the beach, year round. North end entrance at Fourteenth Street, jetty entrance at Seaside Road, open twenty-four hours. Cove entrance at end of Lagoon Boulevard open 7:00 A.M. to 7:00 P.M.

Nowadays, saltwater anglers need to pay as much attention to the rules of their sport as the freshwater counterparts do. Again, the following regulations are subject to frequent change. For the very latest information, consult local newspapers and up-to-date reports of the New Jersey Division of Fish, Game & Wildlife. We include the most recent rules as a guide to which species are already regulated:

Possession and Minimum Size Limits (per Day) for New Jersey (1997)

Species	Open Season	Minimum Length	Limit
Summer flounder	No closed season	14½"	10
Winter flounder	March 1–May 31 Sept. 15–Dec. 31	10"	None
Bluefish	No closed season	None	10
Weakfish	No closed season	14"	14
Tautog	No closed season	13"	None
Cod	No closed season	19"	None
Pollock	No closed season	19"	None
Striped bass	Del. R. & tribs (Trenton Falls to Salem R. & tributaries) Mar. 1–Mar. 31 and June 1–Dec. 31	28"	2
	Del. R. & tribs upstream of Trenton Falls Mar. 1–Dec. 31		
	Atlantic Ocean No closed season (0–3 miles from shore)		
	All other waters: Mar. 1–Dec. 31		

Saltwater anglers have experienced increasing regulation of their sport, but it's not a new phenomenon. The Maryland Department of Natural Resources says the first rules on striped bass fishing date to 1639, when the Massachusetts Bay Company passed a ukase that the fish should not be used as fertilizer for corn and squash.

CAPE MAY COUNTY

Delaware Bay has been called "the other Jersey shore" because, when Philadelphians speak of going "downnashore," they mean only one place— the South Jersey coast, not the salt meadows and beaches of Salem and Cumberland counties.

We'll begin our review of the wonderful New Jersey coast at historic Cape May and work our way northward to the Mullica River.

CAPE MAY

Cape May is a National Historic Landmark that, during the summer months, becomes a nasty place to get into and out of by car. Get there by taking the Garden State Parkway to its southern terminus, or, if you have a lot of time of your hands, Route 47, the Delsea Drive. No matter which route you take, it all comes down to a crawl once you drive down the Cold Spring bridge over the Cape May Canal.

Actually, you don't have to go anywhere else to start fishing. On the left are a number of head boats, and on your right are the docks for the Miss Chris Fishing Center, (609) 884-3939. (A left turn takes you to the popular Lobster House restaurant and seafood market.)

"I love bluefish . . . (but) don't mess with them unless you're ready for combat."
    —NICK ZAFFARY, outdoors writer for the *Reading Eagle*

Night bluefishing can be one of the most exciting types of saltwater angling. It requires heavy tackle and a strong back to bring big slammer blues into the boat. The night boat from the Miss Chris Fishing Center in Cape May costs $35, plus $2 if you want to enter the pool. It leaves at 7:00 P.M. and usually returns after 3:00 A.M. The young mates work hard for you. But it's a long ride home to the Philadelphia area, so be careful.

It was 6:00 P.M. on a late August evening when we boarded the Miss Chris II to pursue monster bluefish. Captain "Butch" left the dock at 7, and we glided through the Cape May Canal for a trip into the Atlantic. The sea was relatively calm, and as evening descended a full, pumpkin-colored moon rose over the ocean to paint the waves with its reflected light. About twelve miles off the cape, the captain anchored up, near several other boats that were also out for blues. Flood lights shone down hard on the water around us, and one of the mates shoveled "chum" over the side. This is ground-up fish, such as mackerel, which puts blues into a feeding frenzy. Our terminal rigs consisted of a large hook attached to

a short wire leader. The twenty-pound test line leading to the leader was threaded to the plastic covering of a "lunker lite," which is a thin little device that emits a greenish glow to attract fish. Above the light was a 4-ounce egg sinker. Our bait was a large chunk of mackerel.

Lines went down, and then we waited . . . and waited . . . and waited. What we didn't know right away was that the problem was our sinkers. The bluefish weren't feeding near the bottom, and the lead was taking our bait way below the cruising depth of our prey. Then, at the boat's stern, Ken Leber tried an experiment. He took off the egg sinker and drifted his bait out into the current. Bam! Ken's line screamed with the telltale sound of a slammer blue, and he finally brought it close enough for the mate to gaff it aboard, making sure he removed Ken's hook with the hand that was protected by a heavy rubber glove.

Sharp-eyed anglers saw what Ken had done and switched their tactics. They, too, began catching fish, although most were hooked from the stern. Others didn't pay attention to what was happening. They stayed with the heavy egg sinkers, and most of them went home without fish. Ken departed early that morning with an extra $60 after winning the pool. —G.I.

When weakies are running, the Miss Chris night boat also heads into Delaware Bay for these beautiful fish, although the huge "tiderunners" are a thing of the past. Many of the fish caught aboard the night boat these days are below the 14-inch minimum, and must be returned.

Dining

Across from the Miss Chris docks, salty Mayer's Bar has decent sandwiches, good New England clam chowder on the menu at times, ice-cold beer, and Patsy Cline on the jukebox. What more could you ask for?

Tackle

Miss Chris Fishing Center has a tackle shop at the dock. Also nearby on the main street leading into Cape May is Jim's Bait & Tackle, 1208 Route 109 at 3rd Avenue, (609) 884-3900. Just before the bridge, where the Garden State Parkway ends, is an excellent shop, Bob's Bait and Tackle, 970 Route 109, Cape May (609) 884-BAIT.

If you drive past the head boat fleets you'll come to a sign that points you to Cape May Point. This is where, during July and August, you will have a good opportunity to catch summer flounder from Sunset Beach, near the Concrete Ship—a.k.a. the SS *Atlantus,* an experimental vessel fabricated near the end of the First World War at a time when steel was in short supply. If you want to see the Concrete Ship, go soon; as Richard Degender, of the *Press* of Atlantic City, wrote, the ship "has been battered by the harsh salty environment for more than seven decades. The *Atlantus* is close to going down to Davey Jones' locker for the last time."

But the summer flounder will be around long after the SS *Atlantus* is nothing more than your grandmother's memory. Use a flounder rig with one hook, and bait it with a tapered strip of squid that wiggles like a small fish. Another tactic is the "open-faced sandwich"—a hook with a squid strip and a live minnow impaled through the lips. Bouncing the rig along the bottom during a good incoming or outgoing tide should get you a fish.

Family members who are unmoved by fishing may collect the famed "Cape May Diamonds" from the beach or watch the sun go down from Sunset Boulevard and the David R. Douglas Park that overlooks Delaware Bay.

For more than six decades, Cape May has been running the Jersey Cape Fishing Tournament. Registration is free, and there are prizes for the top three fish in each category, plus a special children's category. It covers fish caught from Ocean City south to Cape May. Information: (800) 227-2297.

Let's go back to the end of the Cold Spring bridge. This time, drive past the fishing fleets and make a left, following the sign that directs you to the beaches. Then make another left and follow the road, Route 604, until you see a sign directing you to the Fishermen's Memorial. You'll make another left and follow the street to its end, where you will see the memorial that's "dedicated to the fishermen lost at sea." Like the Vietnam Memorial, the names of these fishermen, from 1897 as late as 1988, are inscribed here.

Once you've paid your respects to the memories of brave men who died trying to make a living, get back on Route 604 and follow it to the Beach Avenue dead-end. Here you can park and walk north up the beach to the Cape May jetty along the canal. There is good surf fishing from the beach along here as well.

Dining in Cape May

The Lobster House is one of those old reliable places we return to year after year and rarely are disappointed. It has a "no reservation" policy, which means one can wait—and we have—for almost two hours for a table. There's also outdoor dining, and visitors can walk down the dock and see the fishing boats unload their catch. The Lobster House Fish Market is a great place to stock up for those who haven't caught their limit and want to take some fresh fish home (and pretend they caught it).

A more formal dining spot is Axelsson's Blue Claw, 991 Ocean Drive, just outside Cape May, (609) 884-5878. Heading south on the Garden State Parkway, make a left before you reach the Cold Spring bridge. The Blue Claw is on the left about a mile down the road. This is one of the best seafood restaurants in South Jersey, offering fireside dining in the winter. Try the Prussian Pearls, fresh oysters topped with caviar, a dollop of sour cream, a tiny slice of red onion, and a splash of vodka. The dessert, "Swan in a snowstorm," is a knock-out. Next door is the Axelsson & Johnson Fish Market, which has fresh and cooked seafood, (609) 884-2277.

Some of the other favorite Cape May dining establishments include the Washington Inn, 801 Washington Avenue, (609) 884-5697; the Union Park Dining Room, Macomber Hotel, 727 Beach Avenue, (609) 884-8811; and the Ebbitt Room at the Virginia Hotel, 25 Jackson Street, (609) 884-5700.

The most memorable New Year's Eve that my friend, Pat Staub, and I ever experienced was in Hong Kong when we heard the noonday gun blast away at midnight, its once-a-year nocturnal discharge. The second most memorable New Year's Eve was a 1996 dinner at the Ebbitt Room of the Virginia Hotel.

The prix fixe dinner (curiously, $70 before 6:45, $85 afterward) began with a spiced lobster and tomato bisque, followed by wild mushroom ravioli and assorted seafood "petite fours," salmon and sea bass "osso bucco," and creme brulee. This lavish meal was accompanied by a bottle of Il Pescatore and, afterward, with a glass of excellent Calvados to ward off the winter ague. —G.I.

The area in and around Cape May offers many attractions for families and especially children.

The Cape May County Park & Zoo, SR 9, two miles north of Cape May Court House, off exit 11 of the Garden State Parkway. This 200-acre facility is open seven days a week, 9:00 A.M. to 5:00 P.M., (609) 465-5271. Sadly, one of the zoo's biggest attractions died in September 1996. A tumor took the life of Max, a five-year-old, four-hundred-pound African lion. His death left the zoo with two older lions, Kimba and Webster.

The Cape May-Lewes Ferry (800-64-FERRY). A nice day trip is to take the ferry from Cape May to Lewes, and take a $4 bus to the outlet stores in Rehoboth Beach on the other side of Delaware Bay. You might even see a whale en route to and from Delaware. A round-trip without your car is $8.50 per person, and the ferry takes about an hour and ten minutes each way. The new MV *Twin Capes,* a 300-foot, five-deck behemoth which underwent a $27 million renovation, began running at the start of the summer 1996 season.

The Emlyn Physick Estate, 1048 Washington Street, an eighteen-room Victorian house and museum, dates from 1879. For tours: (609) 884-5404.

The Cape May Lighthouse on Lighthouse Avenue in Cape May Point, (609) 884-8656, open to the public. You can climb all 199 stairs.

The Washington Street Mall for shopping.

Cape May Bird Observatory, (609) 884-2736. This facility is operated by the New Jersey Audubon Chapter, and Peter Dunne is the director. The observatory offers many programs, including a tour of osprey nests by boat and weekly guided field trips. Recommended: a Sunset Birding tour.

Cape May offers the best birding in New Jersey, although mindless development in recent years has taken a toll on habitat. In the past quarter-century, this area has seen half of its bird habitat destroyed. Spring and fall migrants stop here to feed, either before crossing Delaware Bay or, in the spring, after making the flight from the south. The birds not only stop here but often remain for several days, waiting for favorable winds before continuing their migration. The result can be spectacular birding. More than 360 species have been identified, and it's not unusual to hear reports of seeing 100 species in a single day. (The Christmas Day Bird Count by the Delaware Valley Ornithological Club usually reports more than 130 species!)

Our favorite locations are the Concrete Ship or the dunes near the lighthouse. There are many ducks and shore birds, but if the wind is from the northwest, you'll likely see hawks in abundance.

Experienced hawk-watchers like to congregate near the lighthouse. The "firepower" they bring—large telescopes, heavy tripods, 8×50 binoculars—makes the sight resemble a launch at Cape Canaveral.

Eavesdropping on the hawk-watchers's conversations can be fun: "Red at 11 o'clock, moving east! Hey, is that a rough-legged at 2,000, one o'clock? No? Damn, that would have been a good one! Watch that kestrel at three o'clock, 400. He's hungry. He's looking. Beautiful."

Amid this chorus, we search the sky and occasionally spot a small,
unidentifiable dot. —R.S.

If you prefer land birds, take New England Road west to Higbee Beach. Across from the parking area several trails lead to a large open field surrounded by trees. The mixed habitat holds many migrants, and provides a pleasant side excursion, before or after fishing.

Historic Cold Spring Village, a nineteenth-century rural village, 720 Route 9, Cape May, open weekends through September, (609) 898-2300.

Cape May Winery and Vineyard, 709 Town Bank Road, Cape May, opens its doors on Sunday, from noon to 5:00 P.M., (609) 884-1169. Cape May took a silver medal from the New Jersey wine industry in 1997 for its 1995 cabernet sauvignon.

The Delaware Bayshore Office of the Nature Conservancy has tours of its wildlife preserves in the Cape May area, (609) 785-1735.

We will leave Cape May and head north on the Garden State Parkway. Not far up the road we'll get off at Exit 6, take Route 147 east to New York Avenue, and stop at Al's Sea & Surf Tackle Shop before walking out on the North Wildwood jetty for some surf fishing.

The Stone Harbor Bird Sanctuary is on the south end of the island, off Ocean Drive. There is a museum and observation tower, (609) 368-6101.

The Wetlands Institute, a Stone Harbor education and research center with emphasis on wetlands ecology, is located at 1075 Stone Harbor Boulevard, (609) 368-1211. The Institute also runs boat tours of the marshes. In 1995, the Institute recorded a "first"—setting up a color video camera at an osprey nest to wait for the fishhawks to return. It seems that something is always going on at the Wetlands Institute, from the "Wonders of Spring" lectures for preschool kids to brown-bag lunch programs. Hours: 9:30 A.M. to 4:30 P.M. Monday through Saturday; Sunday: 10:00 A.M. to 4:00 P.M.

For more than fourteen years, one of the most interesting annual events has been the Wings 'n Water Festival, a fund-raiser for the Wetlands Institute. Governor Christie Whitman has called the festival New Jersey's premier ecotourism event. Stone Harbor, Cape May Court House, and Avalon team up for the festival, which takes place in September. There are wildlife demonstrations, tours, cruises, exhibits, nature walks, food, and a lot more for the entire family.

The Hereford Inlet Lighthouse and Village, First and Central Avenues, is one of the last working lighthouses in America. It's open to the public, and there's a museum.

Tackle

Smuggler's Cove, 370 83rd Street, Stone Harbor, NJ 08247, owned by a master rod builder, Lou Bachmann, (609) 368-1700.

Fish Tales, 9836 Third Avenue, Stone Harbor, NJ 08247, (609) 967-3100.

AVALON

In Avalon, charters and party boats can be found at the Avalon Fishing Center, Fourteenth and Ocean Drive. The boats here include *Miss Avalon II,* captained by Jerry Hurd. Half-day trips run from 8:00 A.M. to noon and from 1:00 P.M. to 5:00 P.M.; (609) 967-7455.

Dining

The Sea Grill, 225 Twenty-first Street, (609) 967-5511.

SEA ISLE CITY

We're back on the Garden State Parkway, heading north. This time we'll get off at Exit 17 and head east to Sea Isle City. Just west of the Sea Isle City bridge, watch carefully for a little sign that directs you to bear right to the Captain Robbins Fishing Center on Ludlam Landing Road. Capt. Neil Robbins: home (609) 263-3942; dock (609) 263-2020.

This Fishing Center is an excellent venue for both novices and experienced anglers. As we've said before, one litmus test of a good boat is the presence of repeat customers, and you will find many of them aboard Neil Robbins's fishing craft.

Weather permitting and with enough customers to make it worth his while, Robbins sails for sea bass from April through December, seven days a week. A full day's trip, 8:00 A.M. to 4:00 P.M., costs $32, and this captain works hard to make sure his customers come home happy. Two alert mates take care of tangles, bait, lost rigs, getting fish off hooks, and getting rid of the ubiquitous sea robins.

From June through September, the "Captain Robbins" also pursues bluefish on night trips, starting at 7:00 P.M.

After your fishing expedition, head east over the bridge to Sea Isle City, which was originally named Ludlam Beach, after Joseph Ludlam, who had the vision near the end of the seventeenth century to purchase the island and its lovely five-mile-long beach. According to the Sea Isle City Tourism Commission, modern-day bathers poking around the sand dunes have occasionally uncovered muzzle-loading pistols, which "may have been left by pirates who hid in the inlets at either end of the island to evade storms or to hide until sighting a hapless ship to plunder."

You can learn all about these and other facets of the island's past by visiting the Sea Isle City Historical Museum at 4228 Landis Avenue. The museum contains old photographs, memorabilia, exhibits, and the ubiquitous gift shop.

For youngsters, it's hard to beat the annual Sara the Turtle Festival, an event designed to help save the female diamondback terrapins that get squashed by the thousands on roadways every June and July en route to laying their eggs.

Dining

One of Sea Isle City's best-kept secrets is the Braca Cafe, which says it has served Italian specialties since 1901. Braca's is on J. F. Kennedy Boulevard, just off the Sea Isle promenade. The food is reasonably priced, but like many places today they hit you upside-your-head for alcoholic beverages. Reservations are necessary during the summer: (609) 263-4271.

For BYOB, we like Marie's Lobster House, Forty-third and the Bay, (609) 263-2526, and the number of patrons leaving with Styrofoam containers is testimony to gargantuan portions. There's also Carmen's Seafood Restaurant nearby, (609) 263-3471. Another sound BYOB: Screnci's, 6208 Landis Avenue, (609) 263-2217. For good bar food in an upscale environment, try The Dead Dog Saloon in the center of town; it's owned by Terry Young, a graduate of Temple University's Department of English and an expert saltwater flyfisherman whose son specializes in fly-tying—what a great combination!

Tackle

Gibson's Tackle, 4200 Park Rd., Sea Isle City, 08243, (609) 263-6540, is one of the area's best tackle shops, with knowledgeable and helpful people.

> *"The most significant development in angling over the last half-century is the advent of catch-and-release."*
> —ANGUS PHILLIPS, *Washington Post* (February 23, 1997)

CORSONS INLET STATE PARK

I went for a walk over the dunes again this morning
to the sea,
then turned right along

the surf
        rounded a naked headland
        and returned
along the inlet shore
                    —from "Corsons Inlet," by A. R. AMMONS (*The Selected Poems*,
                                expanded edition, W.W. Norton & Co., 1986)

Leaving Braca's, we won't head west to return to the Parkway. Instead, we'll make a right on Ocean Drive ("Follow the flight of the gulls") and motor to Corsons Inlet State Park, one of the most scenic little places in Cape May County, but one for which there seems to be no consistency in punctuation: maps, brochures, and road signs refer to Corson's Inlet, Corsons Inlet, and Corsons' Inlet. All the saltwater angler has to remember, however, is that this is an incredibly productive fishing spot.

Your first stop will be at the Strathmere side of the Inlet. Just before crossing the fifty-cent draw bridge, bear to the right. (A hard left takes you to the Deauville Inn, and a hard right puts you on a collision course with the ocean.) Where the road dead-ends you'll find some limited parking spaces among the residential properties and a sign that points you to a narrow path between the bay berry bushes. Take the path to the left, which will put you along a stretch of beach just northeast of the draw bridge. If you've brought your gear and bait, some exciting fishing awaits you along the beach, around the rips of the inlet, and onto the ocean side. In late spring, portions of the beach will be off-limits to protect nesting piping plovers.

This is one of our very favorite spots along the Jersey coast. One Saturday morning in October 1996, an angler using a fly rod and a homemade saltwater fly dragged a thirty-inch striper onto the beach on the Strathmere side of the inlet. Anything can happen here—sea bass, fluke, blues, stripers, kingfish, weakies—and it usually does. For boat rentals, there's Frank's at Bayview Drive and Whittier Road, (609) 263-6913.

For me, there is a special incentive to fish the Strathmere side of Corsons because my friend, Joe Marshall, the legendary retired Temple University law professor, and his wife, Kaki, live across from the entrance to the south end of the park. When he sees my car parked outside his house early in the morning, Joe will walk down the beach and invite me back for breakfast. If it's later in the day, he'll slip down the beach with a bottle of

*Beck's bier which, when consumed with Joe's sage conversation, is simply
the best way to end any fishing excursion. —G.I.*

Before crossing the toll bridge, we'll make a stop at the Deauville Inn
on Willard Road at the bay, (609) 263-2080. This place can be inconsistent,
but during the summer the Deauville has dockside dining, including an
unbeatable special—clams on the half shell for thirty cents apiece. Another
good dining spot is Mildred's, an old standby just down the road to the
south.

Now let's cross over the bridge. As you drive, listening to your tires
drum on the rickety surface, look to your left. Just below a radio tower you'll
see the remnants of an old dock. Once over the bridge, slow down. On the
right will be a salt pond that's a favorite haunt of mallards, herons, and
egrets. On the left, watch for a dirt road that will take you right past the
tower to the bulkhead and a "hot spot" for local sharpies with saltwater fly
rods. Just past the tower there's room for several cars to park; at low tide,
you can also pull up on the gray sand opposite an old concrete boat launch.

Standing at the bulkhead, you can cast out toward the Deauville across
the inlet. Using Rapala lures, diamond jigs, or top and bottom rigs baited
with squid or cut mackerel, you'll have a good chance to catch stripers and
blues on an incoming tide or after the top of high tide.

One of the most effective lures we've found for casting from the shore
is the Crippled Herring, made by Luhr-Jensen in Hood River, Oregon. The
green and blue versions in 1-ounce and 3/4-ounce sizes, tipped with a strip
of squid, have consistently out-fished other saltwater lures.

You can reach the best spot for fishing by taking a very short walk westward along the sod banks to a place where a little salt creek meanders out
of the meadows. Try fishing above, in front of, and below the creek mouth.
On good days, this place can thrill you. But get there early, before the clods
on jet skis arrive and ruin the ambience as well as your fishing.

*Overcast Sunday morning in mid-October. Sky the color of a plump oys-
ter. Incoming tide. From the south, a mild wind. I pull up at the radio
tower in Corsons Inlet State Park. Half asleep, I rig up my new Orvis #9
saltwater fly rod with a rust-and-red-colored Deceiver lure, then squish
along the sod banks flanking the inlet across from Strathmere.*

I'm lucky this morning, because the jet skis are still asleep, and no other fishers are out here yet. Suddenly I hear fish splashing—it's a feeding frenzy all anglers dream about.

At first, I think these are voracious blues chasing terrified baitfish into the bank.

But they aren't bluefish. On my second cast I hook into a feisty "schoolie" striper of about 15 inches. It's a beautiful fish when I finally bring it in, but it's not large enough to keep. I carefully unhook it, then watch the silvery streak disappear into the dark water. Flushed, I feel like composing a haiku poem to commemorate my first fish on a saltwater fly rod! —G.I.

One place that deserves the attention of anyone interested in saltwater fly-fishing and fly-tying is J.B.'s Fly Trap at 34 Elmwood Drive, Pittsgrove, NJ 08318, (609) 358-1903; fax (609) 358-1573. The Fly Trap's Robert Schaffer is a friendly chap who is eager to help out novices. We've been using some of his shrimp flies, which are reasonably priced at $2.50 each, to pursue weakfish in the inlets around Ocean City, N.J.

Now drive back out the dirt road and resume your trip north on Ocean Drive. This route takes you parallel to, and directly across from, the Strathmere beach you fished earlier. Along this road on the right side are ample places to pull off and fish the inlet.

When you get to the Rush Chattin Bridge, you have a number of alternatives. First, you can park on the left before crossing the bridge and walk under the span to fish for tog that prowl like sunken trolls under the bridge pilings.

Or you can cross the road and walk down to the boggy bank on the right. If you've brought a large plastic can or portable seat, you can fish the inlet from here.

Another option is to park on either side of the bridge and walk to one of the four fishing bays that project outward. On quiet days, these locations are also great for birding. You just might see a kingfisher resting on the railings. In the marshes are egrets, white and great blue herons, and, in the spring, migrating glossy ibises marching like an army of prospectors as they poke their long bills into the mud.

Corsons Inlet offers a smorgasbord of fish—flounder, weakfish, blues, stripers, sea bass, skate, and other saltwater creatures that can be caught from the inlet, beach, and Rush Chattin Bridge.

A reminder about fishing from the bridge: First, be careful about dropping a line in the channel, because boats are always coming in and out of the inlet. Second, remember that, for a location in the salt marshes, Rush Chattin is a relatively high span. Several years ago, when we were fishing from one of the bridge bays, we caught a three-pound bluefish. From the time it hit our hook until we hoisted the wriggling critter over the railing, it felt like we had been reeling for an hour. Third, there are trash containers for paper waste. Use them, but don't consider them as garbage dumps for fish entrails or unused squid.

From the north side of the bridge, you can walk a path to the ocean or follow the east side of the inlet beach and surf fish all the way to the tip of the sandspit. Minnows work well for summer flounder here, and you can catch zillions of minnows with traps placed in the salt creeks. The north side of the sandspit is also a favorite spot for fishers in beach buggies, who gain access from Fifty-ninth Street, at the south end of Ocean City.

Just be alert to the fact that you'll need a special State Mobile Sportfishing permit to enter the park with a four-wheel drive. These $25 permits are only issued in person or by mail through the Belleplain State Forest Office in Belleplain, and they are just for fishing, not all-terrain vehicles. (For directions to Belleplain State Forest, see the section on Freshwater Fishing, Cape May County.)

And the rules are strict. Beach access is limited to the gate off Central Avenue and Fifty-ninth Street in Ocean City, near the old fishing pier on the south end. There's no access from May 15 to September 15. During any twenty-four-hour period, only seventy-five vehicles are allowed on the Corsons Inlet beach. Access can be closed at any time because of high tides, erosion, "or other emergencies." Permit decals must be on the front and rear bumpers before you enter the beach. The beach speed limit is 15 mph. No alcoholic beverages are allowed, and if you're on the beach between midnight and 4:00 A.M., you'd better "be actively engaged in fishing activities" and not any other entanglements.

But wait, as they say in those cable TV infomercials, there's more!

Here is the mandatory equipment you must carry in your vehicle, and it helps to have it when you apply for a permit:

—Fishing equipment and bait/tackle for each person over twelve years old
—Tire gauge
—Spare tire
—Workable jack and board/support for the jack in the sand (the minimum is a 3/4" by 12" by 12" plywood square)

—Tow chain or snatch line

—Shovel

—Flashlight

—Fire extinguisher

—Auto first-aid kit

—Litter or trash bag

—A minimum of 1/4 tank of fuel

The Division of Parks and Forestry on the New Jersey Department of Environmental Protection also "highly" recommends that you carry aboard a current tide chart.

It sounds like a lot of bureaucratic hassling, but fishing from a dune buggy at night or early morning on Corsons Inlet will make you forget all about it.

OCEAN CITY

Ocean City has long been a great vacation spot for families, and its irrepressible public relations man, Temple alumnus Mark Soifer, always keeps things interesting. For example, there's the mid-August Weird Contest Week, which in 1996 included saltwater-taffy sculpting, french-fry sculpting, artistic-pie eating, wet T-shirt throwing, and the "first annual" Miss Miscellaneous Pageant.

This island offers many opportunities for surf fishing, from the south end where, someday, the Fifty-ninth Street Fishing Pier will be restored, to the north, where a jetty runs along the Great Egg Harbor Inlet. In between, the Fifth Street jetty has given up big striped bass, weakies, and blues.

It was late morning on an early October Saturday when I sauntered down to the beach at Fifty-first Street. Surf fishers were lined up north and south as far as the eye could see, but no one was reeling anything in.

I noticed that everyone seemed to be casting as far out into the water as they could. But, with the tide high, I could see what looked like fins cutting through the water only twenty-five yards out into the suds.

I cast my surf rig, baited with a triangular strip of squid, close to shore. Suddenly something took my line with the power of a freight train. At first, I thought I'd foul-hooked a porpoise!

After fighting the fish for twenty minutes, I finally horsed it onto the beach. It was a huge bluefish. My friend, Pat Staub, had left briefly to get a ruler, but by the time she returned I had already gutted and be-headed the fish. Even so, it still measured thirty-four inches from tail to the severed headline! But I was disappointed: the other fishers ignored the fight and landing of my monster bluefish. After all that, I wanted some recognition. —G.I.

One of the secret spots for back-bay fishing in Ocean City can be found at the south end of the island. From Thirty-fourth Street, head south on West Avenue to Fifty-first Street. Turn right and follow Fifty-first Street until it becomes a black-dirt road, and follow it all the way to the Inland Waterway channel between Pecks Bay and Corsons Inlet. Drive carefully along this "road"—you won't want to take your BMW or restored '57 Chevy back here. But the locals know that stripers, fluke, weakies, and sea bass can be caught from the sod banks along the channel. Fishing is best early in the morning or in the evening when boat traffic is quiet and those who use jet skis aren't around.

For jetty fishing, try the Fifth Street Jetty, or drive to the north end, park at the metered places just before crossing the Ocean City-Longport Bridge, and walk eastward up the beach to the jetty. In a few years, this area on Ocean City's northern side should be another good place to fish. There are plans to build a new $40 million Ocean City-Longport Bridge over the Great Egg Harbor inlet, just east of the existing, and very aging, draw-bridge. The replacement span, between the north end of Ocean City and Fish Factory Island in Atlantic County, will be sixteen feet wider than the old bridge. Cape May County has asked the U.S. Army Corps of Engineers to convert the northern section of the old bridge on Route 656 into a well-lit fishing pier.

If you're looking for an open boat, there's the *North Star* with Capt. Paul Barrus, (609) 399-7588. The *North Star* has all-day wreck fishing trips on Wednesday, Saturday, and Sunday, and charters are available.

Novices who aren't sure that saltwater fishing is their "thing" should opt for a half-day trip for sea bass on the *Challenger*. It is docked at the Ocean City Marina & Fishing Center at Bay Avenue near Third Street, where you can rent a boat from Lemont's, (609) 399-1787.

Here you'll also find one of the best charter sportfishing guides in the area. Captain Norman Hafsrud pilots the *Viking*, a twenty-two-foot Aqua-sport, and few people know the back bays of Ocean City as well as this veteran salt, who also takes clients on relatively close off-shore trips. In 1996,

Hafsrud was getting $60 for a half-day of back-bay fishing, with a maximum of four passengers. That's $15 a person, which is hard to beat. He specializes in trips for albacore, bluefish, bonito, flounder, kingfish, and weakfish—and he supplies all equipment. Call (609) 399-8835.

Finally, there are a number of places along the causeway between Somers Point and Ocean City where families can pull off and cast a line into the back bays. We've caught schoolie stripers, weakies, small sea bass, and blues from these little pull-offs. Just be sure to watch your speed on the causeway. It's 40 mph, and the Ocean City police take it very seriously.

Tackle

On the island's south end, the most convenient place is The Sea Gull Shop on Fifty-fifth Street, just east of West Avenue. An elderly couple runs this shop, and they have the latest information about what's biting and where.

Our favorite place was Fin-Atics Marine Supply, Ltd., 1325 West Avenue, Ocean City, NJ 08226, (609) 398-2248. This was a full-service store with friendly personnel who were eager to help newcomers. During the regular fishing season, Fin-Atics had a large blackboard set up outside the store, with chalk-written information on the best baits, best locations, and best times to catch fish. A two-alarm fire in February 1997 gutted Fin-Atics and caused an estimated $150,000 in damages. Owner Bill Wiggins says the old Fin-Atics location will be open by 1998. In the meantime, his shop is located at Tenth Street and the Bay, a second-floor venue he plans to keep after the reopening on West Avenue.

We also like Fishin' Stuff Tackle Shop, 621 Bay Avenue, (609) 398-6996. Owner Bob Johnson even includes his home phone on the business card.

Dining

The Airport Diner at the Ocean City airport on Bay Avenue (formerly Augie's) is a good, cheap place for breakfast. Its creamed chipped beef on toast can stand up with that of any place along the South Jersey coast.

But of all the many places for breakfast in Ocean City, we're partial to Sunnyside at Fifty-fifth Street. Try Karlyn's Creation (Number 11 on the menu), a version of Eggs Benedict. Some of the friendliest, warmest people in the food business own this establishment, and after you visit a few times you'll become part of their extended family. A bonus: Sunnyside is smoke-free. Open on weekends in off-season, closed in winter; (609) 391-9292.

Ed Hitzel, a former *Atlantic City Press* restaurant critic who now publishes a monthly newsletter on South Jersey dining, recommends Ready's on Eighth Street as one of the best breakfast sites. An advantage of going to Ready's is that it's only a few doors from Mark's, at Eighth Street and Central Avenue, where those of us who have newspaper monkeys on our backs can get a "fix" with copies of the *New York Times*, the *Washington Post*, and the always entertaining *New York Post*. Down the street from Sunnyside is Wawa, where many of these papers can be purchased, but you've got to get there early before they sell out.

The Fourth Street Cafe at 400 Atlantic Avenue, (699) 399-0764, has some of the most outrageous scones in the world at a place operated by Mike and Jennifer Bailey.

Mangia, an Italian deli and grille at Fortieth Street and West Avenue, (609) 391-0405, is worth your visit, even if Ocean City laws forbid BYOB. Mangia's shrimp puttanesca—when it's on the menu—is top-notch.

Several other worthwhile places to visit are the Ocean City Historical Museum at Seventeenth Street and Simpson Avenue in the west-central section of town, (609) 399-1801 and, for the kids, the Sand Castle Playground at Thirty-fourth Street and West Avenue.

ATLANTIC COUNTY

SOMERS POINT

It's not technically in Somers Point—Egg Harbor Township is its correct address—but the Klingener Fishing Pier is an excellent and accessible place for saltwater fishing. It is just west of the Somers Point-Longport Bridge, across from the Reef Port.

There are rental boats at Somers Point, and this is a good launching point for some fine fishing. In August 1996, the *Press* reported that an angler caught a fluke that was nearly thirteen pounds. Using a bucktail with a strip of white flounder belly, he caught the fish at dead low tide in Ship Channel, between Ocean City and Somers Point.

Somers Point also has a municipal fishing pier off Bay Avenue. It's a perfect spot for young anglers, because they can dip a line baited with strips of squid and pull up hungry, juvenile sea bass by the bushel.

Another favorite is the beach area of Drag Island, between Atlantic and Cape May counties, in the Great Egg Harbor River. To reach the island, you must avoid the Garden State Parkway bridge between Somers Point and Upper Township. Instead, take the decrepit Beasleys Point Bridge and, from Somers Point, turn left onto a dirt road before the toll booth ($0.50). Drag Island Channel offers shoreline fishing for flounder, blues, perch, weakfish, and stripers, as well as small sea bass, plus such "nuisance" critters as the repulsive oyster cracker.

Anglers who cross the Beasleys Point Bridge into Marmora and Cape May County will soon have another venue for fishing the Great Egg Harbor River. Atlantic Electric is restoring the old public fishing pier near the B. L. England Generating Plant. The original pier, which was built some two decades ago, fell into disrepair. Its replacement will be almost twenty feet wide and about thirty-three feet long.

Dining

The Waterfront, owned by Jay Lamont, director of the Temple University Real Estate Institute, is located on the site of the old Bayshores and across from the old Tony Mart's, which is now called Brownies on the Bay. If you must ask "What are Bayshores and Tony Mart's," then you're too young to remember Chubby Checker! Try a bottle of Jersey Shore Gold, brewed by the Hunterdon Brewing Company of Califon, N.J.

Another of our favorite postangling hangouts is Smith's Clam Bar. Buy a six-pack of beer at Circle Liquors, drive to Smith's on Bay Avenue, sit down at the outdoor clam bar, and stuff yourself on ice-cold, raw top-neck clams on the half shell and red or white clam chowder. You'll be a better person for it.

Also on Bay Avenue is the Anchorage, which dates to 1888. This once-sleepy little taproom was taken over by new owners in 1993. It offers steamed clams, decent crab-cake sandwiches, and "Buffalo" shrimp, which come out of the kitchen two ways—"spicy" or "blistering." In late spring and summer, the Anchorage's front porch is a pleasant place to sit and look out at the bay and the Ocean City-Longport Bridge.

Other restaurants in the area include the consistent Mac's on Shore Road (their shad roe in the springtime is excellent—watch for the sign advertising this seasonal special in the parking area on the west side of Shore Road); Gregory's, next door to Mac's at 900 Shore Road, a Somers Point fixture since 1946 that now features lobster specials and, according to *Atlantic City* magazine, has "the best bar menu," (609) 927-6665; the Crab Trap on the Somers Point circle, (609) 927-7377; and Hatteras Coastal Cuisine, 801 Bay Avenue, (609) 926-3326.

If you hanker for sushi, go to Tokyo Palace on the Somers Point-Longport Boulevard. It's much better than the outside facade looks.

The Gourmet Garage, on Shore Road, is the place to buy pots, pans, and a wide variety of cooking wares.

Tackle

Try the Dolfin Dock on Bay Avenue for a well-stocked emporium and sound advice on fishing. Or go a little north to Campbell Marine, Inc., (609) 641-0489, outside Northfield on the way to Margate.

If you want to take home fresh clams (and, during the season, fresh oysters, mussels, and crabs), bring your cooler to Woodburn's Clams in Somers Point. Going north on the Garden State Parkway, make the first right after paying the toll over the bridge at the Great Egg Harbor River. At the bend in the road, on the right, you'll see a sign for clams. Fifty top-necks, which are perfect for eating raw or steaming, cost $12, and oysters are $4 a dozen. Woodburn's also sells clam pies, made by a gentleman in Millville, for $5. Don't stop by when the Indy 500 is running, because the place will be filled with local folks in baseball caps, all intently watching the race on TV, and it may take awhile to get served. When you do stop by, tell Sid that we sent you.

Aficionados of raw seafood should not miss the annual Bayfest, centered on Bay Avenue in Somers Point. It features antiques, crafts, and plenty of clams on the half shell.

For a bit of local history, visit the Somers Mansion, which dates to around 1725 and sits on a hill next to a Chinese restaurant, overlooking the bay. The address is 1000 Shore Road. Phone: (609) 927-2212.

The adventurous may drive from Somers Point to Ocean Heights Avenue, turn right toward Bargaintown, and go to Brownie's, which is not to be confused with Brownie's on the Bay, across from The Waterfront. This Brownie's often has Harleys parked outside, and there's down-home country music played inside. Outside, the big sign says "Bar Open 10 A.M. to 4 A.M.," and they ain't lyin'.

For more refined dining, continue past Brownie's to Cousin's Country House, at Fire and Zion Roads, in Bargaintown, (609) 927-5777.

Back on the coast, the Longport Bridge has long been a favorite of saltwater fishers, especially those who pay their dues with long nights in search of striped bass. Another popular spot is the Longport Jetty, where a nighttime angler caught a thirty-eight-pound striped bass in August 1996.

Dining

Try the Longport Inn for a casual Sunday brunch. It's at Thirty-first Street and Atlantic Avenue, (609) 822-5435.

MARGATE

In Margate, Cap'n Andy's Fish 'n Fun IV makes a "guaranteed no sea sickness" promise. This pontoon boat is fifteen feet wide and forty-five feet long, and family fishing is a specialty. Gear and bait are included for the $14 cost for four hours of fishing in the back bays.

Departures are at 8:00 A.M. and 1:00 P.M., seven days a week during the season from Captain Andy's Marina in Margate. You'll be drifting for fluke and flounder, using squid and minnows. Ralph Stork owns the marina. Charters are also available.

It had been a long negotiation between Temple University's faculty and administrators, but settlement was reached before expiration of the union contract. Both sides were elated, and the former adversaries in collective bargaining did what came naturally—we planned a fishing trip together to celebrate.

The boat was chartered from Captain Andy's Marina in Margate. From the administration team, the "crew" included C. Robert Harrington, our chief and associate vice president for personnel resources; Dean Robert Smith; and myself. Among the faculty colleagues were Bob Marler, professor of English, and Ralph Towne, professor of Speech.

Because we had to drive from Philadelphia, I had booked the boat for a half-day afternoon trip that left the dock at noon. It was a beautiful calm day in late May, and off we went through the Great Egg Harbor Inlet, loaded with gear and beer, in pursuit of offshore bluefish.

When we were several miles from the beach, the young captain slowed down to prepare for trolling. The outriggers were set, and, like good negotiators, we agreed among ourselves who would have the honor first to take responsibility for the rods.

We were chugging along at a medium-slow troll when it appeared. A large shark, fifteen to twenty feet long, emerged from the depths and began swimming alongside our boat. The young captain, a yellow-booted chap who was an English major at Widener University, began calling other boats in the immediate area as the boat-load of professors and administrators rushed to the port side to see Moby Shark.

"I remember," Marler said later, "looking over at the gray back of the still creature and thinking, 'I must step over the side and walk on its

back; I must.' It was like standing on a cliff or a balcony of a tall building and wanting to jump."

Fortunately for Bob, the shark didn't stay for longer than a few seconds. But what an awesome sight it was before it plunged into the ocean and disappeared.

"Wow!" we all exclaimed. "What an experience!"

Several days later, it was obvious that someone had tried to capitalize on the incident. Across the top of the Philadelphia Inquirer *was this six-column story by writer Fen Montaigne, under this headline:*

WAS IT A GREAT WHITE? SHARK HUNT HAS JERSEY SHORE ABUZZ
ATLANTIC CITY—At least three times in as many weeks, a very large fish has been sighted off the coast here. The old salts agree on one thing: The creature is a shark—and a big one at that. . . .

The next afternoon, Ronald Rookstool, 23, was in the area of the first sighting, captaining another of Stork's charter boats. On board were about eight Temple University professors and administrators. Rookstool said he spotted a 15-foot shark and maneuvered the boat alongside the massive, gray-brown fish.

"His mouth was open as wide as a trash can," recalled Rookstool. "That's no exaggeration. He was right against the boat, and all the professors and the dean were looking right at him. They were astonished. They were a little scared, to be honest. One asked me if the shark would attack the boat, and I said, Well, anything's possible."

—*G.I.*

We move from one monster to another. For children, one of the great sights on the entire New Jersey coast is Lucy the Elephant—all six stories, sixty-five feet and ninety tons of her—at Decatur Avenue and the beach in Margate. A developer built Lucy in 1881 as an attraction for his real estate wares. Today, every youngster deserves a trip to see Lucy. In the words of several advertising slogans, Lucy is a memory that will last a lifetime. Tours are available, (609) 822-6519.

When I was a young, green reporter for the Press of Atlantic City, *I worked from 3:00 P.M. to midnight on the Atlantic County desk for a kindly editor named Bill McMahon—kindly, only because he didn't fire*

*me after discovering very quickly how inexperienced I was. In the early
1960s, Atlantic City was a beguiling place for a single reporter, no matter how unseasoned. Sometimes, after getting off work, I would join City
Editor Jack Steele and other staffers for a drink at the Beach Bar in Margate. And at 3 o'clock in the morning when I had had enough beer, I
would stroll outside, walk to Lucy, place my right hand on one of her
beautiful gray legs, and think profound, existential thoughts while listening to the pounding surf. —G.I.*

In addition to pontoon fishing, the *Duke 'o Fluke*, captained by Brook
Koeneke, runs nature excursions into the back bays behind Margate, taking
tourists to see ospreys, gulls, egrets, herons, and other creatures that call
the marshes their home. Call (609) 822-2272.

VENTNOR

Daily and seasonal rates are available for anglers who want to use
the Ventnor Fishing Pier at Cornwall Avenue and the Boardwalk, (609)
823-7944.

ATLANTIC CITY

By all that's holy and right, Atlantic City shouldn't hold much interest
for the serious fisher. More than twenty years ago, New Jersey residents
made a fatal error by voting to bring casino gambling into the aging resort
town. (At the same time, Americans voted into office a great trout fisherman and peanut farmer from Georgia. Only history will judge Jimmy Car-
ter's effectiveness in the Oval Office, but if nothing else, he sure can lay
down a nice fly line and then do a good job of writing about it later.)

For Atlantic City, casinos have spawned greed, a farm club for Gam-
blers' Anonymous, and a rabid, ill-considered explosion of off-shore development. Unsuspecting voters were told gambling would be a boon to the
city; the truth is that there have been few real benefits for the residents, who
still pay high property taxes, who still must confront nasty pockets of slums,
and who still experience a surprisingly large number of jobless people: in
1995, the unemployment rate for Atlantic City proper (15 percent) was
almost three times that of the national average, and almost 230 percent
higher than the average rate for the State of New Jersey. (On the positive
side, Atlantic City still has one of the Garden State's few free beaches.)

Yet, despite the glitz, despite the unending stream of tour buses loaded with folks eager to part with their money, and in spite of its social problems, Atlantic City remains a great place for anglers.

It was on the Vermont Avenue jetty where Al McReynolds caught his world-record, 78.8-pound striped bass while casting a bluish-black Rebel lure during a raging storm. And the concrete Municipal Jetty facing Absecon Inlet is one of the those places that continues to attract families. Fathers and mothers bring their sons and daughters there to fish, and, years later, those grown-up sons and daughters bring their children, like swallow families returning to Capistrano. On weekends during the summer, boat traffic from the Farley State Marina makes serious fishing dicey, but there are still fish to be caught in the inlet.

Near the municipal jetty is Gardiner's Basin, located at the end of Maine Avenue in the inlet section of Atlantic City and the site of an annual summertime Seafood Festival. Here you'll find the *Applejack* docked, and a good way to introduce youngsters to deep-sea fishing is to take them on a half-day outing with Captain Andy Applegate aboard the *Applejack*. Applegate's specialty is fishing for sea bass, ling, and tog over wrecks that aren't far off the coast. In the springtime, he sails for mackerel, but we don't recommend a mackerel trip for youngsters out on their first saltwater trip.

When mackerel are really hitting—and in recent years it appears that the glory days of catching these sleek and attractive creatures are over for awhile—fishing becomes very intense; lines get incredibly tangled, and the language can be X-rated. We've even seen diamond jigs hanging from ear lobes when the action becomes furious, and anglers go on a feeding frenzy to fill up their burlap sacks with the wriggling fish.

During the regular fishing season, the *Applejack* runs two trips daily: 8:00 A.M.–noon and 1:00 to 4:00 P.M. There are also special off-shore trips by reservation only. Reach Captain Applegate at (609) 345-4077 or (609) 652-8184.

Mackerel can be an easy fish to catch, especially during the annual spring run. The time-honored mackerel rig is a "Christmas tree" of several hooks "baited" with plastic tubes of red, green, or other colors. Tie your line to the swivel at one end of the Christmas tree and place a sinker on the bottom. The weight of the sinker will depend on how strong the current is running, but 6–8 ounces is usually a starter. To find the depth of the fish, let the sinker hit bottom, then slowly retrieve it while jigging the rod at different levels. You'll want a fairly durable rod with line rated at about twenty-pound test because, when the macks are really hitting, it's not unusual to haul up three or four wriggling creatures at a time.

But we haven't seen that in a while. By 1996, mackerel fishing had fallen off precipitously. Twenty years ago, the "run" of these beautiful fish could last for weeks at a time, as they swam north along the New Jersey coast. In recent years, there has hardly been a run at all.

The decline caused alarm bells to go off among party boat captains early in 1997 when the New Jersey Marine Fisheries Council recommended that a Russian "mother" ship be permitted to anchor in Delaware Bay and haul aboard some five thousand metric tons of mackerel caught by the State's commercial fishermen. At a hearing, Captain Applegate pleaded for a denial of the request. "We used to have an eight-week mackerel season. Now we don't catch any mackerel," he was quoted in a January 5, 1997, report in the *Press* of Atlantic City.

In February 1997, Governor Christie Whitman turned thumbs down on issuing the Russians a permit, much to the delight of recreational fishers and to the consternation of the commercial anglers. "The proposed venture with the Russian processing ship would have dispersed and depleted the inshore mackerel stock on which New Jersey's springtime recreational fishing industry depends," the governor declared. "I am not willing to jeopardize the tourism potential and the enjoyment of New Jersey's recreational fishing enthusiasts."

It remains to be seen if the decision will help depleted mackerel stocks (spring 1997 looked like a turn-around season), but here is what mackerel fishing in New Jersey used to be like:

My friend George Leber and I went out on a "magic hour" mackerel trip from Point Pleasant, N.J. The Norma K *left the dock at 3:00 P.M., and we returned at 8:00 P.M. with two huge burlap sacks filled with fish.*

We drove home and proceeded to gorge ourselves on the mackerel's omega-3 fatty acids. We filleted and broiled several. Then we tried a recipe the "locals" had given me during a previous outing in Brielle, N.J.: lathering each fillet with mayonnaise, topping it with a coating of bread crumbs, and baking it in the oven until the covering disappeared into the fish.

Next, we sautéed several filets. Then we poached a couple in white wine. Finally, around midnight, and after more than a few beers, we ate them sashimi-style, with soy sauce and, for extra flavor, some chopped onions on top. It was a memorable fishing and eating trip .—G.I.

Fresh mackerel, placed immediately on ice after being pulled from the ocean, is a real delight, despite complaints of uninformed people that this beautifully sleek fish is too "oily." The critics include the editorial writer for the *Press* of Atlantic City, who wrote this hogwash on January 13, 1997, right after the Marine Fisheries Council approved, by a 5–0 vote, that plan to sell mackerel to the Russian fish-processing boat anchored in Delaware Bay:

"The Russians actually want to eat these fish," wrote the editorialist in endorsing the vote. "Mackerel are skinny, oily unappetizing little fish—but, hey, the Russians like them."

Ignorance *is* bliss. The editorial writer should try some broiled fresh mackerel. Or taste the fish's subtle and delicate roe fried gently in butter. An indignant letter writer responded several days later that "fresh mackerel freshly prepared are delicious, and their nutritional value is well-documented. There is no reason to bad-mouth this southern New Jersey food product."

Perhaps the author of the editorial had been subjected to frozen mackerel, which should be avoided as table fare at all cost. We salt and freeze whole, uncleaned spring mackerel, but with the intention to use it as bait later in the season. Cut frozen mackerel—sliced in long slivers, especially from the silvery under belly—is a wonderful enticement for blues and stripers.

Here is one way to prepare fresh mackerel for the table. It comes from a March 1, 1995, article by Mark Bittman in the *New York Times*:

Mackerel fillets in soy sauce

1/2 cup soy sauce
1/2 cup water
1/2 cup dry sherry
2 tablespoons rice or white wine vinegar

5–6 thin slices of peeled ginger
3–4 crushed garlic cloves
4 mackerel fillets, about 1 pound total, with
    skin on

Mix together all the ingredients except the fish in a large skillet. Bring to a boil and simmer uncovered over medium heat for about five minutes.

Add the mackerel, skin side down.

Cover and simmer about 7 minutes, or until fish is cooked through. To serve, spoon some sauce onto a mound of white rice.

Dining

A nice way to end a half-day Applejack trip is to walk a few feet to the Flying Cloud Cafe, 800 N. New Hampshire Avenue, where even fishy anglers are welcome to sip a cold beer and eat a cheeseburger or soft-shell crab sandwich. Flying Cloud's owners, Ross and Marianne Constantino, are involved in a major remodeling project so that every diner will have a view of the water. The Flying Cloud's number is (609) 345-8222.

The city has a plethora of excellent and high-priced dining establishments, many of them ensconced, not unsurprisingly, in the casinos. Notable dining places include the Old Waterway Inn, 1700 W. Riverside Drive, Venice Park, (609) 347-1793; Peking Duck House, 2801 Atlantic Avenue, (609) 344-9090 or (609) 348-1313, which offers some of the city's best Chinese cooking; and the neighborhood Angelo's Fairmount Tavern, 2300 Fairmount Avenue, (609) 344-2439.

It may be a tad over-rated, but one of the hidden culinary treats of in Atlantic City is Chef Vola's. It's a 48-seat family Italian BYOB place on a little street called South Albion Place that you won't find on the Monopoly board. Jim Quinn, a Temple graduate and food critic for the *Philadelphia Weekly*, pointed out that the restaurant "does not advertise, anywhere, ever. It does not accept credit cards. It has no liquor license (bring your own), no outside sign (except for a small brass plaque by the entrance door in its alley) and no listed telephone number." Stan Hochman, restaurant reviewer for the Philadelphia *Daily News*, swears that owner Michael Esposito serves "the best veal chop in town." The bad news: "You've got a better chance of hearing from Elvis if you're seeking a table on a weekend between Memorial Day and Labor Day." Chef Vola's is open for dinner Tuesday through Saturday. For reservations, (609) 345-2022.

On the other end of the culinary scale is the famous White House Sub Shop, 2301 Arctic Avenue, (609) 345-1564. Whenever possible, we get our hoagies for a saltwater fishing trip from one of two places—the White House or Greenman's on Levick Street in Northeast Philadelphia.

BRIGANTINE

"I walked to the Absecon Inlet jetty through the fog, and as it slowly came into view, silhouettes of fishing rods could be seen poking out from every direction."
—STEPHEN C. SAUTNER, *New York Times* (August 31, 1994)

Brigantine has a long jetty at the south end, from which weakfish, blue-fish, kingfish, and stripers can be caught. There are a few skillful geezers who take tautog by working the rocks at the very end of the ocean side of the jetty.

My son, George, his friend, Ken Leber, and I were fishing from the Brig-antine jetty one morning. We looked up the beach, to the north, and saw a "cloud" of gulls hovering over the water about a half-mile away. Screeching and diving, the gulls came closer, telegraphing a fortuitous "bluefish blitz" along the beach as the voracious critters devoured schools of mullet. The blues chugged south, turned at the jetty, headed to the end of it, then turned and headed west along Absecon Inlet, as scores of us hurled lures into the water—and with almost every cast we retrieved a fighting blue. A blitz is an angler's heaven! —G.I.

Another favorite spot is at the remnants of the old Brigantine Bridge, on both sides of Absecon Inlet. Here you can fish while contemplating the folly of gambling—didn't Samuel Johnson describe it as a "tax on fools"?—and watching construction of even more gambling palaces on what was once, ironically, Atlantic City's municipal dump.

One of the most popular family stops on the island is the Sea Life Museum/Marine Mammal Stranding Center, at 3625 Brigantine Boule-vard, (609) 266-0538, with an observation tank and marine life exhibits.

The north end of the island is where an increasing population of red foxes has gained headlines because they are munching on the eggs of nest-ing piping plovers. You can still take a surf rod and walk all the way to Little Egg Inlet to fish, if you want, or pay for a beach buggy permit and drive up the beach, avoiding the plovers.

For family fishing, try The Fish Finder, a 35-foot boat captained by Joe Fumo, (609) 589-1452, from the Bayside Marina, 4401 Brigantine Blvd.

ABSECON

Leaving Brigantine, we'll return to Absecon Boulevard and then take the White Horse Pike to Absecon. At Shore Road, we'll note the Black Cat Bar, with its big ebony feline staring at us. The Black Cat, incidentally, is another one of those local hangouts where you can pick up tips on crabbing and fishing. Nearby, Absecon Creek is a good place to catch snapper blues in the summer and early fall, as well as hard-shell crabs. Try by the metal bridge, just south of the Pike on Shore Road, or at the bulkhead by the boat launch along Absecon Creek.

There are many versions of the saltwater sinker, but the two basic types are the bank and the pyramid. The pyramid—a hunk of lead shaped like an inverted version of Cheops' monument in Giza—is used on the beaches because its point bites into the sand and helps keep the bait in place when the tide and current are moving swiftly. The bank sinker is shaped like one of Al Capp's schmoozes. It is useful when the area in which you're fishing has a muddy, oozy bottom. All you want the sinker to do is lie there nicely with no penetration.

I learned the difference between these sinkers the hard way one day. Armed with a brand new fiberglass surf-fishing rod and reel, I drove north on Shore Road in Absecon to East Faunce Landing Road, where I made a right-hand turn and came down to the bulkhead along Absecon Creek as the tide was rising. For terminal tackle, I had a fish-finger rig, which allows the line and baited hook to move through a small piece of plastic above a connection for an anchoring sinker.

I snapped on a pyramid sinker to this rig, baited the hook with a nice tapered strip of squid, and cast it way out into Absecon Creek—and down into its muddy bottom.

My knowledge of the different uses of sinkers was expanded enormously when the rod twitched from a hit, and I began reeling in the line to check the bait. Unfortunately, my pyramid had hit the mud and stayed there. It is probably still there, because I had to break the monofilament line in order to retrieve it. As Ben Franklin once said, "Experience is the best teacher, but only fools have to learn from it." —G.I.

Tackle

The Absecon Bay Sportsmen Center, 81 Natalie Terrace, Absecon, NJ 08201, (609) 484-0409, fax (609) 646-8171. This little place is surprisingly well-stocked for its size. The owners are Judith and David Showell. To get there, drive north on Shore Road in Absecon to Natalie Terrace; make a right, go to the dead end, and turn into the parking lot.

Resuming your trip north on Shore Road, you may want to stop for a sandwich, a cold beer, and the children's menu at McGettigan's 19th Hole,

(609) 652-6476. Owned by Mannis McGettigan, one of a number of brothers who came from the old sod to open taverns in the area, the 19th Hole is so named because it's across the street from the former Seaview Country Club, now called the Marriott Seaview, which has an excellent brunch.

From McGettigan's, it's a short ride up Shore Road (U.S. 9) to the Edwin B. Forsythe National Wildlife Refuge, headquartered on Great Creek Road off U.S. 9 in Oceanville. This wonderful wildlife area encompasses more than 42,000 acres in Atlantic and Ocean Counties. The cost to enter is $4 per car, but a new plan will offer annual passes to birdwatchers and nature lovers for only $12. Those who purchase a federal duck stamp—the $15 Migratory Bird Hunting and Conservation Stamp—will still have access to Forsythe whenever they want to. A quarter of a million people visit this national treasure each year. Phone: (609) 652-1665.

Near the entrance to Forsythe is the Noyes Museum on Lily Lake Road in Oceanville. Its exhibits range from those of area artists to duck decoy makers and the history of oystering in South Jersey. Well worth a visit, the Museum is open Wednesday through Sunday, 11:00 A.M. to 4:00 P.M. Admission is only $3, and those under 18 are free. Seniors pay $2. Call (609) 652-8848.

Dining

The Pitney Tavern & Restaurant, where the locals hang their hats, at 200 S. Pitney Road, Absecon Highlands, (609) 652-1550. Good spot for a cold beer and a sandwich.

The Oyster Creek Inn, at the end of Oyster Creek Road, is an old standby for seafood dinners.

Like the Oyster Creek Inn, the Mott's Creek Inn just north of Oyster Creek can be reached by car or boat. Once just an old bar, it has been revitalized and renamed as the Mott's Creek Inn and Frankie's Great Bay Cafe. It is at the end of Motts Creek Road, off U.S. 9, north of Smithville, (609) 652-1444. A joint effort of Chef Doug Braun and Frank Florence, the place had been closed for several years until it reopened in the Spring of 1996.

THE MULLICA RIVER

Heading north on U.S. 9, just before the turn off for Chestnut Neck Boat Yard, near the banks of the Mullica River and the beginning of Great Bay, you will see a large monument to the Minute Man. It was placed there in 1916 by the Daughters of the American Revolution to honor patriots who raided British ships during the Revolutionary War, especially whose who died in a skirmish with the Redcoats on October 6, 1778.

Sometime in 1998, when the new home and museum of the Port Republic Historical Society opens, you will also be able to see artifacts of the audacious era of privateering. This facility will become a reality as a result of the U.S. Department of the Interior, which donated the property, and to lobbying efforts by former Congressman Bill Hughes and history-minded local citizens and organizations.

After reading the monument's inscription and pausing for a moment to praise brave men, you will proceed to the Chestnut Neck Boat Yard, whose official address is 758 Old New York Road in Port Republic. Ann Bruno, Mary Ann Bruno, and other relatives of a great local man, the late Nuncie Bruno, hold court here, selling squid, minnows, grass shrimp, artificial lures, gas, tackle, and hard-shell crabs in season. The Chestnut Neck Boat Yard is about three miles north of Smithville, (609) 652-1119, fax (609) 652-5610.

One of our favorite fishing spots is right under the Garden State Parkway bridge over the Mullica. To get there, make a right from the entrance to the boat yard and continue on down the road until it ends at a dirt cul-de-sac. (Don't make a right into a private lane.) Park as close to the reeds as possible, because fishermen who use the Chestnut Neck's boat launch drive down here to turn their trailers around. Gather your gear and walk down a dirt path to the base of the Parkway bridge.

In recent years, slobs have littered this spot with beer cans, empty six-pack cartons, old fishing line, and other assorted debris. Make sure you take out whatever you bring in. By casting out into the Mullica, we have caught weakfish and even catfish here, and stripers are a good possibility as well. You can walk out on the sod banks, too, but watch out for an underwater cable on the west side of the bridge. It must be adorned like a Christmas tree, with many lures, hooks, and sinkers from unsuspecting anglers.

As with other shore fishing holes, plan to get here early or late, because the jet-ski enthusiasts are a menace on the Mullica, too.

You can guarantee that no jet skis will bother you if you come to Collins Cove, off the Port Republic Wildlife Management Area, west of the bridge, when winter becomes nasty enough to congeal these waters into a hard freeze.

Then the only invaders are ice fishermen, who converge on Collins Cove and other nearby Mullica spots for white perch. When the tasty perch are running, they can be caught by the bucketful (once you find the right depth of the fish) on hooks baited with small minnows, little pieces of bloodworm or jigs. The best bait, however, is grass shrimp, which is often available at the Chestnut Neck Boat Yard.

> *It was during a bitter winter in the mid-1970s, and Collins Cove was under a heavy mantle of ice. My son George and I were driving on the Garden State Parkway over the Mullica River one Sunday when we noticed scores of ice fishermen working their jigs and tip-ups. It looked easy, so we parked and, dressed in normal winter clothes, grabbed the rods that we always kept in my car and strode out on the ice. We had no auger, but it was easy to find a hole that had been vacated by earlier anglers and not re-frozen. We fished for all of five minutes, until the cold wind blowing across the frigid ice turned our unprepared feet to frozen stumps and drove us to the safety of our car. The lesson we learned that day was to be prepared when you go ice fishing.* —G.I.

Collins Cove in the Port Republic Wildlife Management Area is located west of the Garden State Parkway. To reach it from the Philadelphia area, take the White Horse Pike to Pomona, turn left at Route 575 and head north to Clarks Landing Road. Turn left, go under the Parkway, and when you see a sign for the WMA, turn right and follow the road to the parking area.

BURLINGTON COUNTY

From Chestnut Neck, head north on the Garden State Parkway and get off at the first exit over the Mullica River. This will put you on U.S. 9, heading north to New Gretna and the best seafood bargain in South Jersey—Allen's Clam Bar, (609) 296-4106.

For more than three decades, Allen's has been providing good seafood at modest prices. Where else can you find six absolutely fresh cherrystone clams on the half shell, properly chilled, for $2.95? Or, "then and now," that traditional South Jersey specialty, clam pie, for $6.95? Best of all, Allen's is BYOB, and there's a liquor store across the street.

Service, however, can clam up when the place is congested with customers. We once watched as a trio of out-of-town customers—including an intrepid chap wearing a Grgich Vineyards T-shirt from Napa Valley—stalked out after waiting an inordinate time for someone to take their orders. If you can bear with it, you'll be rewarded with some of the most reasonably priced seafood the shore offers. An example: one Sunday in the summer of 1996, two of us were fishing the Mullica River. We stopped at Allen's at 11:30 for lunch, and the place already was filling up. Between us, we ate four dozen superb clams on the half shell, an outstanding soft crab sandwich, a side order of French fries, a cup of Manhattan clam chowder, and a platter of fried clams. The tab: $27.48. Is this Heaven or not? (We've always been partial to the classic Allen's T-shirt: "Eat Clams, and Come Again.") Open Tuesday–Sunday, 11:00 A.M.-9:00 P.M.; closed Monday.

COD, BLACKFISH, AND WHITING IN THE WINTER

If fishing through the ice for perch doesn't sound like an appealing way to relax in the winter, try fishing for cod, whiting, or blackfish from a head boat. For cod, your best bet is to put on many layers of warm clothing and head north. We've fished aboard the 125-foot *Jamaica* out of Brielle, and it's a fine boat, captained by Howard Bogan, (908) 528-5014. Early in the winter season, we have loaded up with whiting on the *Norma-K II*, out of Ken's Landing in Point Pleasant, (908) 892-9787. And all the way south, the Miss Chris fleet, docked in Cape May, offers twelve-hour wreck trips during the winter for blackfish and cod on a reservation-only basis, (609) 884-3939.

These fish are among the tastiest saltwater denizens, with firm, white flesh. Here are some of our favorite ways to serve them:

Cod fillets with red peppers and onions

(from the American Institute for Cancer Research)

1 tablespoon olive oil
1 sweet red pepper, cut into thin strips
4 slices red onion
1 tsp minced garlic

1/2 tsp dried oregano
1 pound cod fillets, cut into four pieces
2 tablespoons chopped fresh parsley
Pepper

In a nonstick skillet, heat oil over medium heat; add red pepper and sauté for three minutes. Separate the onion into rings and add to the pan with garlic and oregano. Sauté for one minute, then push vegetables to the edge of the pan.

Add cod fillets, cover and cook three minutes. Turn the fish, cover the pan, and cook 2–3 minutes longer, or until fish is opaque. Sprinkle cod with parsley and season with pepper to taste. Spoon the red pepper mixture over the fish and serve. Four servings.

Bacalas (salted, dried codfish): George Ingram's Sunday breakfast

1-pound bacala filet
1 small shallot, minced
1 small garlic clove, minced
3 tablespoons unsalted butter
2 tablespoons flour

1 cup milk
Pinch of Old Bay Seasoning
1 bay leaf
Chopped fresh parsley
Half cup reserved poaching liquid

Cut bacala into one-inch pieces and soak in water for twenty-four hours, changing water often. (Don't use a metal container.) Place fish in a large pot and cover with water. Add the bay leaf. Bring to a boil and then simmer for five minutes or until bacala is tender. Drain, reserving one-half cup of the poaching liquid.

In a large saucepan, melt butter and add shallot and garlic. Sauté gently until they are translucent. Add flour and stir continuously with a wooden spoon for several minutes. Remove from heat.

Heat the milk in a saucepan. Add reserved poaching liquid and Old Bay. Just before milk boils, add it to the butter-flour mixture, put the pan over high heat and stir until the sauce is thickened. Lower heat, add the bacala and cook until the fish is heated through. Top with chopped parsley.

Serve over home-fried potatoes or toast points.

Blackfish (Tautog) stew *(New York Times, May 6, 1990)*

2 tablespoons extra-virgin olive oil
1/2 cup chopped onions
1 cup finely julienned leeks, white and light-green part only
2 cloves garlic, crushed
1/2 pound potatoes, peeled and sliced thin

2 cups milk
Salt and freshly ground black pepper to taste
Pinch nutmeg
1-1/2 pounds blackfish fillets, in 2-inch chunks
1 tablespoon minced fresh chives

Heat oil in a three- to four-quart casserole. Add onion and sauté over medium-low heat until soft but not brown. Stir in leeks and garlic, sauté a minute or two longer, and stir in potatoes.

Add milk, bring to a low simmer, cover and cook until potatoes are just tender, about ten minutes. Season with salt and pepper to taste, then stir in the nutmeg. (Recipe can be prepared up to one hour in advance up to this point.)

Reheat milk and vegetable mixture to a low simmer. Add blackfish, cover and simmer about ten minutes, just until fish is cooked through. Check seasonings and sprinkle with chives. Serve in soup bowls. Yield: four servings.

Whiting—frost fish—is probably the most versatile fish you can catch for the table. It is delicious smoked, deep fried, sautéed, steamed, or baked—and it's an easy fish to clean and fillet. Here is a recipe for steamed whiting from food writer Florence Fabricant, of the *New York Times*:

Steamed Whiting with scallions and ginger

(*New York Times*, May 6, 1990)

4 whole whiting, about one pound each, cleaned
3 tablespoons sesame oil
1 bunch scallions

A slice of ginger, one inch thick, peeled and slivered
2 tablespoons white soy sauce
3 tablespoons rice vinegar

Put a Chinese steamer basket over a wok. Into the basket place a heat-proof plate that can hold the fish. Oil the plate with one tablespoon of the sesame oil. Pour an inch of water into the wok and bring to a boil while preparing fish.

Remove roots from the scallions and quarter them lengthwise. Then cut them into three-inch lengths.

Scatter half the scallions and half the ginger in the basket. Put some of the scallions inside each fish and scatter the rest over the top.

Cover the steamer with a lid or double thickness of heavy-duty foil and steam fish about fifteen minutes.

Carefully remove fish and transfer to a serving platter. Drain all but a few spoonfuls of liquid from the plate, reserving the scallions and ginger. Scrape the reserved liquid, scallions, and ginger into a dish, add soy sauce, vinegar, and remaining sesame oil. Stir and spoon over fish.

Crabbing

🦐 Crabbing is still one of the great family recreational, and egalitarian, activities that can be practiced from bridges and tidal creeks all over the salt and brackish waters of New Jersey and even Pennsylvania. In recent years, the blue claw crab has migrated farther up the Delaware River than ever before, at least in modern memory. At one time, crabs were being caught as far north as Neshaminy Creek in Bucks County and along the Delaware below Trenton. This phenomenon was probably the result of years of drought, which moved the river's salt line closer to New Jersey's capital city.

In Philadelphia, savvy crabbers have also caught the *Callinectes sapidus*—"beautiful swimmer"—on the Schuylkill River below the Philadelphia Museum of Art.

It's easy to catch crabs. Purists will tell you that only hand lines are acceptable, with a chicken back tied to one end of the line and a waiting net as you slowly bring the bait to the surface. But those of us who want to take crabs home for the pot still rely on collapsible metal traps. The bait may be a piece of chicken, squid, or moss bunker attached by heavy string or thin wire to the bottom of the trap. Our own preference is the skeletal frame of a filleted flounder, one that still has some fish flesh on it. A chunk of oily mackerel or a piece of squid are also good. Just remember to change the bait from time to time. When it becomes "washed out," it doesn't do a good job of attracting hungry crabs.

In New Jersey, your hardshell crab must be 4-1/2 inches from point to point of the shell. Don't rely on memory of what you think 4-1/2 inches is because, when the crabs are being brought up, it's easy to imagine that they're bigger than they really are. That oversight has cost many crabbers a fine from the warden. The easiest trick is to take an inexpensive plastic ruler, cut it off at the required length, and put it in your pocket. Here's another trick you'll have to learn from experience: measuring the crab's shell without getting a bloody finger from one of its pincers.

No license is needed for hand lines or regular crab traps. New Jersey issues a noncommercial crabbing license for the use of not more than two commercial-style crab pots (those large plastic traps that stay in the water for up to seventy-two hours) or two trot lines. You can only possess one bushel of crabs, and crabs harvested with this license can't be sold. The license costs $2, and applications are usually included in the May edition of the *New Jersey Fish and Game Digest*, published by the Division of Fish, Game & Wildlife. Licenses are also available at most coastal bait and tackle shops or by calling (609) 748-2031. A crab pot "shall mean a cube or rectangular shaped device not larger than 30 inches on a side with openings inward for the entrance of crabs."

When it comes to recreational crabbing, everyone has a preferred method. Some folks like to go out on a moonlight night in the back marshes after drenching themselves in insect repellant (note: recent research suggests that smelly feet attract mosquitoes) and use a net to scoop up crabs that swim along the surface of the water. Some crabbers like only the incoming tide while others swear by the outgoing tide. The truth is that crabs can be caught any time, even on dead-low water. But from our experience the incoming tide is best, right up to flood tide.

Where can you crab? The choices are virtually limitless.

In Atlantic County, one of our favorite spots is in the Forsythe National Wildlife Refuge. Heading north on U.S. 9, take Route 618 right after the Oceanville United Methodist Church and follow the paved road as it curves right and then left until you see a sign, "Scotts Landing Road." If you are driving from the north, make a left off Route 9 at the alternate Route 561, just past where the Smithville shops are located. Scotts Landing is 1.5 miles from the Route 9 turnoff. But watch out for the bodacious Canada geese, who believe they own the road. After making the turn into Scotts Landing, the paved road changes to a dirt road that leads down to a dock and boat launch. Park on the left and crab along the dock to your right and front.

Scotts Landing is open from 4:00 A.M. to 9:00 P.M., April through October. (This is a popular launching place for New Jersey duck hunters in October.) From November through March, the hours are 4:00 A.M. to 7:00 P.M. During the summer, bring plenty of insect repellant, because the mosquitoes and greenheads can be fearsome at times.

Another good location is the banks of the Mullica River, near Chestnut

Neck. From the Chestnut Neck Boatyard, continue on the blacktop road until it ends at the base on the Garden State Parkway bridge over the Mullica. Gather your gear and walk down a dirt path to the concrete embarkment under the bridge. Crabbers drop their nets here, or walk out on the marshes to the left or right. Just make sure the tide is high enough for comfortable crabbing—and please take your trash with you.

In Seaview, Galloway Township, take the road next to McGettigan's 19th Hole until it dead-ends at the bay. Farther south on U.S. 9, try Brown Avenue, north of Absecon. The dirt road is pretty beaten up, but a four-wheel drive vehicle should get you out onto the salt marshes, where crabbing can be very good. There are bridges along White Horse Pike, between Absecon and Atlantic City, where you can crab.

Rental boat locations for crabbing include Somerset Cove Marina & Rich's Bait and Tackle, Somers Point–Mays Landing Rd., (609) 927-9393; Dad's Place Marina, 501 W. Ocean Dr., North Wildwood, (609) 522-3911.

Delaware Bay offers many crabbing spots, including Dividing Creek Boat Rentals on Route 553, (609) 785-2828; Beaver Dam, also on Route 553; and the Newport Landing Marina ($45 per boat).

Eating Crabs: A Health Caution

According to New Jersey officials, you should avoid eating the crab's hepatopancreas, which has the highest levels of chemical contaminants. This part of the crustacean is commonly called the "green gland" and is located under the gills. You should also discard the cooking liquid and not use the green gland "in any juices, sauces or soups."

But if you eat crabs . . .

George Perrier, owner of one of the greatest restaurants in America, Le Bec-Fin on Walnut Street in Philadelphia, created a great crab cake recipe that uses shrimp mousse as a binder. This one will never get a seal of approval from the American Heart Association.

George Perrier's crabcakes with shrimp
(*Philadelphia Inquirer,* October 14, 1992)

1 pound lump crabmeat
3/4 pound unshelled shrimp
1 whole egg
3/4 heavy cream
Salt and freshly ground pepper to taste
1/2 cup minced scallions

1 tablespoon Dijon-style mustard
1 teaspoon Worcestershire Sauce
1/4 teaspoon hot pepper sauce
1/2 cup vegetable oil
Parsley Butter Sauce (see recipe)

Pick over crabmeat to remove cartilage and shell, leaving lumps as large as possible. Shell and devein the shrimp. Place shrimp in processor or blender, add the egg, cream, salt and pepper, and puree as smooth as possible. Use a rubber spatula to scrape down sides of blender container. Transfer puree to a mixing bowl.

Add the crabmeat, scallions, mustard, Worcestershire, and hot pepper sauces. Stir gently but thoroughly. Shape the mixture into ten cakes. Heat two tablespoons of oil in a nonstick skillet. Sauté crab cakes, several at a time, adding oil as needed. Cook over medium heat about three minutes on each side or until golden brown. Remove and keep warm. Serve with Parsley Butter Sauce.

Parsley butter sauce

3 tablespoons finely chopped shallots
2 tablespoons sherry vinegar
1/4 cup dry white wine
1/2 cup fish broth or clam juice
1/2 cup heavy cream

3 tablespoons butter
Salt and freshly ground pepper
  to taste
1 tablespoon coarse mustard
1/4 cup finely chopped parsley

Combine shallots, vinegar, and wine in a saucepan; bring to a boil and reduce by half. Add the broth and cream; bring to a boil. Cook at a rolling boil about forty-five seconds. Whisk in butter. Add salt and pepper. Stir in mustard and parsley. Spoon over crab cakes. Makes about 3/4 of a cup.

Here's an easier recipe, from the Maryland Department of Agriculture, Seafood Marketing Program:

1 pound crabmeat
1/2 cup cracker crumbs or bread crumbs
2 eggs (or 1 large)
1/4 cup mayonnaise

1 teaspoon seafood seasoning (such as Old
  Bay, Wye River)
1/4 teaspoon white pepper
2 teaspoons Worcestershire sauce
1 teaspoon dry mustard

Remove cartilage from crabmeat. In a bowl mix together eggs, mayonnaise, seafood seasoning, white pepper, Worcestershire, and dry mustard. Add crabmeat, mixing gently and evenly. Add cracker crumbs evenly. Shape into six cakes. Deep fry in oil at 350 degrees F. for 2–3 minutes until golden, or sauté in a frying pan with a little oil for five minutes on each side.

There's a continuing controversy over the way hardshells should be cooked. Marylanders like to steam their crabs, but Philadelphia natives say that method produces a dry crab. They prefer their crabs boiled.

Here's how Maryland's Seafood Marketers recommend cooking crabs:

1/2 cup seafood seasoning

1/2 cup salt

3 cups white vinegar

3 cups beer (or water)

3 dozen live hardshells

Mix seasonings, vinegar, and beer. Put half the crabs in a very large pot with rack and tight fitting lid. Pour half the seasoning mixture over top. Add rest of crabs and remaining liquid. Cover and steam until crabs turn bright red.

(Note: the Maryland marketing folks recommend 20–30 minutes; we Philadelphians say that's a recipe for a dry crab. Try 10–15 minutes.) Serves 9–12, depending on size of crabs.

Our friend, Anthony Petaccio, owner of the Rose Garden Flower Shop in the Port Richmond section of Philadelphia, cooks his crabs this way:

Anthony's garlic crabs

Put live crabs in the refrigerator for several hours until they become "sleepy" and won't attack your fingers. Take them out, one at a time, and clean them by removing the top shell and the "dead man" gills. Break in half and rinse and pat dry. Heat a large skillet over high heat, add olive oil, sliced garlic cloves, and red pepper flakes. Add as many crabs as will fit into the pan. Sauté until the shells are red, turning the crabs several times. Sprinkle with lots of fresh chopped Italian parsley—and have plenty of paper towels.

If you don't want to take the trouble to catch your own crabs, there are many wonderful places in Philadelphia and New Jersey to sample cooked "beautiful swimmers." Here are only a few:

PHILADELPHIA CRAB HOUSES

The best crab place in the city is a private club called the POLISH-AMERICAN CITIZENS' HARMONIA AND OSWIATA CLUB at Orthodox and Aramingo Avenue. A membership costs $5, and it helps to be Polish. Cindy, Ed, and Mark Kasprzak are carrying on the tradition begun by their late father, the legendary crab cooker Eddie Kasprzak; (215) 533-4390.

CHICKIE AND PETE'S CAFE, 4010 Robbins Avenue (Robbins and Mulberry Street). Pete Ciarrochi is carrying on the hardshell tradition begun by previous owner Wally Nowacki. "My crabs are unique," says Pete. "It took me years to perfect my sauce." This is a very popular stop, and on weekends it can be almost impossible to get a table. But Pete always can be counted on to put a smile on your face, no matter how hectic things get; (215) 338-1190.

FATHEAD'S, 6171 Torresdale Avenue. This is a Philadelphia taproom from the old school—narrow entrance, shuffleboard, long bar, and good seafood. Fathead's crabs are served similar to those at nearby Chickie and Pete's, in a red sauce; (215) 624-9423.

CAP'N CHET'S BLUE POINT INC., 5301 Harbison Avenue. This venerable establishment has been serving decent crabs for many years; (215) 288-2438.

BONCELA'S CAFE AND RESTAURANT, 2372 Orthodox Street, at Milnor Street. For years there's been a friendly rivalry between the Harmonia Club and Boncela's. In fact, Eddie Kasper at one time left the Harmonia and cooked for owner Joanne Clements; (215) 537-8039.

BYRNE'S TAVERN, 3301 Richmond Street. This is a comfortable Irish pub, set in a Polish neighborhood of Lower Northeast Philadelphia, and specializing in hardshells. Owner Frank Byrne is an environmentalist who cares deeply about the future of the crab industry; (215) 634-8707.

BONK'S BAR, Richmond and Tioga Streets. Just north of Byrne's on Richmond is this quintessential taproom, complete with a ladies' entrance on the side. The crabs can be pricey, but they're darn good; (215) 634-9927.

DINARDO'S, 312 Race Street. This family restaurant and bar in Philadelphia's Olde City section, is near some of the City's most famous historic sites. Well worth a trip; (215) 925-5115.

NEW JERSEY CRAB HOUSES

GRABBE'S, 19 Delsea Dr., Westville, has a long-established reputation; (609) 456-3594.

CRABBY'S, on Route 50 in Belcoville, just south of Mays Landing, may just be the best crab house in South Jersey; (609) 625-2722.

BOOKS AND INFORMATION ON CRABS AND CRABBING

Cottrell, Ernest J., Frank J. Mellaci, and John B. Cottrell. *Successful Crabbing* (Camden, Maine: International Marine Publishing Company, 1976).

Warner, William. *Beautiful Swimmers*. A classic.

Horton, Tom. *An Island Out of Time* (1996), a beautiful and unromanticized portrait of the people of Smith Island, near the border between Maryland and Virginia.

Marty's Crabbing Directory is a mimeographed, fourteen-page list of places that rent boats for crabbing, from Ocean Gate to Delaware Bay, as well as recipes and tips for catching the "beautiful swimmers." Complete with misspelled words, it is available by sending $3.00 to Martin Trani, P.O. Box 342, Bensalem, PA 19020; (215) 638-0106. For neophytes only.

Dobarro, Joe, and Bill Figley. *New Jersey's Blue Crab*, a brochure published by the state of New Jersey.

FINISHING OFF

Somewhere in the world there is probably another discussion of crabs such as the one above, but we doubt it. One of us doesn't even like crabs in any form other than the picked-clean meat, but so what? That same person can't move through tiny waves or slight swells without chumming over the side. But, even if he turns green, gray, or white, he always keeps fishing. One of us is the turkey who goes birding when he should be fishing, so readers get stuff on birds that for the other two of us is occasionally stuff for the birds. And another of us should probably enroll in the Culinary Institute of America just to learn to chop better than his son.

Having skipped beloved creeks, ignored some folks' favorite lakes, bypassed great eateries, erred about bait (maybe), and sat happily in a downwardly mobile bar, we know that—despite the omissions and our eccentricities—we have produced a fishing and happiness book. We are neither rich nor poor. We love good fun and good food, and we are willing to get into small arguments about fishing spots. We have indulged our own tastes in hopes that we can help you indulge yours. Two of us will never show you a reach cast; one of us does a tuck cast that looks like a fighter plane crashing. Another thinks a roll cast happens in dark alleys. Yet the three of us have had lifetimes of wonderful fishing pleasures, and we would like for you and your family or group to have the joy.

There are snobs in every sport, especially the social sports, such as tennis, golf, and fishing. One of us carries everything he owns for hunting and fishing in his vehicle every day of his life; he has never unloaded, and there are flies in there that must have once belonged to someone's great grandfather. Another still uses a glass fly rod sometimes. Once in a local tavern, we briefly joined several people, who had seen the stuffed vehicle and the glass rod. They themselves were expensively dressed and outfitted with truly expensive equipment. They laughed at us openly, even though we had outfished them earlier two to one. To ease the tension, we actually bought those fellows a bottle of bordeaux, a good but relatively inexpensive bottle. Can you believe it? We overheard the sneers about cheap bordeaux. You cannot win over people like that, and we openly admit failure.

Here instead is how it should go. Fly fishing a trophy zone with Joe Humphreys (one of the best in the nation), we watched Joe, with his concentration and famous tuck cast, catch and release five or six trout to our one. It was a fine demonstration for three poorly performing but experienced fishers. Joe must have known how we felt, but he did what he does best, and he did it to show us how to do it best. Then he looked up, grinned, and said without a trace of condescension, "Let's go fishing."

That's our book! "Let's go fishing!"

Appendix

WHERE TO LOOK FOR MORE INFORMATION

The National Weather Service provides updated information about the Delaware River flow and the creeks that empty into it. Call 1-800-431-4721.

The Delaware River Basin Commission maintains a Website with important information on water quality, flood conditions, and other things you want to know: **http://www.state.nj.us/drbc/info.htm**.

PENNSYLVANIA DAILY NEWSPAPERS

Bucks County Courier Times, Levittown, Pa. **Joe Punchello** writes the "Open Spaces" column for Sunday editions. The *Courier Times* also runs stories by the outdoor columnist for the Calkins newspapers, **Elmer Anderson**.

Daily Local News, West Chester, Pa. **Tom Tatum** writes an outdoors column about hunting and fishing each Tuesday.

The Mercury, Pottstown, Pa. **Bob Ballantyne** is the paper's hunting and fishing correspondent, while **Jim Loe** writes a "Salt Spray" fishing column during the season.

The Morning Call, Allentown, Pa. The *Call* publishes one of the best outdoors pages in the region, and its outdoors editor, **Tom Fegely**—a former biology teacher—is one of the best of the breed. He writes with authority on hunting, fishing, and such engaging subjects as watching Eastern phoebes while float-fishing down the Delaware River.

The Times-Leader, Wilkes-Barre, Pa. Outdoors editor **George Smith** gives readers a full page of hunting and fishing news of the area on Sundays.

The Pocono Record, Stroudsburg, Pa. **John Serrao** writes the "Poconos Outdoors" nature column, and **Tom Eveland** writes "Wildlife Watch" in the Sunday paper.

The Patriot-News, Harrisburg, Pa. Outdoors columnist is **Scott Weidensaul**, and **Capt. Charley Zaimes** writes a column on saltwater fishing.

The Philadelphia Daily News. Each Thursday during the regular season, this tabloid paper publishes an advertising section, prepared by **Lou Rodia**, on saltwater fishing.

The Philadelphia Inquirer. **Conrad Grove** has been this paper's outdoors writer since 1996. His columns, which are always intelligent and well-informed, appear on Sundays. **Steven Morgan**, a freelancer, supplements the *Inquirer's* Sunday outdoors page with news about hunting and fishing in Pennsylvania and New Jersey. The "Weekend" section on Fridays has a freshwater and saltwater fishing report compiled by retired *Inquirer* outdoors writer **Ben Callaway**. During the regular fishing season, the column includes a map and a "tip of the week."

The Reading Eagle, Reading, Pa. **Nick Zaffary**, the paper's wire editor, writes an engaging Sunday column on hunting and fishing, in addition to articles by **Doyle Dietz**.

The Times Herald, Norristown, Pa. Outdoors columnist is **P. J. Reilly**.

PENNSYLVANIA WEEKLY NEWSPAPERS

The River Reporter, Main Street, Narrowsburg, NY 12764. Good upper Delaware reports by **Pat Camuso** and **Harold Novick**.

NEW JERSEY DAILY NEWSPAPERS

Burlington County Times, Willingboro, N.J. **Steve Carpenter** is the author of a Sunday column on the outdoors.

The Courier-Post, Cherry Hill, N.J. **Ben Callaway**, retired outdoors writer for the *Philadelphia Inquirer*, writes a Friday fishing column.

Gloucester County Times, Woodbury, N.J. **Ralph Knisell**, owner of a sporting goods store, and the *Fisherman's* Delaware Bay correspondent, writes a fishing column every Thursday.

The Press of Atlantic City. *Press* Sports Editor **Mike Shepherd** writes a fishing column on Friday and in The Outdoors Page, which runs on Sunday along with **Kevin Post**'s "Nature's Way," **Lou Rodia**'s "Life Outdoors" columns, and **Fred Schaaf**'s excellent report on astronomy. On Friday, Shepherd's "Shep's Hot Spot" provides reliable information about bay, coastal, and offshore fishing. Reporter **Richard Degener** does an excellent job of covering environmental issues. The *Press* also publishes tide tables, which are available at many tackle shops throughout South Jersey.

Finally, the newspaper sponsors a free Press Fishing Contest each year (1997 was the forty-third annual one), offering almost $1,800 in prizes in twenty-seven categories of saltwater and freshwater fishing.

The Times, Trenton, N.J. A comprehensive weekly report on salt and freshwater fishing is prepared by **Russ Wilson**, contributing editor of the *Fisherman*. It appears on the back page of the Sports section on Fridays. **Bill Garry** writes a boating column, and senior editor **Arnold Ropeik** contributes weekly little gems about his fishing experiences.

The Trentonian, Trenton, N.J. **Robert Brunisholz** writes an informative outdoors column for this tabloid newspaper on Tuesdays, Fridays, and Sundays.

The Star-Ledger, Newark, N.J. The old-timer **Howard Bryant** covers hunting and fishing for the *Star-Ledger*, one of the Garden State's most respected newspapers. **Al Ristori** writes a Sunday column devoted to saltwater angling.

Asbury Park Press, Asbury Park, N.J. **John Geiser**, a resident of Wall Township and the author of three books on saltwater fishing, writes a column about freshwater and saltwater fishing and hunting, primarily in central and northern New Jersey. The *Press* also offers Web browsers an excellent site for all kinds of fishing and hunting links at this URL: **http://www.app.com/fishing/fishlink.htm**.

OTHER DAILY NEWSPAPERS

The New York Times, New York, N.Y. **Nelson Bryant**, the best in the business, writes only occasional pieces now in semi-retirement. During the regular fishing season, the *Times* sports section also publishes a report, "Fishing in Local Waters," which often covers as far south as Atlantic City. Other outdoors pieces are written by freelancers.

The New York Post, New York, N.Y. **Ken Moran** is the *Post's* knowledgeable outdoors writer, but the focus of his pieces, of course, is on the North Jersey-New York City area, where most of his readers reside. His column appears Wednesday, Friday, and Sunday.

The Washington Post, Washington, D.C., doesn't generally cover fishing in our region, but outdoors writer **Angus Phillips** is one of the best in the business, and he can always be counted on for a good hunting or fishing yarn.

WEEKLY PUBLICATIONS

The Fisherman, New Jersey, Delaware Bay Edition, 1622 Beaver Dam Road, Point Pleasant, NJ 08742; (908) 295-8600. Managing Editor: **Pete Barrett**. Weekly, except for two weeks in December. 1 year (50 issues), $25. Single issues, $1.25. For both the novice and the experienced fisher, this is an essential publication. The New Jersey/Delaware Bay edition has how-to and where-to stories on saltwater and freshwater fishing in New Jersey, Delaware Bay, and the Delaware River. The *Fisherman* also provides product information and advice on equipment in the "Tackle Doctor" column by Contributing Editor **Russ Wilson**. "Salty Fly Corner," written by Associate Editor **Mark Marquez**, addresses this increasingly popular sport.

The *Fisherman* sponsors a special fund for reef building, shore access, and conservation. It is an effort that deserves your support. Send donations to the *Fisherman* Sportfishing Fund, 1622 Beaver Dam Road, Point Pleasant, NJ 08742.

The Sandpaper, 600 West Avenue, Ocean City, NJ 08226; (609) 398-7964 (free). During the regular fishing season, **Captain Henry Bender** writes an entertaining column about saltwater and freshwater fishing opportunities in the area. We like any fishing column that begins with these words: "Let the reader beware. This column, as well as all future columns, may contain falsehoods, lies, rumors and/or pieces of gossip that are by no means intentional."

Cape May County Gazette-Leader, Wildwood, N.J. **Boyd Tyler** writes the "Tightlines" fishing column.

MAGAZINES

Pennsylvania Outdoors (formerly *Pennsylvania Afield*), a monthly newsprint magazine published by the *Altoona Mirror* newspaper, P.O. Box 2008, 301 Cayuga Avenue, Altoona, PA 16603; (814) 946-7356. Single copies, $1.50; one-year subscription, $13.95. An interesting guide to hunting and fishing in Pennsylvania, with an editorial perspective that addresses the concerns of rank-and-file hunters and fishers.

Field & Stream, published by Times Mirror Magazines, Inc., 2 Park Avenue, New York, NY 10016. Single issue, $2.50; 1 year, $15.94; website: www.fieldandstream.com. E-mail for subscription information: stream@neodata.com. A publication that covers hunting and fishing, with a targeted special section for Northeastern readers.

Outdoor Life, published by Times Mirror Magazines, 2 Park Avenue, New York, NY 10016. Single issue: $2.50; 1 year, $15.94. E-mail address for subscription inquiries: Outlife@Neodata.com. Like its sister publication, *Outdoor Life* has a regional "East" section that includes Pennsylvania, New Jersey, and Delaware.

Sports Afield, published ten times a year, P.O. Box 7166, Red Oak, IA 51591. $13.97 for one year. The *Washington Post* has said that *Sports Afield* and *Gray's Sporting Journal* (see below) publish "some of the best nonfiction writing these days. . . . These are well-crafted magazines in which hunters pursue life as well as death, fishermen release their catches and some characters don't eat any meat at all," wrote the *Post's* magazine columnist, Linton Weeks (September 10, 1996).

Gray's Sporting Journal, published seven times a year by Morris Communications Corporation, 713 Broad Street, Augusta, GA 30901. Subscription: $36.95 per year.

National Fisherman, published by Journal Publications, 120 Tillson Avenue, Suite 201, P.O. Box 908, Rockland, ME 04841-0908. Subscriptions: (800) 959-5073; fax (207) 594-8978. Single issues, $2.50; 1 year, $22.95

This publication primarily targets the Atlantic and Pacific commercial fisher. A sample article: "Getting the most out of your gillnet." But it's still a fascinating read for the recreational angler who wants to find out the concerns of the people who make a living doing what we do for fun.

Pennsylvania Angler and Boater, published by the Pennsylvania Fish & Boat Commission, 3532 Walnut Street, Harrisburg, PA 17109. Single copies, $3.00; 1 year subscription, $9.

We were annoyed when the monthly *Pennsylvania Angler* became the bimonthly *Pennsylvania Angler and Boater* in 1997. It is still an indispensable publication for the Keystone State freshwater fisher. Its articles are informative and intelligent—even if you're not interested in the boating pieces. We wouldn't be without it—and neither should you.

Fly Fisherman, published six times a year by Cowles Magazines, Inc., 6405 Flank Drive, Harrisburg, PA 17112-2753. Subscription: 1 year, $24. A fine publication for the serious fly-fisher.

American Angler, The Magazine of Fly Fishing and Fly Tying, published bimonthly by Abenaki Publishers, Inc., 126 North Street, P.O. Box 4100, Bennington, VT 05201-4100; (802) 447-1518. Subscription: $19.95 for six issues; (800) 877-5305.

Fly Rod & Reel is published six times a year (January-February, March-April, May-June, July-August, September-October, and November-December) by Down East Enterprise, Inc., Rockport, ME 04856. The publication calls itself "The Magazine of American Fly-Fishing," and its contributing editors include such notables as Ted Williams, Dave Hughes, and Ted Leeson. Subscriptions cost $16.97 for one year.

Eastern Outdoors is a free monthly newsprint publication, the outdoors equivalent of those "shoppers" in local communities. One of the most worthwhile features is the ads. Subscriptions are available for $9.75 for 12 issues by writing to P.O. Box 532, Cape May Court House, NJ 08210. It is edited by **Lou Rodia**.

Mid-Atlantic Fly Fishing Guide is another free publication. It appears 10 times a year and provides guide charts to hatches and their dates for all of the major streams in New York, Pennsylvania, and New Jersey. Such experts as Lefty Kreh, Bob Clouser, Charles Meck, and Cathy and Barry Beck are often among the contributors.

New Jersey Outdoors, published quarterly by the New Jersey Department of Environmental Protection, Bureau of Revenue, CN 417, Trenton, NJ 08625-0402. To subscribe, call 1-800-645-0038. Subscriptions: 1 year, $15; two years, $26. Stories about the environment and freshwater and saltwater fishing in the Garden State.

Trout, the official magazine of Trout Unlimited, published in January, April, July, and October. Membership in Trout Unlimited ($30) includes a 1-year subscription to *Trout* Magazine: Membership Services, Trout Unlimited, 800 Follin Lane S.E., Suite 250, Vienna, VA 22180-4959; (703) 281-1100. Anyone who is serious about trout fishing should belong to Trout Unlimited.

Flyfisher: Magazine of the Federation of Fly Fishers, the official publication of the Federation of Fly Fishers (FFF), appears four times a year. The organization emphasizes conservation, education, and restoration through fly fishing. The magazine is free to members of the Federation, a growing organization that is increasingly effective in its efforts to protect trout fisheries and educate anglers. We endorse it wholeheartedly. To join: Federation of Fly Fishers, P.O. Box 1595, Bozeman, MT 59771; or call (406) 585-7592.

REPORTS

The Delaware Estuary Plan, "Discover its Secrets," a draft Comprehensive Conservation and Management Plan for the Delaware Estuary (1994), was prepared under the Water Quality Act Amendments of 1987. For a copy of the entire 300-plus page report or an executive summary, call 1-800-445-

4935 or write to the Delaware Estuary Program, Public Participation Coordinator, c/o Pennsylvania Environmental Council, 1211 Chestnut Street, Suite 900 Philadelphia, PA 19107.

The Delaware Estuary Program has several other valuable publications: "The Delaware Estuary Public Access Guide," 3rd printing, October 1994, is a series of maps showing the location of public access sites, recreational facilities, and historic and cultural sites from Trenton Falls to Cape May; and

"Birding Guide to Cumberland County, N.J.," October 1993, is a comprehensive review of birding in one of New Jersey's least developed counties along Delaware Bay. It was funded in part by the Delaware Estuary Program, with the support of County resources.

A new publication of the Division of Fish, Game and Wildlife is "Inventory of New Jersey Lakes and Ponds" (Vol. 1, No. 1). The first volume covers twelve public lakes, including Amwell Lake, Hunterdon County; Colliers Mill Pond, Ocean County; Furnace Lake and Merrill Creek Reservoir, Warren County; Union Lake, Cumberland County; and Wilson Lake, Gloucester County. It reports on fish populations, water depths, and water quality. To order, send a $3 check, payable to "New Jersey Division of Fish, Game and Wildlife," to Lake Inventories, New Jersey Division of Fish, Game and Wildlife Bureau of Freshwater Fisheries, Box 394, Lebanon, NJ 08833.

DELAWARE RIVER FISHING GUIDES

J. B. Kasper, 400 Hillside Avenue, Morrisville, PA 19067; (215) 295-1502. Kasper, who writes for the *Fisherman* magazine, guides Delaware River anglers for smallmouth, largemouth, stripers, shad, walleye, and crappie. He'll also take you for New Jersey trout and Pine Barrens pickerel, as well as on one- and two-day float trips on the Delaware.

John Brylinski, Muskie Daze Guide Service, P.O. Box 160, Layton, NJ 07851; (201) 948-4724.

Anthony Ritter, Gone Fishing Guide Service, Narrowsburg, NY 12764; (914) 252-3657 or (212) 866-6398. A New York state-licensed guide, Ritter has McKenzie drift boat trips, full and half-day, down the Delaware for trout, smallmouth bass, and walleye.

Michael Padua, Sweetwater Guide Service, Narrowsburg, NY; (914) 252-3439.

Bill Fraser, Upper Delaware Outfitters, Box 1, Hankins, NY 12741; (914) 887-4853.

Big River Charters: Rich Hanson & Sons, Box 103, Columbia, NJ 07832; (800) 362-0433 or (908) 496-4688. Shad, muskie, walleye, stripers.

Ray "Peewee" Serfass, full and half-day trips for smallmouths, muskie, walleye, channel catfish, shad. P.O. Box 194 Heath Lane, Pocono Summit, PA 18346; (717) 839-7736.

MAPS

The Delaware River Basin Commission has a set of recreational maps on coated paper for the 200-mile, nontidal stretch of the river from Hancock, N.Y., to Trenton, N.J. There are 10 maps in all, and they show river depths, channels, and the International Canoe Federation's Scale of River Difficulty. They even come in a waterproof, zipper-lock bag. Cost: $10 per set. Send a check or money order, made out to the DRBC, to the Commission at P.O. Box 7360, West Trenton, NJ 08628. (The DRBC also offers a set of Schuylkill River recreational maps, from Tamaqua Dam to the Fairmount Dam in Philadelphia, for $8.)

Good county maps of all the areas covered by this book are published by Alfred B. Patton, Inc., Swamp Road (Route 313) and Center Streets, P.O. Box 857, Doylestown, PA 18901-0857. Call (215) 345-0700 for a free map catalog.

Lake Survey Fishing Maps Guide, a Fishing Guide for All Seasons, published by Comtech Lithographics, Inc., P.O. Box 536, 7300 Route 130 North, Building 20, Pennsauken, NJ 08110; (609) 665-8350.

Discovering and Exploring New Jersey's Fishing Streams and the Delaware River, Comtech Lithographics (see above).

Complete New Jersey Trout Waters: A Guide for Trout Anglers, published by Gogal Publishing and Alfred B. Patton, Inc. ($6.95)

BOOKS

"Some of the best fishing to be found anywhere is to be found in print."
—ARNOLD GINGRICH, *The Joys of Trout*

Books by Women

Women are entering the sport of angling in large numbers. Although women authors write from a woman's perspective, much of what they say is equally useful for men. It should be noted that the first book in English about fly-fishing, published in the fifteenth century, is credited to a woman!

Berners, Dame Juliana. *A Treatise on Fishing with a Hook*, translated by William Van Wyck (North River Press, 1979, orig. 1496).

Beck, Cathy. *Cathy Beck's Fly-fishing Handbook* (Lyons and Burford, 1996).

Wulff, Joan. *Joan Wulff's Fly-casting Techniques* (Lyons and Burford, 1987).

Wulff, Joan. *Fly-fishing Expert Advice from a Woman's Perspective* (Stackpole, 1991).

Pennsylvania Angling

The Keystone State is blessed with some of the finest trout streams in the country, three noble rivers, the upper part of a saltwater bay, and access to one of the Great Lakes. It is not surprising that writers have found it a muse with inexhaustable charm. These books will help you find your way into the Pennsylvania literature.

Guide to Public Fishing Waters and Boating Access in Pennsylvania (Harrisburg: Pennsylvania Fish and Boat Commission, 1993).

Fox, Charles. *The Wonderful World of Trout* (Freshet Press, 1971, revised edition).

Kasper, J. B. *The Delaware River and Its Fisheries* (Gogal Publishing Co.).

Kasper, J. B. *The Delaware River Fishing and Structure Map Set* (Gogal Publishing Co.).

Landis, Dwight. *Trout Streams of Pennsylvania: An Angler's Guide* (Hempstead-Lyndell, 1991).

Meck, Charles. *Pennsylvania Trout Streams and Their Hatches* (Backcountry Publications, 1989).

Sajna, Mike. *Pennsylvania Trout & Salmon Fishing Guide* (Frank Amato Publications, 1988).

Angling in New Jersey

With the Atlantic on its east coast, the Delaware River and Bay on the west, and smaller streams in the north, New Jersey has a great deal to offer the angler. Here are some books that we have found helpful.

Dale, Frank. *Delaware Diary: Episodes in the Life of a River* (Rutgers University Press, 1996).

Luftglass, Manny. *Gone Fishin' in Spruce Run Reservoir* (Luftglass, Box 280, Somerville, NJ 08876, 1995).

New Jersey Department of Environmental Protection. *Guide to New Jersey's Wildlife Management Areas* (Division of Fish, Game and Wildlife, revised periodically).

New Jersey Department of Environmental Protection. *A Guide to Health*

Advisories for Eating Fish and Crabs Caught in New Jersey Waters (Division of Science and Research, revised periodically).

How-to Books

Introductory books on fishing are like apples: a new crop appears annually. Check the most recent to learn about the latest developments in lures, lines, and rods. Here are a few we have found to be of lasting value.

Humphreys, Joe. *Joe Humphreys' Trout Tactics, Updated and Expanded* (Stackpole Books, 1993).

Rosenbauer, Tom. *The Orvis Fly-fishing Guide* (Lyons & Burford, 1988).

Rosenbauer, Tom. *Prospecting for Trout* (Delta, 1993).

McClane, A. J. *McClane's New Standard Fishing Encyclopedia and International Fishing Guide* (Holt, Rinehart Winston, 1977).

How-to in Salt Water

Barrett, Pete. *Saltwater Fishing Guide* (Fisherman Library).

Caputi, Gary. *Fishing for Striped Bass* (Fisherman Library).

Kamienski, Don. *Fishing for Fluke* (Fisherman Library).

Venturo, Captain Greg. *How to Fish Wrecks, Lumps and Rockpiles* (Fisherman Library). The address of the Fisherman Library is The Fisherman, 1620 Beaver Dam Road, Point Pleasant, NJ 08742; (800) 553-4745.

Kreh, Lefty. *Fly Fishing in Salt Water* (Lyons & Burford, 1988).

Kumiski, Captain John. *Saltwater Fly Fishing* (Fisherman Library).

Lyman, Henry. *Bluefishing* (Lyons & Burford, 1987).

Tabory, Lou. *Inshore Fly Fishing* (Lyons & Burford).

History, Ethics, Conservation, and Tradition

Fishing has a tradition and literature that rivals, and perhaps surpasses, that of any other sport, including baseball. For some writers it is an escape, for others a technical exercise, and for a few it is a drama, a metaphor for life. In this brief list we have tried to include some of the best contemporary work as well as an introduction to the classics. If you can't find a specific title in your bookstore or library, almost any book written or edited by Ernest Schwiebert, Nick Lyons, John Merwin, Joe Brooks, or John Gierach will occupy an evening if you absolutely must stay indoors.

Brooks, Joe. *Trout Fishing* (Harper & Row, An Outdoor Life Book, 1972).

Cordes, Ron. *Pocket Fly Fishing Guide* (Greycliff Publishing, 1992).

Gierach, John. *Another Lousy Day in Paradise* (Simon & Schuster, 1996).

Haig-Brown, Roderick L. *A River Never Sleeps* (Crown Publishers, 1974).

Hersey, John. *Blues* (Alfred A. Knopf, 1987).

Leeson, Ted. *The Habit of Rivers* (Lyons & Burford, 1994).

Lyons, Nick. *The Seasonable Angler* (Funk & Wagnalls, 1970).

Maclean, Norman. *A River Runs through It and Other Stories* (University of Chicago Press, 1976).

Merwin, John. *New American Trout Fishing* (Macmillan, 1993)

Montgomery, M. R. *The Way of the Trout* (Avon, 1991).

Oplinger, Carl S. and Robert Halma. *Poconos: An Illustrated Natural History Guide* (Rutgers University Press, 1988).

Schullery, Paul. *American Fly Fishing* (Lyons & Burford, 1992).

Schwiebert, Ernest. *Death of a Riverkeeper* (Dutton, 1980).

Traver, Robert. *Trout Magic* (Crown, 1974).

Walton, Izaak. *The Compleat Angler, or the Contemplative Man's Recreation,* illustrated by Arthur Rackham (Weathervane Books, 1975).

Walton, Izaak and Charles Cotton. *The Compeat Angler,* edited by John Ruxton, introduction by John Buchan (Oxford World's Classics, 1982).

Wright, Leonard M., Jr. *The Fly Fisher's Reader* (Simon & Schuster, A Fireside Book, 1990).

Books about What to Do with Your Catch (besides releasing it)

Among the vast library of fish cookbooks are these:

The Grand Central Oyster Bar and Restaurant Cookbook, Crown (1977).

The Encyclopedia of Fish Cookery, A.J. McClane, Holt, Rinehart Winston (1977).

Howard Mitchum's Seafood Cookbook

Fish & Shellfish, James Peterson (Morrow).

BOOKLETS

Return of a Native: Shad in the Lehigh River, a fifty-two-page booklet written by Dennis Scholl, president of the Delaware River Shad Fishermen's Association. Send a check for $5.75, made out to DRSFA, to 502 Magnolia Road, Hellertown, PA 18055. Proceeds benefit the association.

ANGLING IN CYBERSPACE

There is a growing number of Websites devoted to fishing. Like most Websites, they vary in quality, and many—including the official state sites—

are not updated often enough. With these caveats, here are some we've encountered:

The Pennsylvania Fish and Boat Commission has a Website at **http://www.state.pa.us/fish**

New Jersey says it has some 4,100 freshwater ponds, lakes, and reservoirs of one acre in size or greater. The problem: much of it is on private property. The state has a Website listing the public access areas, the nearest town, acreage of the fishing area, and whether there are boat ramps and outboards are allowed. It's all there, by county, just by clicking on **http://state.nj.us/dep/fgw**. The Pennsylvania Fly Fishing home page is **http://www.easetech.com/pafish** Click on map of Pennsylvania for NOAA weather reports.

Trout Unlimited's Web Page is **http://www.tu.org/trout/**

Online Sportsman is a free publication for Internet users interested in hunting and fishing. Its URL: **http://www.onlinesportsman.com**

Anglers Online, The Fishing Yellow Pages, has everything from ice fishing to fly-fishing dealers: **http://www.streamside.com/index.html**

Daiwa's Home Page: **http://www.daiwa.com/**

Bass Pro Shops' Outdoor World Online: **http://www.basspro.com/**

New Jersey Division of Fish, Game & Wildlife: **http://www.state.nj/us/dep.fgwweb/htm/welcome.htm**

Delaware River Shad Fishermen's Association: **http://mgfx.com/drsfa**

Map of Delaware River Boat Launch Sites for New Jersey, Pennsylvania, and New York: **http://mgfx.com/fishing/regions/delaware/articles/delmap.htm**

Delaware River Home Page: **http://mgfx.com/fishing/regions/delaware/index.htm**

The New Jersey Pineland Commission has a home page: **http://www.state/nj.us/pinelands**

For shore tide tables, consult *The Press* of Atlantic City at **http://www.pressplus.com**

RADIO AND TELEVISION

"Delaware Valley Outdoors" can be seen on a number of cable channels in Bucks, Montgomery, and Philadelphia Counties, including Suburban, Bridge, Lower Bucks, Comcast, and Adelphia cable systems. It is hosted by Bob Murray.

VIDEOS

The quality of how-to-fish videos varies enormously. We have seen some real clunkers that nonfishing friends and relatives have given us as gifts. Here are a few we especially like:

"Fly Fishing Made Easy" (Scientific Anglers, 3M, 1993) is an excellent introduction to the sport, with tips for bass, panfish, and trout.

"Billy Pate's Saltwater Fly Casting" (1994) is part of the "Hooked on Fly Fishing" series. If you are considering getting into the fast-growing sport of saltwater fly-fishing, this is the one video to buy.

"Joe Humphreys' Nymphing Tactics" (1996).

The Fisherman Library also offers videos, including "Fluke Fishing" with Captain Al Lorenzetti, a 90-minute VHS tape that costs $29.95, and "Fluke Fishing: Improving Your Catch," with Don Kamienski, a 50-minute VHS tape for the same price. We haven't had the opportunity to view these videos, but if they are comparable in quality to the Fisherman books (see above), they should be worthwhile.

ORGANIZATIONS

If you are serious about fishing and environmental issues, you should belong to the righteous organizations that represent your interests. Here are some of them:

American Littoral Society

American Littoral Society, Sandy Hook, Highlands, NJ 07732; (908) 291-0055. The ALS needs the support of every serious fisher. This dedicated group works on behalf of wetland protection, water quality of estuaries and coastal waters, and coastal wildlife habitat. The Society also sponsors a number of fun field trips and even a Maryland crab feast. Dery W. Bennett is its tireless executive director. Individual membership (includes family) is $25 a year.

An important affiliate of the ALS is the Watershed Association of the Delaware River and the Delaware Riverkeeper Network. For information contact Riverkeeper, P.O. Box 753, Lambertville, NJ 08530; (609) 397-4410.

Delaware River Shad Fisherman's Association

Anyone who fishes for shad on the Delaware should belong to this organization, founded in 1974 and "dedicated to the preservation of the

American shad and the Delaware River." Membership starts as low as $5 a year. Meetings are held on the third Wednesday of each month (excluding July, August, and December) at the Se-We-Co Fire Company Social Hall on Route 378 in Lower Saucon Township, north of Easton, Pa. President: Dennis Scholl. Shad Hot-Line for up-to-date information during the season: (610) 954-0577 or (610) 954-0578.

Trout Unlimited

The organization describes itself this way: "Trout Unlimited's mission is to conserve, protect and restore North America's trout and salmon fisheries and their watersheds." When you join the national, you are enrolled in the chapter nearest you. This is the pre-eminent national organization for anglers. They publish *Trout,* a quarterly.

Trout Unlimited, 1500 Wilson Boulevard, Suite 310, Arlington, VA 22209-2404.

Federation of Fly Fishers

The Federation, like Trout Unlimited, is dedicated to conservation, restoration, and education, specifically through the sport of fly fishing. Throughout the United States, there are Councils that support the organization and its goals. The Federation publishes a quarterly, *Flyfisher.*

Federation of Fly Fishers, P.O. Box 1595, Bozeman, MT 59771.

American Birding Association

An organization for active birders. Its mission is "to bring all the excitement, challenge, and wonder of birding to you." Their regional guides are specific, accurate, and indispensable for birders.

American Birding Association, P.O. Box 6599, Colorado Springs, CO 80934.

The National Audubon Society

The society has a system of sanctuaries, a network of local clubs in many states, and an elegant headquarters in New York City that was designed to demonstrate environmentally friendly urban architecture. Their extensive publication program includes *Audubon* magazine and a newsjournal, *Audubon Activist.*

The National Audubon Society, 700 Broadway, New York, NY 10003.

South Jersey Fly Fishers

South Jersey Fly Fishers, P.O. Box 95, Salem, NJ 08079; (609) 935-0020. Individual membership—$25 annually, plus a one-time "joining fee" of $10 for new members. Membership includes a monthly newsletter. Family membership is $35 a year.

New Jersey Conservation Foundation

The Nature Conservancy—Pennsylvania and New Jersey
New Jersey Field Office, Elizabeth D. Kay Environmental Center, 200 Pottersville Road, Chester, NJ 07930.

In recent years the Nature Conservancy has acquired some 4,200 acres of pinelands in Burlington and Ocean counties, and expanded the Gandy Beach Preserve and Manumuskin Preserve in Cumberland County. This organization deserves our generous support. The Nature Conservancy Delaware Bayshores Office, (609) 785-1735.

The New Jersey Beach Buggy Association

Membership Secretary, P.O. Box 186, Collingswood, NJ 08108.

Recreational Fishing Alliance

This relatively new organization aims at becoming for saltwater fishers and private boat owners what the National Rifle Association is for hunters and gun enthusiasts. Big commercial fish operations are wary of this group, but the RFA asserts that it is not against commercial fishing per se. Membership is $25 for one year, $60 for three years.

Recreational Fishing Alliance, P.O. Box 308, New Gretna, NJ 08224; (888) SAVE FISH.

The Friends of the Wissahickon

This is an organization of people "concerned for the preservation and restoration of the Wissahickon portion of Fairmount Park and its protection through balanced use."

The Friends of the Wissahickon, 8708 Germantown Avenue, Philadelphia, PA 19118-2717; (215) 247-0417.

New Jersey Federation of Sportsmen's Clubs, Inc.

With 150,000 members, the Federation represents the Garden State's hunters and fishers. A $25 membership includes a monthly newsletter and insurance. Information: NJFSC, P.O. Box 751, Chester, NJ 07930-0751.

Estuary Action Group for a Lasting Environment (EAGLE)

This conservation organization was formed recently to protect the Delaware estuary of Salem, Cumberland, and Cape May counties. Membership is $5 and $2 for students. EAGLE can be reached at (609) 455-1257.

South Jersey Fly Fishers

These folks meet at the Salem County Sportsman's Club, Route 40, Carney's Point. For information, (609) 339-4465.

RIVER ACCESS

The Delaware River Basin Commission has a list of all river access areas from Balls Eddy, Pa., to Trenton, N.J. It is available by writing to the commission at its headquarters, P.O. Box 7360, West Trenton, NJ 08628.

The Pennsylvania Fish & Boat Commission publishes a handy, one-page map of all the public boat launch sites on the Delaware, from Balls Eddy in Wayne County to the Commodore Barry Bridge in Chester.

The handout also gives the distances between sites and offers tips on how and where to catch fish. (Examples: "For walleye and muskie, try the big hole at Narrowsburg. . . . [In Philadelphia] striper action starts in May, peaks in early July with the mouths of Pennypack Creek and Poquessing Creek hotspots.") The map also shows the location of nine public launch sites on the New Jersey side of the river, from Worthington to Mercer County.

Write to the commission at P.O. Box 67000, Harrisburg, PA 17106-7000.

Also, the Fish Commission provides newspapers with drawings to help anglers recognize the difference in brook, rainbow, brown, and palomino trout stocked in the Commonwealth's waterways.

INFORMATION ON FRESHWATER LICENSES

New Jersey (1997)

Seniors—Persons 70 years of age and older may purchase a lifetime fishing license for a one-time processing fee of $2. Contact the Trenton office of the Division of Fish, Game & Wildlife at (609) 984-0547.

Licenses are valid from purchase to Dec. 31 of each year.

Resident Family Fishing-Parents—$27.50

Supplementary, each child 14–18—$2.25
Resident—$16.50
Junior-Senior Resident (ages 14, 15 and 65–69)—$7.75
Resident Trout Stamp—$7.75
Nonresident Trout Stamp—$15.50
Nonresident or Vacation Fishing (7 days)—$16.50

Garden State licenses are required *upstream* of each of the following locations:

Cape May County

—East Creek: 100 feet below East Creek Dam in Eldora
—Tuckahoe River: first northerly tributary downstream of lower Route 49 Bridge (McNeals Bridge)
—West Creek: 100 feet below West Creek Lake Dam (at Pickle Factory Pond)

Cumberland County

—Cedar Creek: 100 feet downstream of Cedar Creek Dam
—Cohansey River: Route 49 Bridge at Bridgeton
—Dividing Creek: Route 555 Bridge
—Maurice River: Mouth of Manumuskin Creek, near Port Elizabeth
—Mill Creek: Tributary of Cohansey—Route 553 Bridge at Fairton
—Muskee Creek: South side of bridge on Weathersby Road
—Nantuxent Creek (Pages Run): Route 553, north of Frames Corner
—Oranoken Creek: Whitecar Mill, north of Beaver Dam
—Riggins Ditch: Route 47
—Stow Creek: Buckhorn Road Bridge, Jericho

Salem County (none required for Delaware River)

—Alloway Creek: Route 5409 Bridge at Alloway
—Oldmans Creek: Route 1-295, Southbound Bridge
—Salem River: DuPont Dam near Cedar Crest Manor
—Salem Canal: Dam at Deepwater

Gloucester County

—Big Timber Creek: whole length
—Delaware River: Commodore Barry Bridge at Bridgeport

—Mantua Creek: whole length
—Raccoon Creek: whole length
—Woodbury Creek: whole length

Camden County

Licenses are required on the Delaware River and on all other waters.

Burlington County

—Bass River: Fir Bridge on Stage Road in Bass River State Forest
—Batsto River: entire length
—Blacks Creek: entire length
—Delaware River: entire length
—Mullica River: Line between 7th Avenue in Sweetwater and the ramp at Crowleys Landing
—Pennsauken Creek: entire length
—Pompeston Creek: entire length
—Rancocas Creek: entire length
—Swedes Run: entire length
—Wading River: Charcoal Landing, Chips Folly Campground

Atlantic County

—Absecon Creek: Dam at Lower Atlantic City Reservoir
—Great Egg Harbor River: Power lines at confluence of Gravelly Run near Mays Landing
—Nacote Creek: Port Republic Dam
—Patcong Creek: Bargaintown Lake Dam
—South River: Power lines immediately below Route 50

Pennsylvania (1997)

Licenses are valid from January 1 to December 31 of each year. They are available at more than 1,700 licensing agents, at the offices of county treasurers, and at regional offices of the Pennsylvania Fish and Boat Commission.

Resident (16–64) $16.25, plus .75 issuing agent fee
Senior Resident (65-up) $3.25, plus .75
Senior Resident LIFETIME (65-up) $15.25, plus .75
Nonresident (16-up) $34.25, plus .75
Seven-Day Tourist (16-up) $29.25, plus .75

Three-Day Tourist (16-up) $14.25, plus .75
Trout/Salmon Permit (16-up) $5, plus .50

Boundaries

—A Pennsylvania and New York license is valid in the Delaware
River, including the West Branch, between New York and Pennsylvania when you are fishing from a boat or from either shore. In
other words, if you have a Pennsylvania license, you may cross the
bridge at Hancock, New York, wade into the Delaware to fish, and
not worry about a citation.

—A Pennsylvania or New Jersey license is valid in the Delaware
River between New Jersey and Pennsylvania when fishing from a
boat or from either shore. In other words, if you have a valid New
Jersey fishing license, you may cross the iron bridge at Bull's Island
State Park, walk up the river at Lumberville, Pa., and legally fish.

Index

Absecon, N.J., 200–02
Absecon Creek, N.J., 200–01
Absecon Highlands, N.J., 149
Absecon Inlet, N.J., 196, 200
Access Areas: information on, 232
Akens Pool, N.Y., 19
Alcyon Lake, N.J., 147
Alder Marsh Brook, Pa., 39
Allentown, Pa., 92, 94, 97; Allentown City
   Park system, 92; Little Lehigh Creek at, 86;
   The Morning Call (newspaper), 94
Alloways Creek, N.J., 158
Alpine Mountain, Pa., 84
Ambler, Pa., 108
American Littoral Society, 166
Analomink, Pa., 84–85
Anecdotes and stories: Ingram, George H.
   Jr., 9, 23, 32–33, 36–37, 37–38, 40, 42, 45–
   46, 55–56, 58, 66–67, 88–89, 97, 98–99,
   125–26, 126–27, 134, 143, 143–44, 144,
   149–50, 160–61, 161–62, 163, 164, 169,
   172, 175–76, 178, 183–84, 184–85, 187–
   88, 193–94, 194–95, 197, 200, 201, 204;
   Marler, Robert F. Jr., 11–12, 22–23, 26–
   27, 32, 43–44, 47–48, 48–49, 50–51, 62–
   63, 81–83; Smith, Robert R., 80–81, 94,
   99–100, 104–105, 113, 117, 179–80
Annual Kids' All American Fishing Derby,
   N.Y., 20
Antique Dealers' Association, 69
Antiques, Pa., 67–69, 110; Castle Antiques
   and Reproductions, 68–69; Country Clas-
   sics, 68
Appalachian Trail, 79–80; Appalachian Trail
   Conference, Inc., 80; *Appalachian Trail
   Guide*, 80
Ashokan Reservoir, N.Y., 29
Assumpink Wildlife Management Area, N.J.,
   135–36
Atlantic City, N.J., 195–99; casino gambling,
   195–96; vehicle access to beaches, 173
Atlantic City Reservoir, N.J., 138
Atlantic County, N.J., 148–52, 190–204; park
   system, 150
Atlantic Electric, 191
Auburn, Pa.: Tulpehocken Creek, 106
Audubon, Pa., 109

Audubon Society, 12
Avalon, N.J., 180–81; Avalon Fishing Center,
   181; vehicle access to beaches, 173
Axelsson and Johnson Fish Market, N.J., 178

B.L. England Generating Plant, N.J., 191
B.P. Exploration and Oil, Inc., 3
Bach Festival, Bethlehem, Pa., 93
Balls Eddy access, Pa., 21–23, 26
Bargaintown, N.J., 192
Barryville, N.Y., 73–74
Bars. *See* Dining and Lodging
Basket Creek, Pa., 35
Bath, Pa., 97
Batsto, N.J., 145
Batsto Lake, N.J., 138
Batsto River, N.J., 145, 148
Batsto Village, N.J., 145
Battle of Trenton: re-enactment of, 135
Bauer's Fishing Pond, N.J., 156
Beasleys Point Bridge, N.J., 190–91
Beaverkill River, N.Y., 18–21, 29, 84
Beaver Run, Pa., 114
Bed and Breakfasts. *See* Dining and Lodging
Belleplain, N.J., 156–57
Belleplain State Forest, N.J., 156–57; mobile
   sportfishing permit, 186
Belvidere, N.J., 121
Berks County, Pa., 108, 116–17
Bethany, Pa., 56
Bethlehem, Pa., 93, 96–97; Shad Festival, 93
Big Bushkill Creek, (Monroe County), Pa.,
   73, 76–77; *See* Bushkill Creek
Big Flat Brook, N.J., 120–21; and Blewett
   Tract, 121; lower stream access, 121
Big Timber Creek, N.J., 138
Biking, 112, 124, 150; *Biking for Bugs*, 150
Birch Grove Park, N.J., 149–50
Birch Run, Pa., 114
Birding, 12, 101, 103–05, 108–10, 112–13,
   151, 195, 202; binoculars for, 12; in Birch
   Grove Park, N.J., 149–50; in Cape May,
   N.J., 179–80; Christmas Day Bird Count,
   179; Delaware Valley Ornithological Club,
   Pa., 179; guides for, 12; in Philadelphia's
   Carpenter's Woods, 108
Birding the Delaware Valley Region, 13

Birds of North America, 12
Blakeslee, Pa., 90
Blewett Tract, N.J.: year-round fly-rod fishing in, 121
Blooming Grove Trout Hatchery, Pa., 70
Blue Marsh Lake, Pa., 116–17; bass fishing, 117; dam, 116
Boats: canoe's value, 10; at Delaware Water Gap, 78; necessity of, 9–10; public launch sites, 232; rental boats at Corson's Inlet, N.J., 183; rental boats for crabbing, 210; on Upper Woods Pond, Pa., 39, winter head boats, 205; *See* Party boats
Brandywine Creek, Pa., 114–15
Breweries. *See* Wineries and Breweries
Bridges, historic: Brooklyn Bridge, 60, 64–65; Delaware Aqueduct, 65; oldest existing wire suspension bridge, 65
Brielle, N.J.: winter head boats, 205
Brigantine, N.J., 199–200; vehicle access to beaches, 173
Brigantine Bridge, N.J., 200
Bristol, Pa., 23, 95
Brodhead Creek, Pa., 8, 82–88
Bryn Athyn, Pa., 103
Buckingham, Pa., 21, 31
Bucks County, Pa., 97–102
Bulls Island, N.J., 9
Bulls Island State Park, N.J., 98, 125–27; and Delaware-Raritan Canal, 131
Burlington City, N.J., 139–40
Burlington County, N.J.: 138–47, 204–07
Burlington County Historical Society, N.J., 140
Bushkill, Pa., 76–78
Bushkill Creek(s), Pa., 8, 73; *See* Little Bushkill and Big Bushkill
Bushkill Falls, Pa., 77
Butler Park, N.J., 123
Butternut Creek, Pa., 8, 72
Byram, N.J., 125–26

Cabin Run Creek, Pa., 101–02
Callicoon, Pa., 31, 35–36
Callicoon, N.Y., 35, 59
Callicoon Bridge, N.Y., 36
Callicoon Creek, N.Y., 36
Camden County, N.J., 145–46
Camelback Mountain, Pa., 86
Camp Dark Waters, N.J., 139
Camp Inawendiwin (Girl Scout's Camp), N.J., 142
Canadensis, Pa., 81–85, 87–88
Canals, 65, 95
Cannonsville Reservoir, N.Y., 15, 21
Canoes. *See* Boats
Cape May, N.J., 175; ferry to Lewes, De., 178–79; lighthouse, 179

Cape May Bird Observatory, N.J., 179
Cape May County, N.J., 151, 155–57, 174–190, 191
Cape May County Park & Zoo, N.J., 156, 178
Cape May Court House, N.J., 156, 180
Capoolong Creek Wildlife Management Area, N.J., 133
Captain Andy's Marina, N.J., 193–94
Carversville, Pa., 98
Catskill Mountains, N.Y., 29, 84
Catskill Park, N.Y., 29
Cedar Lake Park, N.J., 153
Center Point Golf Club, Pa., 110
Central Perkiomen Valley Park, Pa., 109
Chatsworth, N.J., 143
Chester County, Pa., 113–16
Chestnut Hill area, Philadelphia, Pa., 107
Chestnut Neck Boat Yard, N.J., 202–04
Children, places to go with: Batsto Village, N.J., 145; Bauer's Fishing Pond, N.J., 156; Belleplain State Forest, N.J., 156–57; *Biking for Bugs*, 150; Birch Grove Park, N.J., 149–150; C. F. Martin and Company, N.J., 96; Cooper River Park, N.J., 145; and fishing, 10; Sand Castle Playground, N.J., 190; *See* Festivals; Lighthouses; Museums and Historic Places; Zoos
Christmas Factory, Pa., 86
Cinnaminson, N.J., 129
Circle Liquors, N.J., 191
Clarks Pond Wildlife Area, N.J., 153
Claws 'N' Paws Wild Animal Park, Pa., 67–68
Clearwater Seafood Store, Pa., 53
Clinton, N.J., 10, 133
Coastal Eagle Point Oil Company, 3
Cocheton, N.Y., 35–38, 59
Cohansey River, N.J., 159
Cohanzick Zoo, N.J., 155
Cold Spring(s), Pa., 22, 39–41, 43, 49
Collegeville, Pa., 109–10
Collins Cove, N.J., 203–04
Colonial Mansion: historical site in Ridley Creek State Park, Pa., 112
Commercial Township, N.J., 163
Concrete Ship (*s.s. Atlantus*), N.J., 176–77, 179
Conshohocken, Pa., 106, 111
Conte's Market, N.J., 142
Coolbaugh Township, Pa., 89
Cooper, James Fenimore: house and writings, 139–40
Cooper River, N.J., 138, 145–46; Park, 145
Corson's Inlet, N.J., 120; State Park, 182–88
Country Classics: antique shop in Hawley, Pa., 68
Crabbing: Absecon, N.J., 210; Atlantic County, N.J., 209–10; books and information,

213–14; Bucks County, Pa., 208; Cape May County, N.J., 210; Chestnut Neck Boatyard, N.J., 210; Delaware River, 208; health caution, 210; how-to, 208–09; licenses, 209; live crabs to buy, 164; McGettigan's 19th Hole, N.J., 210; Mullica River, N.J., 209–10; Newport Landing Marina, N.J., 162; Smithville, N.J., 209; where to go, 209–10; White Horse Pike, N.J., 210; Wildwoods, N.J., 210
Crabhouses: New Jersey, 213; Philadelphia, 212–13
Cranberry Lake, N.J.: stocked northern pike, 121
Crescent Lake, N.J., 150
Cruises: sunset, 159
Cumberland County, N.J., 152–55
Cumberland Pond, N.J., 153–54
Cyberspace: angling in, 228

Damascus, Pa., 35–38, 59
Dams: New York, 15
Darby Creek, Pa., 8, 105
David R. Douglas Park, N.J., 177
Day's Bakery, Pa., 54
Deckers Eddy, Pa., 19
DeLargy, Chef Chuck, 120–30
Delaware and Hudson Canal, Pa., 65
Delaware and Hudson Canal Company, 55
The Delaware and Its Fisheries, 59
Delaware and Raritan Canal: at Bull's Island, N.J. 131, 134
Delaware Aqueduct, Pa. and N.Y., 65
Delaware Bay, N.J., 22, 154, 158–64, 169, 174, 176–79; Nature Conservancy office at Delaware Bayshore, 180
Delaware Canal, Pa., 95–96
Delaware County, Pa., 111–13
Delaware Delicacies Smoke House, N.Y., 27–28, 30
Delaware River: autumn fishing, 9; best river fishing, 119; and Brodhead Creek at East Stroudsburg, Pa., 84–85; Buckingham, Pa., access, 21; Callicoon, Pa. and Cohecton, N.Y., 36; Damascus, Pa., access, 21; East Branch, 27–31; East and West Branches, 3, 15, 19; East and West Branch junction at Junction Pool, 26–28; 121; at Easton, Pa., 95; Equinunk, Pa., 32–34; and fishing guides, 56–57, 68, 223–24; insects, 24; Kingwood, N.J., access, 124; and Lackawaxen River, 59–60, 66; from Lackawaxen to the Two Bushkill Creeks, 73–78; at the Lehigh River for shad, 94; at Long Eddy, 35; at Narrowsburg, N.Y. and along N.Y. Route 97, 59; Philadelphia Airport Area, 104; and Poconos, Pa. area, 58; reports

and guides, 222–24; and Shehawken, Pa., access, 25–26; and Sussex County, N.J., access, 120; toxic discharges, 3; Upper Delaware, 24, 97; water conditions hot-line, 19; watershed, 3; West Branch, 18–21; West Branch, main stem, 14
The Delaware River, 76
Delaware River Basin Commission, Pa., 28–29: river access areas, 232; website, 217
Delaware River Shad Fishermen's Association, Pa., 93
Delaware Riverkeeper Network, N.J., 138
Delaware State Forest, Pa., 72, 76, 84
Delaware Valley: triangle defined, 3
Delaware Valley College, Pa., 100
Delaware Valley Ornithological Club, Pa., 179
Delaware Water Gap, 15, 78–81, 85, 86
Delaware Water Gap National Recreational Area, 74, 76, 78–80; camping, 79; housing, 79–80; Information Center, 78–79; Van Campens Brook, 122
Delco Anglers, N.J., 112
Delran Township, N.J., 140
Dennisville Lake, N.J., 155
Department of Environmental Resources, Pa., 100
Depew Island, 78
Deposit, N.Y., 18–20
Depue Island, 78
Dingman's Creek, Pa., 8
Dingman's Falls, Pa., 81
Dingman's Ferry, Pa., 76
Dining and Lodging: Airport Diner, 189; Al's Bait House, 162; Allen's Clam Bar, 204–05; The American Grill, 98; The Anchorage, 191; Angelo's Fairmount Tavern, 199; Angler's Roost and Hunter's Rest, 61; The Apple Jack Bar, 98–99; Autumn Inn, 36; Axelsson's Blue Claw, 177–78; Baimondo's Ristorante and Pizzeria, 20; Balconic Cafe, 145; Barley Creek Brewing Company Restaurant, 86; Barryville Hotel, 74; Bateman's Live Crabs, 164; Beaverkill Valley Inn, 20; Benjamin's, 154; Best Western Inn (Pond Eddy), 74; Black Bass Hotel, 98, 125, 129–30; Black Cat Bar, 200; Braca Cafe, 182; Brass Rail, 94; Brownies, 191–92; The Buck, 151–52; The Cafe at Rosemont, 131; Carmen's Seafood Restaurant, 182; Carole's Bar, 22–23; Carverville Inn, 98; Cascades Restaurant, 69, 97; Cavallo's Country House, 96; CC's Cafe, 69; Cedar Creek Brewery and Restaurant, 149; Centre Bridge Inn, 98, 127; Chadds Ford Inn, 115; Champs Sports Bar, 110; Cheers Bar, 36–37; Chef Vola's, 199; Chet's, 151; Cisco's

Bar, 108; Club 97, 36; Cock 'n Bull Restaurant, 129; Corbin Cafe, 152; Corbin House, 152; Corbin Manor Inn, 152; Cordaro's, 57; Cousin's Country House, 192; Crab Trap, 191; Crabby's, 151; Cuckoo's Nest, 66; The Cuttalosa Inn, 98; De Thomasi's, 152, The Dead Dog Saloon, 182; Deauville Inn, 183–84; Delaware River Club Fly-Fishing Resort, 21; Dilly's Ice Cream, 127; Dilly's Corner, 98; Dilworthtown Inn, 115; Dionysus Restaurant, 157; Ebbitt Room of the Virginia Hotel, 178; Eddies, 141; Edelweiss, 90; Edgewater Restaurant, 74; Ehrhardt's Lakeside Restaurant, 72; Equinunk, Pa., Fire Company Barbecue, 35; Fairfield Inn, 159; Falls Port Restaurant and Hotel, 69; Fife and Drum Motor Inn, 57; The Fireplace Restaurant, 41; Fireside Inn, 38, 48–49; Fisherman's Inn Restaurant, 141; Flat Brook Tap House, 121; Flo's, 141; Flying Cloud Cafe, 199; Forge and Anvil, 131; Forks Inn, 148; Fourth Street Cafe, 190; Francesco's 146–47; French Manor, 90; Frenchtown Inn, 124; Fuji's, 129; Ginger's Country Restaurant, 35; Godfrey Daniel's Coffee House, 93; Grand Cafe, 69; Green Bank Inn, 143–44; Greenman's 199; Gregory's Restaurant, 191; H & H (Jazz Bar) 135; Hallowich Log Cabin, 151; Hankins House, 35; Hatteras Coastal Cuisine, 191; Hazzard's Raintree Restaurant, 91; Higbee's Marina and Restaurant, 160–61; Hot Dog Johnny's, 122; The Inn at Egg Harbor, 148; Inn at Peck's Pond, 73; The Inn at Sugar Hill, 151; The Inn at Woodloch Pines, 73; Jack Trainer's, 57; Kupetz Bar, 152; Lackawaxen House, 66; Lambertville Station, 9; Le Gorille, 74; Lemont's, 188; Lobster House, 175, 177; The Lobster House Fish Market, 177; Log Cabin Hotel and Bar, 19; Longport Inn, 192; Lorenzo's, 135; McGettigan's 19th Hole, 201–02; McGowan's Buckingham Mountain Brewing Co. and Restaurant, 102; McNally's, 108; Macomber Hotel, 178; Mac's, 191; Main Street Beanery, 57; Mangia, 190; Marie's Lobster House, 182; Marriott Seaview, 202; Mayer's Bar, 176; Meil's Restaurant, 128; Mendenhall Inn, 115; Mildred's, 184; Mimi's, 103; Mott's Creek Inn and Frankie's Great Bay Cafe, 202; Mountain House, 79; Myers Marina Restaurant, 162; Narrowsburg Holiday Inn, 59; Narrowsburg Inn, 58–59; National Hotel, 124; Nethercott Inn Bed and Breakfast, 30; New Hedger House, 143; Oak Table, 20; Old Mill Stream,

69; Old River Tavern, 151; Old Waterway Inn, 199; Olver's Bed and Breakfast, 57; Oyster Creek Inn, 202; Patricia's Waterfront Cafe, 162; Peking Duck House, 199; Penn York Bed and Breakfast and Lodging Association, 30; Perna's, 72; Petrizzo's Italian-American Restaurant, 77; Pic-a-lilli Inn, 142–43; Pine Knob Inn 81–84, 87–88; The Pitney Tavern, 202; Ram's Head Inn, 149, 159; Ready's, 190; Reber's Castle Inn, 74; Red Schoolhouse, 38, 41, 56; Riverview Inn, 21, 25; Robert Christian's, 90; Robin Hood Diner, 20; Roebling Inn on the Delaware, 66; Rohman's Inn, 74; Rosemont's Victoria, 132; Rub 'n Grub, 121; Screnci's, 182; The Sea Grill, 181; Seafood Festival: Bridgeton, N.J., 155; Seafood Festival: Atlantic City, N.J., 196; Seafood Festival: Mauricetown, N.J., 154; Sergeantsville Inn, 132; Settler's Inn, 55, 62–63, 69–70; Shellpile Restaurant and Raw Bar, 163; Ship John Inn, 159; Ship's Inn, 124; Skytop Lodge, 87; Smith's Clam Bar, 191; Spring Valley Inn, 93; Starlight Inn, 30; Starlight Lodge, 30; Sterling Inn, 90–91; Stockton Inn, 127; Sunnyside, 189; Sweetwater Casino Restaurant, 148; Tabernacle Inn, 142; Tanglewood Lodge, 71; Ten Mile River Lodge, 59; Tokyo Palace, 191; Townhouse Diner, 57; Triton Bar, 152; Turbine Restaurant, 69; Two Guys From Italy, 57; Union Park Dining Room, 178; Valley Green Inn, 107–08; Vega Grill, 93; The Villa Restaurant, 53; Village Tavern, 142; Vinnie's, 103; Virginia Hotel, Ebbitt Room Restaurant, 178; Washington Inn, 178; The Waterfront, 191; The Wayne Hotel, 54; West Branch Angler and Sportsmen's Resort, 18–19; White Eagle, 140; White House Sub Shop, 199; White Owl Tavern, 66; Wolfe's Pioneer Motel, 59; Woodbine Inn, 141; Woodburn's Clams, 193; Youell's Oyster House, 96
Disabled access: Loch Lomond, Pa., fishing pier, 81
Dismal Run, Pa., 112
Dolfin Dock, N.J., 192
Dorflinger/Suydam Wildlife Sanctuary, Pa., 68
Downsville, N.Y., 28
Doylestown, Pa., 99–102
Drag Island, N.J., 190
Drag Island Channel, N.J., 191
Duck Harbor Pond, Pa., 35, 38
Dulcimers, 113
DuPont Chemical Company, 3
Dyberry, Pa., 23

Dyberry Creek, Pa., 8, 22, 35, 38, 54; East
  Branch, 39, 43; West Branch, 39, 41, 44,
  49, 51, 52; Middle Branch, 40–41; Proper,
  Delayed Harvest, Fly-fishing Only, 41–42
Dyberry Village, Pa., 48, 52

East Branch, Pa., 28
East Creek Lake, N.J., 138
East Creek Pond, N.J., 156
East Greenville, Pa., 108
Easton, Pa., 76, 94–96; Canal Museum, 95;
  dining, 96; junction of the Delaware, Le-
  high & Morris Canals, 95; Morris R. Wil-
  liams Center for the Arts, 94; State The-
  atre, 94
Easton Dam, Pa., 94
East Stroudsburg, Pa., 84–86; The Gorge, 85
East Stroudsburg State University, Pa., 85
Edward G. Bevan Wildlife Management Area,
  N.J., 152–53
Edwin B. Forsythe National Wildlife Refuge,
  N.J., 202
Eels, 15, 42–43
Egg Harbor, N.J., 148–49
Egg Harbor Lake, N.J., 148
Egg Harbor Township, N.J., 190
Elk Mountain, Pa., 30
Ellis Pond, N.J., 153
Emilio Carranza Memorial, N.J., 142
Environmental and fishing organizations,
  229–32
Environmental Protection Agency (EPA),
  100, 137
Equinunk, Pa., 22–23, 31
Equinunk Creek, Pa., 33–34
Erie Canal, Pa., 95
Estell Glass Works, N.J., 150
Evansburg State Park, Pa., 109–10

Fairmount Park, Philadelphia, Pa., 107
Farley State Marina, N.J., 196
Federal Wild and Scenic Rivers Act, 154
Festivals: Bayfest, 192; Sara the Turtle Fes-
  tival, 182; Seafood Festival, 196; Wings 'n
  Water, 180; See Dining and Lodging
Field Guide to North American Birds, 12–13
A Field Guide to the Birds East of the Rockies, 12
Fifth-Street Jetty, N.J., 188
Fifty-ninth Street Fishing Pier, N.J., 187
Fisher, definition of a, 2
The Fisherman, 119
Fishermen's Memorial, N.J., 177
Fishing: bibliography of books, magazines,
  etc. 220–28; children and, 10; derbies, 20;
  float-tube, 87; maps available, 224; news-
  paper coverage, 217–20; organizations re-

lated to, 229–32; television, radio, and
  video programs, 229
Fishing guides, 55–57, 68; list of, 223–24
Fishing licenses: freshwater license informa-
  tion, 233–35; reciprocal border agreement
  among New Jersey, New York, and Pennsyl-
  vania, 18; state boundaries for, 235
Flat Rock Dam, Pa., 94
Flat Rock Park, Pa., 106
Flatbrook Creek, N.J., 76
Flatbrookville, N.J., 120
Flemington, N.J., 132
Flies and Hatches: Upper Delaware River,
  24–26; See specific locations
Fly fishing classes, Pa., 25, 87, 115
Forsythe National Wildlife Refuge. See Ed-
  win B. Forsythe National Wildlife Refuge
Fort Delaware, N.Y., 58
Fortescue, N.J., 160–62
Franklin Smelting and Refining, 3
Franklin Township, N.J. 123
French Creek, Pa., 113–14
French Creek State Park, Pa.: hiking, historic
  iron works, picnics, 113–14
Frenchtown, N.J., 123–25
Freshwater fishing: licenses, 9; Northeastern
  Pennsylvania, 14; Northern New Jersey,
  119

Gardens, Pa.: model eighteenth-century, 110;
  Longwood Gardens, 116
Gardiner's Basin, N.J., 196
General Edgar Jadwin Dam, Pa., 49
Geographic coverage of this book, 3
Giampietro Lake Pond, N.J., 153
Giampietro Park, N.J., 153
Gibraltar, Pa., 106
Gladwyne, Pa., 94, 106
Glenmore, Pa., 115
Gloucester County, N.J., 146–47
Glyphosate, 159
Golf courses: Skytop Lodge, 87; Stroudsburg
  area, 86
The Gorge, Pa., 85
Gourmet Garage, N.J.: discount cookery
  store, 192
Gravelling Point, N.J., 131
Gray, Pearl Zane, 64
Great Egg Harbor Inlet, N.J., 187
Great Egg Harbor River, N.J., 150–51, 190–92
Greater Pinelands (New Jersey) Dulcimer So-
  ciety, 113
Green Lane, Pa., 109
Green Lane Reservoir, Pa., 108–09
Greenwich, N.J., 159–60; Christmas house
  tour, 159–60

Grey, Dolly, 64
Grey, Zane, 60, 64; Zane Grey Mansion and
   Museum, Pa., 60, 63, 64
Guides, Delaware River fishing, 56–57, 68,
   223–24
Guitars: Martin, 96

*The Habit of Rivers: Reflections on Trout Streams
   and Fly Fishing*, 6
Hale Eddy, N.Y., 18
Halfway House, Pa., 84
Hamlin, Pa., 67
Hammonton, N.J., 149
Hammonton Lake, N.J., 148
Hancock, N.Y., 3, 15, 18, 27–28, 30–31, 35
Hancock Bridge, 15, 18–19, 21, 27
Hankins, Pa., 35; canoe rentals, 35
Harley-Davidson, 96
Harrisonville Lake, N.J., 147
Harrisville Lake, N.J., 138
Hatchery truck, 43–44
Hatches, II, 24–25
Hawley, Pa., 55–58, 60–63, 67–70, 72–73
Hawley Antique Exchange, Pa., 68
Hay Creek, Pa., 8
Henry, Arthur, 84
Henryville House on Brodhead Creek,
   Pa., 84
Hereford Inlet Lighthouse and Village, N.J.,
   180
Higbee, Howard William, 72
High Bridge, N.J., 133
Hiking, 113, 115, 122
Himalayan Institute, Pa.: classes in medi-
   tation, yoga, diet and nutrition, self-
   rejuvenation, and biofeedback, 56; holistic
   therapy program, 56
Hirshhorn, Joseph, 90; and Hirshhorn Mu-
   seum, 90
Historic Cold Spring Village, N.J., 180
History of American fly-fishing, 84
Holley Ross Pottery, Pa., 91
Hollister Creek, Pa., 36
Hone, Philip, 55–56
Honesdale, Pa., 11, 38, 49, 53–58, 60, 65,
   67–68
Honey Brook, Pa., 115
Hooks, barbless, 7
Hopewell Furnace, Pa., 113
Hopewell Village, Pa., 114
Hotels, *See* Dining and Lodging
Hudson River, 29
Humphreys, Joe, viii, 24, 87, 215
Hunterdon County, N.J., 123–135
Huntingdon Valley, Pa., 103
Hurricane Diane, 85

I. L. A. Guns and Ammo, Pa., 115
Ice fishing, 39, 40
Inland Water Way, 188
Inns. *See* Dining and Lodging
Insect hatches: Upper Delaware River, 14
International Map Company, 72

J. T. Baker Company, 3
Jersey Cape Fishing Tournament, N.J., 177
John Heinz Tinicum National Environmen-
   tal Center, Pa., 105
John Heinz Tinicum Preserve, Pa., 105
Jones Creek, Pa., 72
Jordan Creek, Pa., 8
Junction Pool, Pa., 26–28, 121; sewage treat-
   ment plant, 28

Kasper, J. B., 9, 76
Ken Lockwood Gorge, N.J., 133
Kimbles, Pa., 61
Kingwood, N.J., 128
Kintnersville, Pa, 97–98
Kittatinny Mountains, 58, 120
Klingener Fishing Pier, N.J., 190
Kunkell Rapids (Delaware River), 59

La Anna, Pa., 91
Labar Island (Delaware River), 78
Lackawaxen River, Pa., 55, 58–67, 70–71;
   and the Delaware River, 66, 73; Pennsyl-
   vania Power and Light hotline, 62; West
   Branch of, 54
Lafayette College, Pa., 94, 96; Morris R. Wil-
   liams Center for the Arts, 94
Lahaska, Pa., 102
Lake Aeroflex, N.J.: stocked trout, 121
Lake Assumpink, N.J., 135–36
Lake Atsion, N.J., 143
Lake Galena, Pa., 99–101
Lake Nockamixon, Pa., 100–01
Lake Nummy, N.J., 138, 156–57; canoeing
   on, 157
Lake Shohola, Pa., 73
Lake Superior State Park, N.Y., 59
Lake Wallenpaupack, Pa., 61–62, 67–68, 70–
   73, 84; Angler's Aid map, 72; campgrounds,
   71; restaurants, 72–73; tackle shop, 81; Vis-
   itor's Center, 72
Lambertville, N.J., 9, 101, 123, 128–29,
   134–35
Lambertville Station, N.J., 9; boat launch, 129
Lambertville Shad Festival, N.J., 128
Landis, Dwight, 19, 24, 52, 72–73, 76, 84–85
Laudenslager's Mill: Little Lehigh, Pa., 92
Leesport, Pa., 106
Lehigh Canal, Pa., 95–96

Lehigh County, Pa., 91–97, 108
Lehigh Creek, Pa., 8
Lehigh River, 8, 94, 97
Lester G. MacNamara Wildlife Management
   Area, N.J., 151
Lewes, De.: ferry to Cape May, N.J., 178–79
Licenses. *See* Fishing Licenses
Lighthouses: Cape May, N.J. 179; Forty Foot
   Lighthouse, N.J., 164; Hereford Inlet, N.J.,
   180
Limits, New Jersey state: saltwater fish per
   day, 174
Linda Slocum Antiques, Pa., 68
Lipari Landfill, N.J., 147
Lititz, Pa., 96
Littering, 10
Little Bushkill Creek, Pa., 73, 76–77
Little Equinunk, Pa., 35–36
Little Flat Brook, N.J., 121
Little Kettle Creek, Pa., 44
Little Lehigh Creek, Pa., 86, 91–94
Little Lehigh Fish and Game Protection As-
   sociation, 92
Little Valley Creek, Pa., 111
Livingston Manor, N.Y., 19–20, 23–29
Loch Lomond, Pa., 81
Lockatong, N.J., 131–32
Lodging. *See* Dining and Lodging
Logging, Pa., 65
Long Eddy, Pa., 35
Longport, N.J.: vehicle access, 173
Longport Bridge, N.J., 192
Longport Jetty, N.J., 192
Long Reach Marina, N.J., 163
Lordville, N.Y., 31, 34
Lordville Bridge, 34
Lower Promised Land Lake, Pa., 72
Lower Woods Pond, Pa., 35, 38–39
Luckenback flour mill, Pa., 93
Lucy the Elephant, Margate, N.J., 194
Ludlam Beach, N.J., 181
Lumberville, Pa., 9, 98–99, 125, 131
Lyndell, Pa., 115

McMichaels Creek, Pa., 85
Magazines. *See* Fishing
Manumuskin River, 154
Manumuskin Preserve, N.J., 154
Manayunk, Pa., 93
Manayunk Farmer's Market, Pa., 93
Maple Lake, N.J., 150
Maps, 4, 5, 16, 118, 224
Maps, available to order: fishing maps, 224;
   Lake Wallenpaupack, 72
Margate, N.J., 193–95; vehicle access to
   beaches, 173

Marine Fisheries Administration, New Jersey
   Division of Fish, Game and Wildlife, 171
Mark's: purchase newspapers in Ocean City,
   N.J., 190
Marmora, N.J., 191
Marshall's Creek, Pa., 77, 86
Martin, C. F. and Company, 96
Mary Wilcox Bridge, Pa., 42, 46, 49
Masthope, Pa., 59–60
Matamoras, Pa., 74–75
Matts Landing, N.J., 164
Maurice River, N.J., 153–54, 163
Mauricetown, N.J.: annual seafood festival,
   154; Mauricetown Park, 154; muskrat din-
   ner in, 154
Meck, Charles, 24, 43, 72–73
Medford Township, N.J., 138–39
Menantico, N.J., 154
Mercer-Monmouth Counties, N.J., 135–36
Mercury, levels in fish, 137–38
Methylmercury, levels in fish, 137
Metztown, Pa., 92
Middle Creek, Pa., 60
Milanville, Pa., 38
Milford, N.J., 123–24
Milford, Pa., 74–75, 120–21
Milford Beach, Pa., 120
Millbrook, N.J., 122
Millrift, Pa. 74
Minisink Battleground Park, N.Y., 65–66
Minisink Ford, N.Y., 65
Miss Miscellaneous Pageant, N.J., 187
Mobil Oil, 3
Mohrsville, Pa., 106
Monocacy Creek, Pa., 96–97
Monocacy Watershed Association, 97
Monroe County, Pa., 73, 76–91
Monsanto Chemical Company, 3
Moon: Full Moon Walk in Peace Valley Park,
   Pa., 99
Moore Brothers Wine Company, N.J., 146
Morris Canal, N.J., 95
Montgomery County, Pa., 106, 108–11
Motels, *See* Dining and Lodging
Mount Holly, N.J., 138
Mount Pocono, Pa., 90
Mount Tammanny, N.J., 79
Mountain Lake, Pa., 84
Mullica Hill Pond, N.J., 147
Mullica River, N.J., 138, 148, 175, 202–04
Mullica Township, N.J., 148
Municipal Jetty, N.J., 196
Musconetcong River, N.J., 123; Abba Vine-
   yards near, 123; public access to, 123
Museums and Historic Structures: The Acad-
   emy of Natural Sciences, 137; Annie S.

Kemmerer Museum, 93; Brandywine River Museum, 115–16; Canal Museum, 95–96; Catskill Fly-fishing Center and Museum, 20; Cumberland County Historical Society, Christmas House Tour, 159; Dorflinger Glass Museum, 68; The Emlyn Physick Estate, 179; Equinunk Historical Society, 34–35; Equinunk Historical Society, Joe Hill Sawmill, 34; Estell Manor, 150; Fonthill Museum, 102; Gemein House, Moravian Museum, 93; Hereford Inlet Lighthouse and Village; High Point State Park, High Point Monument, 120–21; Hopewell Furnace, 113–14; Howell Living History Farm: ice harvest, 135; Independence National Historic Park, 34–35; James Fenimore Cooper House, 139–40; The James A. Michener Art Museum, 102; Joe Hill Sawmill, 34; John Sebastian Goundie House, 93; Longwood Gardens, 116; The Mercer Museum, 102; Michener Art Museum, 102; Minisink Battleground Park, 60, 63, 65–66; Moravian Museum, 93; The Moravian Pottery and Tiles Works, 102; Morris Arboretum, 107; National Park Service Information Center, Narrowsburg, N.Y., 58; Noyes Museum, 202; Ocean City Historical Museum, 190; Old Barracks Museum, 135; Peace Valley Nature Center, 99; Philadelphia Museum of Art, 106; Phillips Mushrooms and Mushroom Museum, 116; Port Republic Historical Society, 203; Prallsville Mill Historic Village, 132; Quiet Valley Living Historical Farm, 86; Roebling Aqueduct, 60, 63–65; Ron Kobli's Decoys and Wildlife Gallery, 124; Roscoe O & W Railway Museum, 20; Sea Life Museum/Marine Mammal Stranding Center, 200; Somers Mansion, 192; Stone Harbor Bird Sanctuary, 180; Stourbridge Lion, 55–57, 67; Trenton Barracks, 135; Valley Forge National Historic Park, 106, 110–11, 114; Washington Crossing Historic Park, 95, 101, 134; Wayne County Historical Society, 54–56; Winterthur, 116; Zane Grey Mansion, 55, 60, 63–64, 66
Music festivals: Wildflower Music Festival at the Dorflinger Glass Museum, Pa., 68

Nakashima Reading Room, at the Michener Art Museum, Pa., 102
Narrowsburg, N.Y., 38, 56, 58–59, 60; launch sites, 59
Narrowsburg Eddy, N.Y., 59
NASA, 166
National Fish and Wildlife Foundation, 21

National Marine Fisheries Service, 165
National Safe Boating Week, 7
National Weather Service. See Weather
Nature Conservancy, 159; Delaware Bayshore office, 180; and Manamuskin Preserve, N.J., 154
Nazareth, Pa., 96
Neshaminy Creek, Pa., 101; and crabbing in, 208
New Britain Township, Pa., 99–100
New Brooklyn Lake, N.J., 138
New Hope, Pa., 95, 101
New Jersey: Atlantic County, 148–52, 190–204; black bear population, 120; boundaries, 235; Burlington County, 138–45, 204–07; Camden County, 145–46; Cape May County, 151, 155–57, 174–90, 191; Cumberland County, 152–55; finest trout lake in, 133; Gloucester County, 146–47; Green Acres program, 142; Hunterdon County, 123–35; licenses, freshwater fishing, 9; Mercer County, 15–36; Monmouth County, 135–36; Northern New Jersey, 119–36; premier trout streams, 120; saltwater fishing regulations, 173–74; state mobile sport-fishing permit, 186; Sussex County, 119–121; Warren County, 119–23
New Jersey Angler Sportmen's Association: competition, 122
New Jersey Beach Buggy Association (NJBBA), 172
New Jersey Department of Environmental Protection, 137–38, 158; Division of Parks and Forestry, 187
New Jersey Division of Fish, Game, and Wildlife, 120, 133, 152–53; Adopt-A-Wreck, 166; Pequest Trout Hatchery and Natural Resource Center Open House, 122; saltwater fishing regulations, 173–74
New Jersey Marine Fisheries Council, 197–98
New York City, N.Y., 65, 67
New York Department of Environmental Conservation, 29, 36
Newfoundland, Pa., 81
Newport Landing Marina, N.J., 162
Newspapers. See Fishing
Newtown Lake, N.J., 138
Night bluefishing, 175
Nixon's General Store, N.J., 142
Nockamixon State Park, Pa., 100
Norristown, Pa., 106
North Wildwood, N.J., 180; vehicle access to beaches, 172
Northampton County, Pa., 91–97; Bushkill Creeks, 76

Northeast Firearms, Pa., 56
Northeast Sports, Pa., 56

Oak Pond, Pa., 146–47
Occidental Chemical Corporation, 3
Ocean City, N.J., 187–90; Corson's Inlet, 120; Longport Bridge, 191; vehicle access to beaches, 173
Ocean City Marina and Fishing Center, 188
Odd-Lot Outlet, Pa., 86
The 100 Best Small Art Towns in America, 94
Organizations. *See* Fishing
Orvis, 20–21, 45–46, 56, 87, 113
Orvis Fly Fishing School (Skytop Resort): schedule, 87; women-only classes, 87
Orvis News, 20

Palm, Pa., 108
Palmyra, N.J., 140
Party boats and charters, 160–62, 169–171, 181; Angler's Choice, Sportfishing Charter Service, 171; *Applejack*, 162, 196–97, 199, Atlantic County Party and Charter Boat Association, 171; *Bonanza II*, 161; *Cap'n Andy's Fish 'n Fun IV* (pontoon boat), 193; Captain Robbins Fishing Center, 181; *Challenger*, 188; *Duke O'Fluke*, 195; *Fortescue Queen*, 61; *Miss Avalon II*, 181; Miss Chris fleet, 205; *Miss Diane*, 164; *Miss Fortescue*, 160; New Jersey directory of charter and party boats, 171; *Norma-K II*, 205; *North Star*, 188, *Viking*, 188–89
Peace Valley Park, Pa., 99
Peaslee Wildlife Management Area, N.J., 153–54
Pecks Bay, N.J., 188
Pemberton, N.J., 141–42
Pemberton Lake, N.J., 141–42
Pennsauken Creek, N.J., 141
Pennsylvania: boundaries, 235; Berks County, 2, 116–17; Bucks County, 2, 97–102; Chester County, 2, 113–16; Delaware County, 2, 111–13, Lackawanna County, 2; Lehigh County 2, 91–97; licenses, 234; Monroe County, 2, 78–91; Montgomery County, 108–11; Philadelphia County, 103–08; Pike County, 2, 59–73, 73–77; Wayne County, 2, 11, 14–57, 71–73.
Pennsylvania Atlas and Gazetteer, 84
Pennsylvania Fish and Boat Commission, 8, 21, 25, 34, 39, 40, 54; public launch sites, 232
Pennsylvania Power and Light Company (PP&L), 72, 89; hydroelectric power plant, 61, 71; Lackawaxen and Lake Wallenpaupack hotline, 62; Lake Wallenpaupack, 61;

Lake Wallenpaupack campgrounds, 71; water release, 63
Pennsylvania Trout and Salmon Fishing Guide, 66, 73, 84
Pennsylvania Trout Streams and Their Hatches, 24, 43
Pennypack Creek, Pa., 103
Pennypack Park, Pa., 103–04
Pennypack Watershed Association, 103
Pepacton, N.Y., 28–29
Pepacton Reservoir, N.Y., 15, 28
Pequest River, N.J., 122–23
Pequest Trout Hatchery and Natural Resource Education Center, N.J., 122; Open House, 122; Wildlife Management Area, 122
Perkiomen Creek, Pa., 8, 108–09
Permission to fish, 10
Permits: New Jersey State Mobile Sportfishing Permit, 186; *See* Fishing Licenses
Philadelphia, Pa., 65, 103–10; Kelly Drive, 86; Philadelphia, 103–04; Philadelphia International Airport Area, 104–05
Philadelphia Museum of Art, Pa.: crabbing at, 208
Phragmites, 159
Pickering Creek, Pa., 8
Pickle Factory Pond, N.J., 156
Pidcock Creek, Pa., 101
Pig Pen Pool, N.Y., 19
Pike County, Pa., 59, 66–67, 69–70, 73–76, 120
Pine Barrens, N.J., 143–44
Plum Creek, Pa., 116
Pocono area, Pa., 58, 67, 81, 86, 88, 91
Pocono Bazaar Flea Market, Pa., 86
Pocono Creek, Pa., 86
Pocono Lake, Pa., 90
Pocono Mountains Vacation Bureau, 86
Pocono Outlet Complex, Pa., 86
Poconos Vacation Guide, 86
Point Pleasant, N.J., 205
Point Pleasant, Pa.: tubing, 98
Pompeson Creek, N.J., 140
Pond Eddy, N.Y., 74–75
Pond Eddy Creek, Pa., 74–75
Poplar Run, Pa., 83–85
Port Jervis, N.Y., 59, 66, 74; and Minisink, 80
Port Norris, N.J., 163–64
Port Republic Wildlife Management Area, N.J., 203–04
Possession and Minimum Size Limits, N.J., 174
Potter County, Pa., 44
Pottery: Holley Ross Pottery, Pa., 91; The Moravian Pottery and Tiles Works, Pa., 102
Pottstown, Pa., 106

Pottsville, Pa., 106
Poxono Island, 78
Preston Park, Pa., 25
Promised Land Lake, Pa., 72
Promised Land State Park, Pa., 72, 84
Prompton Lake, Pa.: bass fishing in, 54
Prompton State Park, Pa., 54
Public Service Electric and Gas, 158–59
Pughtown, Pa., 114

Quakertown, Pa., 100

Radio programs. See Fishing
Railroad history: Honesdale, Pa., 55–56
Ralph Stover State Park, Pa. 101
Rancocas Creek, N.J., 139, 141
Rancocas State Park, N.J., 141
Rancocas Watershed Conservancy, 138–39
Raritan River, N.J.: Ken Lockwood Gorge,
    133; South Branch, 10, 133
Ratzman Access, N.J., 121
Raven Rock, N.J., 125
Reading, Pa., 106, 116
Recipes: Angler's Trout, 70; Anthony's Garlic
    Crabs, 212; Art Michael's Fried Fish Strips,
    57; Bacalas (salted, dried codfish): George
    Ingram's Sunday Breakfast, 206; Blackfish
    (Tautog) Stew, 206; Braised Roe with Leeks,
    Tarragon and Capers in White Wine, 130;
    Cod Fillets with Red Peppers and Onions,
    205; George Perrier's Crabcakes with
    Shrimp, 210–11; Mackerel Fillets in Soy
    Sauce, 198; Maryland Department of Agri-
    culture Crabcakes, 211; Maryland Seafood
    Marketer's Hardshell Crabs, 212; Parsley
    Butter Sauce, 211; Peppered Shad Fillet,
    130; Settler's Inn Angler's Trout, 70; Shad
    and Shad Roe recipes, 129–30; Steamed
    Whiting with Scallions and Ginger, 207
Red Hill, Pa., 108–09
Reeves Brothers: crab sellers, N.J., 164
Rehoboth Beach, De., 178
Resica Falls Boy Scout Camp, Pa., 77
Resorts. See Dining and Lodging
Restaurants. See Dining and Lodging
Revolutionary War: Minisink massacre, 66
Ridley Creek, Pa., 111–13
Ridley Creek State Park, Pa., 112–13; Colo-
    nial Mansion, 112
Rileyville, Pa., 38, 49; Grange Hall flea mar-
    ket, 35
Rinebeck, N.Y., 29
Rising Sun Lake, N.J., 136
Ritz Theater, Pa., 55
Rivell, Thom, 61, 81–83, 90–91
Riverside, N.J., 140

Riverton, N.J., 140–41
Riverton Yacht Club, N.J., 140
Roche Vitamins, 3
Rockland, N.Y., 19, 29
Roebling, John Augustus, 63–65
Roebling, Washington, 65
Rohm & Haas Company, 147
Roscoe, N.Y., 19–20, 28–29
Rose Pond, Pa., 38
Rosemont, N.J., 131
Round Valley Reservoir, N.J., 133–34
Round Valley Wildlife Management Area,
    N.J., 133
Royal Delaware River Yacht Club and Ma-
    rina, N.J., 140
Rush Chattin Bridge, N.J., 185–86

Salem Nuclear Power Plant, N.J., 158, 164
Saltwater fishing: autumn fishing, 8; practical
    tips, 166–169
Sara the Turtle Festival, N.J., 182
Savona Foods Inn, N.J.: Italian food ware-
    house, 141
Saw Mill Lake, N.J., 121
Saw Mill Pond, N.J., 121
Sajna, Mike, 66, 73–74, 84
Schaefer Spring Creek, Pa., 92
Schuylkill Haven, Pa., 106
Schuylkill River, Pa., 86, 94, 105–07, 109–11
Sea Isle City, N.J., 181–82; vehicle access to
    beaches, 173
Sea Isle City Historical Museum, N.J., 182
Sea Isle City Tourism Commission, N.J.,
    181–82
Sergeantsville, N.J., 132
Shad Festival, Pa., 93
Shad migrations, 94
Shark, Great White?, in N.J., 193–94
Sharp's Run, N.J., 139
Shawness Islands, 78
Shaws Mill Pond, N.J., 152–53
Shehawken Creek, Pa., 25
Shehawken Launch, Pa., 25–27
Ship Channel, N.J., 190
Shohola, Pa., 73–74
Shohola Creek, Pa., 73–74
Shohola Falls, Pa., 73–74
Skinners Falls, Pa., 38
Skippack, Pa., 110
Skippack Creek, Pa., 109–10
Skippack Trail, Pa., 110
Skytop, Pa., 84
Smithville, N.J., 202
Snyder Pond, Pa., 36
Somers Point, N.J., 190–92; Bayfest, 192
Somers Point-Longport Bridge, N.J., 190

South Sterling, Pa., 90–91

Spirit of Paupack, 71

Spruce Run Reservoir, N.J., 133

Starlight, Pa., 25, 30

Starlight Lake, Pa., 30

State borders, 18

State Theatre, Pa., 94

Still Swamp Run, Pa., 89

Stockton, N.J., 9, 101, 123, 127–28, 131–32; Stockton area, Phillips Fine Wines and Liquors, 127

Stone Harbor, N.J., 180; vehicle access to beaches, 173

Stone Harbor Bird Sanctuary, N.J., 180; museum and observation tower, 180

Stone Tavern Lake, N.J., 136

Stourbridge Rail Line, Pa., 54–55, 70

Strathmere, N.J.: beaches, 183–85

Stream Map of Pennsylvania, 72

Street Names of Philadelphia, 107

Stroudsburg, Pa., 74, 84–86

Sturgis Pretzel House, Pa., 96

Sullivan County, N.Y., 69

Sunset Beach, N.J., 176–77

Surf fishing, N.J., 172–74

Susquehanna County, Pa., 30

Sussex County, N.J., 119–21

Sylvan Lake, N.J., 140

Tackle shops: Absecon Bay Sportsmen Center, 201; Al's Bait House, 162; Al's Sea and Surf Tackle Shop, 180; Barton's Bait Shop, 160; Best in Philadelphia, 103; The Beaverkill Angler, 19; Blackwater Sports Center, 155; Bob's Bait and Tackle, 176; Brandywine Outfitters, 115; Brinkman's Bait and Tackle, 103, 162; Campbell Marine, Inc., 92; Cap's Bait and Tackle, 140; Chip's Bait and Tackle, 115; Cortland Pro-Shop, 113; Dan's Sport Shop, 133; Delaware River Fly Shop, 19, 21, 30; Dolfin Dock, 192; Dunkelberger's Sport Outfitters, 86; Eyler, Inc., 113; Fin-Atics Marine Supply, Ltd., 189; Fish and Fur Sporting Goods, 147; Fish Tales, 181; Fishin' Stuff Tackle Shop, 189; Fur, Fin and Feather, 19; Gibson's Bait and Tackle, 182; Gordon's Sports Supply, 115; Harry's Army and Navy, 144; Hook-Line and Sinker, Inc., 147; Howard's Sporting Goods, 147; J.B.'s Fly Trap, 185; Jim's Bait and Tackle, 176; Jim's Outdoor Sportsman, 140; King's Bait, Tackle and Accessories, 145; Larry's Fisherman's Cove, 147; Longreach Marina, 163; Mick's Canoe Rental, 144; Mike's Sportsmen's Den, 144; Miss Chris Fishing Center, 175–76; North-

east Flyfishers, 56; Oliver's, 133; Orvis Shop (Philadelphia), 94; The Reel Doctor, 147; Ricky's Army and Navy Store, 145; The Sea Gull Shop, 189; Smuggler's Cove Bait and Tackle, 181; Sportsman's Paradise, 147; Sportsman's Rendezvous, 121; The Sportsmaster, 104; Sportsmen's Center, 144; Thom Rivell's Fly Fishing Tackle Shop; Wild Bill's Bait and Tackle, 160

Tafton, Pa., 71

Tanners Falls, Pa., 41, 43, 44, 49, 50; murder at, 51–52

Tannersville, Pa., 86

Taverns. *See* Dining and Lodging

Teeter's Funiture Store, Pa., 69

Television and video programs. *See* Fishing

Temple University, Pa., 14, 25, 30, 82, 96, 106–07, 110

Theodore Roosevelt State Park, Pa., 95

tidal boundaries, 9

Titusville, N.J., 134–35

Tobyhanna Creek, Pa., 8, 77, 88–91

Tobyhanna Lake, Pa., 88–89, 91

Tobyhanna State Park, Pa., 91

Tocks Island, 78

Tohickon Creek, Pa., 101

Tom's Creek, Pa., 76

Toxic Fish Alert: Delaware River, 138

Toxins, 137

Trash, 10

Trenton, N.J., 65, 134–35, 208; Marine Terminal, 135; *Trenton Times*, 135; Trenton Thunder (team), 135; *Trentonian*, 135

Trexlertown, Pa., 92

Trout habitat: destruction of, 29

Trout stream management, 112

Trout streams: best autumn streams, 8

Trout streams of Pennsylvania, 19, 24, 76, 84–85

Trout Tactics, vii, 87

Trout Unlimited, 20–21. 29, 112; Beaverkill Restoration Project, 21; Brodhead Chapter, 85; Lehigh Chapter, 91; Monocacy Chapter, 97; successful opposition to the Delaware Water Gap Dam, 78; Tulpehocken Chapter, 116; Valley Forge Chapter, 111

Tubing: Bucks County River Country, Point Pleasant, Pa., 98

Tuckahoe Cheese Factory, N.J.: cheesecake, 152

Tuckahoe River, N.J., 151

Tulpehocken Creek, Pa., 106, 116–17; delayed harvest area, 116

Tunkhannock, Pa., 41

Turkeys, fresh: Bush's Turkey Farm, N.J., 142

Tusten, N.Y., 59

Twin Capes, N.J., 179
Tyler State Park, Pa., 101

Uhlertown, Pa., 124
Union Lake, N.J., 153; mercury in, 138
United States Army Corps of Engineers, 29, 85, 116–17, 188
United States Department of the Interior, 203
United States Fish and Wildlife Service: study, 2
United States National Park Service (NPS), 33–34
United States Steel Fairless Works, Pa., 3
Upper Black Eddy, Pa., 124
Upper Delaware River, 14–18; East Branch area, 29; water conditions, 15; West Branch, 18–27
Upper Delaware Scenic and Recreational River, Pa., 74
Upper Woods Pond, Pa., 35, 38–40

Valley Creek, Pa., 110–12
Valley Green, Pa., 108
Valley Greens Association, The, 113
Van Aucken Creek, Pa., 54
Van Put, Ed, 24
Van Campens Brook, N.J.: Delaware Water Gap National Recreational Area, 122
Vehicles: on the beach, 172–73
Ventnor, N.J., 195; vehicle access to beaches, 173
Ventnor Fishing Pier, N.J., 195
Vineland, N.J., 153

Wading River, N.J., 138
Wallenpaupack Creek, Pa.: West Branch, 72
Wallenpaupack Dam, Pa., 71–72
Wallenpaupack, Lake. See Lake Wallenpaupack
Wallpack Bend, 76, 78
Walpack Wildlife Management Area, N.J., 121; Walpack Center, 121; lower Big Flat Creek access, 121
Walton, Izaak, 115
Warren County, N.J., 119–23
Washington Street Mall, N.J., 179
Watauba River, Tenn., 24
Water Gap
Water safety, 7
Water Wheel Junction, N.Y., 20
Wayne County, Pa., 11, 14, 25, 38, 40, 49, 69, 71

Wayne County Chamber of Commerce, Pa., 55–56
Wayne County Fair, Pa., 38, 52–55
Wayne County Fair Grounds, Pa., 49, 52
Weather information, 217
Websites: fishing related, 228
Weird Contest Week, N.J., 187
West Chester, Pa., 113
West Pond, N.J., 155–56
Wetlands Institute, N.J., 180
Weymouth, N.J., 150
Weymouth River, N.J., 150
Wheaton Village, N.J., 154
White Clay Creek, Pa., 8
White Mills, Pa., 68
White Township, N.J., 121–23
Whitemarsh, Pa., 107
Wickecheoke, N.J., 132
Wild and Scenic Act. See Federal Wild and Scenic Act
Wildflower Music Festival at the Dorflinger Museum, Pa., 68
Wildwood, N.J.: vehicle access to beaches, 172
Willowemoc River, N.Y., 18–23, 29, 84
Wilmington Trail Club, Pa., 115
Wilson Lake, N.J., 138
Wineries and Breweries: Abba Vineyards, 123; Balic Winery, 151; Barley Creek Brewing Company, 86; Cape May Winery and Vineyard, 180; Cedar Creek Brewery and Restaurant, 149; Chaddsford Winery, 115; Clover Hill Vineyards and Winery, 92–93; Egg Harbor City Microbrewery and Restaurant, 149; Franklin Hill, 93; Hunterdon Brewing Company, 191; McGowan's Buckingham Mountain Brewing Company and Restaurant, 102; Renault Winery, 148–49; River Horse Brewery, 129; Tomasello's, 149
Wings 'n Water Festival, N.J., 180
Winslow Wildlife Management Area, N.J., 146
Wissahickon Creek, Pa., 107–08
Wister, Owen, 64
Women fishers, 2; women-only fly-fishing school, 87
Woodbine, N.J., 157
Wulff, Lee, 20

Zoos: Birch Grove Park, 149–50; Bridgeton Zoo, 155; Cape May County Park and Zoo, 156, 178; Claws 'N' Paws Wild Animal Park, 67; Cohanzick Zoo, 155

About the Authors

GEORGE H. INGRAM JR., is a Temple University administrator, Temple alumnus, and freelance outdoors writer who lives on the Delaware and has published hunting and fishing articles in *The New York Times, The Wall Street Journal, The Philadelphia Inquirer, Pennsylvania Game News,* and other magazines and newspapers.

DR. ROBERT F. MARLER JR., retired as a Temple University professor of English in 1994 after teaching at the institution for twenty-eight years. A long-time fly-fisher, he lives on a farm in Benton, Pennsylvania, not far from Fishing Creek, with his wife, Jan; his daughter, Mary Beth; and an aging Chevy pickup truck.

DR. ROBERT R. SMITH retired as Dean of the School of Communications and Theater at Temple University in 1996, after serving in that position for almost eighteen years. A fishing and birding enthusiast, he is an authority on the literature of fly fishing. He now resides on Trout Farm Lane in Plympton, Mass., with his wife, Suzanne.